Sociolinguistics and Deaf Communities

How do people use sign languages in different situations around the world? How are sign languages distributed globally? What happens when they come in contact with spoken and written languages? These and other questions are explored in this new introduction to the sociolinguistics of sign languages and Deaf communities.

An international team brings insight and data from a wide range of sign languages, from the USA, Canada, England, Spain, Brazil, and Australia. Topics covered include multilingualism in the global Deaf community; sociolinguistic variation and change in sign languages; bilingualism and language contact between signed and spoken languages; attitudes toward sign languages; sign language planning and policy, and sign language discourse.

Sociolinguistics and Deaf Communities will be welcomed by students of sign language and interpreting, teachers of sign language, and students and academics working in linguistics.

ADAM C. SCHEMBRI is Associate Professor on the Linguistics program and director of the Centre for Research on Language Diversity at La Trobe University.

CEIL LUCAS is Professor Emerita in the Department of Linguistics at Gallaudet University.

Sociolinguistics and Deaf Communities

Edited by

Adam C. Schembri

and

Ceil Lucas

 CAMBRIDGE
UNIVERSITY PRESS

2099

KH

CAMBRIDGE
UNIVERSITY PRESS

University Printing House, Cambridge CB2 8BS, United Kingdom

One Liberty Plaza, 20th Floor, New York, NY 10006, USA

477 Williamstown Road, Port Melbourne, VIC 3207, Australia

314-321, 3rd Floor, Plot 3, Splendor Forum, Jasola District Centre, New Delhi - 110025, India

79 Anson Road, #06-04/06, Singapore 079906

Cambridge University Press is part of the University of Cambridge.

It furthers the University's mission by disseminating knowledge in the pursuit of
education, learning and research at the highest international levels of excellence.

www.cambridge.org
Information on this title: www.cambridge.org/9781107663862

© Cambridge University Press 2015

First published 2015

A catalogue record for this publication is available from the British Library

Library of Congress Cataloging in Publication data
Sociolinguistics and deaf communities / edited by Ceil Lucas and Adam C. Schembri.
    pages   cm
ISBN 978-1-107-05194-2 (Hardback) – ISBN 978-1-107-66386-2 (Paperback)
1. Sign language.   2. Deaf–Means of communication.   3. Sociolinguistics.
I. Lucas, Ceil, editor.   II. Schembri, Adam C., editor.
HV2474.S6194 2015
306.44087´2–dc23   2014030970

ISBN 978-1-107-05194-2 Hardback
ISBN 978-1-107-66386-2 Paperback

10/20/20

Contents

Figures

Tables

Contributors

ROBERT ADAM is Research Associate at the Deafness Cognition and Language Research Centre, University College London. His research interests include sociolinguistics, bilingualism, and Deaf interpreters; his doctoral studies focused on language contact between two sign languages.

ROBERT BAYLEY is Professor of Linguistics at the University of California, Davis. He has conducted research on variation in English, Chinese, Spanish, ASL, and Italian Sign Language as well as ethnographic studies of US Latino communities.

JORDAN FENLON is a Mellom Postdoctoral Fellow within the Department of Linguistics at the University of Chicago. He was previously a research associate at the Deafness, Cognition and Language Research Centre where he assisted in the development of the British Sign Language (BSL) Corpus (www.bslcorpusproject.org) and BSL Sign Bank, a corpus-based dictionary for BSL (www.bslsignbank.ucl.ac.uk).

JOSEPH C. HILL is Assistant Professor in the Specialized Education Services department at the University of North Carolina at Greensboro. His areas of interest in socio-historical and sociolinguistic aspects of African-American variety of American Sign Language and attitudes toward signing varieties in the American Deaf community.

CEIL LUCAS is Professor of Linguistics, Emerita at Gallaudet University, where she taught (1982–2013). She is a sociolinguist with broad interests in the structure and use of sign languages. She has co-authored and edited many articles and books, including *The Linguistics of American Sign Language*, 5th edn (with Clayton Valli, Kristin Mulrooney, and Miako Villanueva).

RONICE MÜLLER DE QUADROS has a Ph.D. in Linguistics and has been a Full Professor at the Federal University of Santa Catarina since 2002. Her research activities focus primarily on sign language acquisition and she also has worked on bilingualism, Deaf education, and sign language interpretation.

JOSEP QUER is ICREA Research Professor at Pompeu Fabra University (Barcelona), head of the Catalan Sign Language Lab and member of the Catalan Academy (Institut d'Estudis Catalans) in charge of Catalan Sign Language issues. His research focuses on the formal analysis of sign and spoken languages (syntax, semantics), but also on sign language planning and policy.

DAVID QUINTO-POZOS has a Ph.D. from the Department of Linguistics at the University of Texas at Austin. David conducts research on developmental signed language disorders, the interaction between language and gesture in signed language, and contact phenomena in signed languages.

CYNTHIA ROY was awarded her Ph.D. in linguistics from Georgetown University. Cynthia is a professor and the Ph.D. Coordinator in the Department of Interpretation at Gallaudet University. Her areas of interest are discourse analysis, sociolinguistics, and research about interpreting.

ADAM C. SCHEMBRI was awarded his Ph.D. in linguistics from the University of Sydney in 2002, and has worked at a number of universities in both Australia and England and published work on both Auslan and BSL. He is now director of the Centre for Research on Language Diversity and teaches on the Linguistics program at La Trobe University in Melbourne, Australia.

ERIN WILKINSON is Assistant Professor in the Department of Linguistics at the University of Manitoba (Canada) and a member of the Executive Team of the National Science Foundation Science of Learning Center on Visual Language and Visual Learning (VL2). Her research interests include cross-language processing in bimodal bilinguals, and she also explores grammatical and typological patterns and the phenomenon of iconicity across signed languages.

ELIZABETH A. WINSTON was awarded her Ph.D. in linguistics from Georgetown University. Elizabeth is the Director of the Teaching Interpreting Education and Mentors (TIEM) Center. Her research and teaching interests include discourse analysis, interpreting pedagogy and assessment, and educational interpreting.

1   Introduction

Adam C. Schembri and Ceil Lucas

In the 2001 volume entitled *The Sociolinguistics of Sign Languages*, edited by Ceil Lucas (Cambridge University Press), it is stated that, since the early 1980s, "the field of sign language sociolinguistics has virtually exploded. There is work to report on from all of the major areas of sociolinguistics: multilingualism, bilingualism and language contact, variation, discourse analysis, language planning and policy, language attitudes, and work that reports on Deaf communities from all over the world" (xvii).[1] That volume provided chapters on all of this work. Lucas went on to observe that

> the earliest sociolinguistic research in Deaf communities was shaped and perhaps limited by at least four interrelated considerations: 1) the relationship between the spoken language of the majority community and the sign language, particularly in educational settings; 2) limited knowledge of the linguistic structure of the sign language; 3) doubts as to the actual status of the sign language as a "real language"; and 4) application of spoken sociolinguistic models to sign language situations. (p. 4)

Turning now to 2015 and the current volume, we attempt here to cover the same basic areas of sign language sociolinguistics. We intend this volume to be used as a text in upper-level undergraduate and graduate sociolinguistics courses, but also hope that it is a contribution which will be of interest to sign language researchers and sociolinguists working on both signed and spoken languages as well as anyone with a desire to know more about the sociolinguistics of Deaf communities. We have come a long way since the 2001 volume! While there is, of course, still a necessary focus on the relationship between spoken languages and sign languages, especially in educational settings, a tremendous amount of work has been done on the relationship between sign languages in the last decade. We see some of this important

---

[1] The term "Deaf" with the upper-case 'D' is used to describe communities of deaf adults and children who share the use of a sign language and Deaf cultural values, behaviors, and traditions. The term "deaf" with the lower-case 'd' is usually an audiological description of a person's level of hearing, and may be used to describe people who do not use a sign language and who do not identify with and participate in Deaf culture and Deaf communities. This deaf–Deaf distinction will be used throughout this volume.

work documented in Chapter 2: "Sign Languages in the World." In Chapter 2, Jordan Fenlon and Erin Wilkinson distinguish *macro* Deaf communities from *micro* ones, the latter including "deaf villages" in which inhabitants, both hearing and Deaf, use a sign language. We see deeper work on the historical relationships between sign languages, and on the effects of sign language colonialism, new technologies, and economic mobility. Chapter 2 also explores the reality of language endangerment that affects sign languages as much as it affects spoken languages. The focus on the relationship between sign languages continues in Chapter 3: "Sign Languages in Contact," by David Quinto-Pozos and Robert Adam, with consideration of contact between sign languages such as Hausa Sign Language and American Sign Language or between Japanese Sign Language and Taiwan Sign Language, and the sign language use that happens at transnational gatherings and in border areas. These studies show us the sociolinguistic features unique to language contact between two sign languages. We now also have a generation of Deaf multilingual signers, i.e., Deaf people who quite comfortably use more than one sign language, in addition to being able to read, write, and possibly speak one or more majority spoken languages. As with the 2001 volume, this work on Deaf communities expands notions of bilingualism and language contact first developed in studies of spoken languages. Studies of gesture that have emerged from sign language studies have also had the same effect of expanding the horizons of the discipline.

Significant amounts of research in the past fourteen years have vastly expanded our knowledge of the structure of sign languages. In 2001, the Lucas *et al.* volume on sociolinguistic variation in American Sign Language (ASL) was just being published. As we see in Chapter 4: "Variation and Change in Sign Languages," by Robert Bayley, Adam C. Schembri, and Ceil Lucas, we now can add descriptions of Black ASL and of variation in Italian Sign Language (LIS), British Sign Language (BSL), Australian Sign Language (Auslan), and New Zealand Sign Language (NZSL) to the original work on ASL. We see how this work informs our overall knowledge of sign language variation and change and also how research methods used for studying variation in sign languages may have implications for the study of variation in spoken languages. In Chapter 5: "Discourse Analysis and Sign Languages," by Cynthia Roy and Betsy Winston, we see how studies on the structure of sign language discourse have expanded and deepened our understanding of signed interaction, and have much to teach us about spoken language interaction too. Finally, Chapter 6: "Language Policy and Planning in Deaf Communities," by Josep Quer and Ronice Müller de Quadros and Chapter 7: "Language Attitudes in Deaf Communities," by Joseph Hill show us that while there have been advances in the thinking about and the recognition of the status of sign languages as "real languages" – with examples from Spain, Catalonia, and Brazil – there are still significant attitudinal obstacles to overcome even now.

Looking back, we see that the four interrelated considerations that shaped earlier research on the sociolinguistics of sign languages have changed or have been replaced. As can be seen in the six chapters in this volume, current and future research will

- have to deal with signing in transnational settings and the outcomes – code-switching, code-mixing, borrowing – that result from the contact between Deaf bilinguals and Deaf multilinguals;
- need to explore the effect of new technologies on discourse structure and on data collection methodologies;
- include analyses of variation in sign languages beyond ASL, LIS, BSL, Auslan, and NZSL, and should begin to explore how so called 'second wave' and 'third wave' approaches to the study of variation (Eckert 2012) can be usefully applied to an understanding of sign language use in Deaf communities;
- focus on the endangerment of sign languages due to colonialism and the rise of medical technologies such as cochlear implants;
- involve the various stances on the recognition of sign languages and analyses of language planning and policy activities;
- be concerned with shifts in attitudes and ideologies concerning sign languages.

These are considerations that research and experience have made possible since 2001. Remarkably, however, the basic underlying motivation for studies of sign sociolinguistics past and present has not shifted. In the 2001 volume, Lucas referred to what guided Stokoe in the preparation of the *Dictionary of American Sign Language* (DASL). As early as 1957, Stokoe was aware of the thinking of George Trager and Henry Lee Smith: "They insisted that it was pointless to study languages alone. Languages, they said, had to be studied along with the cultures of their users. One must examine not just the forms and structures of a language but also its actual use and content" (Stokoe 2001: 59). This sociolinguistic perspective clearly guided the inclusion of Croneberg's groundbreaking appendices in the DASL, appendices that showed how language, culture, and deafness worked together to form unique communities. The importance of studying the sociolinguistics of Deaf communities remains the same: first, the recognition that sign languages have sociolinguistic lives like other systems that we recognize as languages reinforces the status of sign languages as "real languages." Second, this recognition and accompanying legitimization of sign languages allows for the discussion of what the medium of instruction should be in Deaf education and to the question of why it should not always include sign languages; it allows for the improvement of services for Deaf people, such as signed/spoken language interpreting, and continues to open new career paths for Deaf people as sign language researchers, teachers of Deaf children and adolescents, interpreters and interpreter trainers, and teachers of sign languages. The study of the sociolinguistics of Deaf communities in all of its aspects contributes to the continuing empowerment of Deaf people all over the world.

REFERENCES

Eckert, P. (2012) Three waves of variation study: The emergence of meaning in the study of variation. *Annual Review of Anthropology* 41: 87–100.
Stokoe, William C. (2001) *Language in Hand – Why Sign Came before Speech.* Washington, DC: Gallaudet University Press.

2   Sign languages in the world

Jordan Fenlon and Erin Wilkinson

Introduction

What is multilingualism?

Multilingualism, the use of two or more languages by an individual or a community is described as a 'powerful fact of life around the world' (Edwards 1994). If we consider that there are an estimated 195 countries in the world today against the 7,106 living languages listed in the *Ethnologue*, we might assume that for most of the world's population, multilingualism is a common occurrence (Lewis, Simons, and Fennig 2013). But what do we mean by multilingualism? Research in this field is interested in how languages coexist alongside other languages and the factors that contribute to the various multilingual environments throughout the world. For example, people who know more than one language may or may not be equally proficient in each of their languages; they may only be as proficient as is necessary and their use of different languages may be confined to specific social settings or groups. The extent to which these language communities interact with one another may also vary. Additionally, some languages may not have any official recognition within the nation states in which they are found, and this may affect how these languages are perceived by others.

When we consider sign languages, we find many examples of multilingualism that parallel those described for spoken languages. In this chapter, we describe how multilingualism is a fact of life for nearly (if not all) signing individuals. We begin with a brief description of sign language as languages in their own right followed by a description of the different environments in which sign languages can thrive and the patterns of transmission that define them so that one can appreciate where, why, and how sign languages exist today. We also describe the types of multilingual environments that characterize the lives of deaf individuals and the factors that contribute to or against multilingualism.

Sign languages are real languages

To begin with, some common myths about sign languages are addressed here. First, sign languages are real languages. Research into sign languages as

5

legitimate languages was hindered at first by the belief that sign languages were visual representations of spoken languages or primitive forms of communication (e.g., Bloomfield 1933). It was not until the work of Stokoe (1960), which demonstrated that signs consisted of sub-lexical components, that the linguistic status of sign languages was taken seriously. Since then, much research has been undertaken across the language sciences highlighting how sign languages provide a valuable insight into the way that languages work (e.g., Emmorey 2002). Second, sign language is not universal. Many believe this myth to be true due to the iconic nature of many signs or the mistaken belief that they are artificial languages. Instead, sign languages are languages that have developed independently from one another within deaf communities around the world and have been demonstrated to be typologically diverse (e.g., Zeshan 2004). We cannot expect that a signer using Australian Sign Language (Auslan) will be able to communicate fluently with a signer using Italian Sign Language (LIS, Lingua dei Segni Italiana).

Once we accept these two facts, that sign languages are real languages and that many of the world's sign languages have evolved independently from one another, we can begin to appreciate the potential for linguistic diversity that sign languages represent. However, formal investigation of sign languages have been historically biased towards Europe and North America, although a growing number of studies are investigating non-Western sign languages (e.g., Zeshan and de Vos 2012). Additionally, efforts to document and describe the world's sign languages are still in its infancy; few sign languages can be said to have a dictionary that is completely representative of its lexicon and large-scale documentation projects (e.g., sign language corpora) have only been possible in recent years due to advancements in video and transcription technology (Johnston and Schembri 2013). For sign languages in non-Western countries, this kind of research effort may not have even taken place.

Official figures for sign languages are also unlikely to provide us with a complete picture of multilingualism within the world's deaf communities. The *Ethnologue*, the most reliable count of the world's languages, lists 137 sign languages and acknowledges that this figure is likely to be inaccurate (Lewis *et al.* 2013) (see Woll *et al.* (2001) for a detailed discussion on the issue of counting the world's sign languages). Census figures describing the general population and the languages that they use are frequently controversial. Usually, such surveys cluster together people with hearing loss without differentiating between signing and non-signing deaf people or they do not ask census participants directly to specify if anyone uses a sign language at home. Official figures from deaf organizations are also questionable; while the World Federation of the Deaf (WFD) estimates there are 72 million deaf people worldwide (World Federation of the Deaf 2013b), it is unclear what this figure is based on. The lack of accurate and detailed longitudinal census surveys severely hinders our attempts to understand the distribution of sign languages in the world. Rather than attempt to quantify the number of the world's sign languages, we aim to describe instead how multilingualism is a fundamental characteristic of deaf communities in the world today. We do this with a look at the past (e.g., what are the factors that lead to a sign language community), the present (e.g., what is the status of these languages today? To what extent do they interact?), and the future (e.g., what changes in the near future are likely to have an effect on the use and distribution of sign languages around the world?).

What factors lead to a sign language community?

What are the general characteristics that contribute to a sign language community? Their emergence is typically spontaneous, independent (to a certain extent) of spoken languages and other sign languages, and often against a changing socio-political background. For ease of explanation, we group sign languages of the world into two broad categories (following Schembri 2010): sign language macro-communities and micro-communities (other terms that have been used to describe these communities include, for example, 'deaf community sign languages' and 'village sign languages' respectively, Padden 2011). Here, we explain the typical social and linguistic characteristics that make up these two communities.[1]

Macro-communities

Sign languages from macro-communities generally refer to sign languages used across nation states. These include, among others, languages such as Auslan, Brazilian Sign Language (LIBRAS, Língua Brasileira de Sinais), British Sign Language (BSL), French Sign Language (LSF, Langue des Signes Française), American Sign Language (ASL), and Japanese Sign Language (NS, Nihon Shuwa). This category may also apply to sign languages located in large urban centres such as Hong Kong Sign Language and Hausa Sign Language.

Sign languages in macro-communities are described as large stable signing communities that emerged from the European tradition, beginning in the late eighteenth century, of bringing deaf children together in residential schools. Although references to the use of signs date back to 1550 in Spain (Plann

---

[1] We do not consider other types of sign languages such as alternate sign systems used by hearing people when the use of speech is forbidden (e.g., the signing observed by Warlpiri Aboriginals, see Kendon 1988) or artificial sign systems created to assist learning (e.g., Cued Speech; see LaSasso, Crain, and Leybaert 2010), since they cannot be described as primary sign languages emerging from deaf communities (the focus of our chapter).

1997) and 1575 in Britain (Sutton-Spence and Woll 1999), linguists traditionally believe that the conditions provided by residential schools acted as a catalyst that led to the stabilization and widespread use of sign languages that we observe today (Schembri *et al.* 2010). Prior to this period, deaf people may have lived in isolated communities with little or no contact with other deaf people and any sign language in use was likely to be highly variable. This historical account means that the age of sign languages in macro-communities is often associated with the establishment of the first deaf school and, as such, are considered young languages when compared to most spoken languages.

The educational policy used in schools during this period varied across the world. Beginning in France and afterwards in other parts of Europe including Spain, Portugal, Sweden, and Italy, deaf children were taught using sign language as the medium of instruction (McBurney 2012). In contrast, the oral method, established at a deaf school in Leipzig, Germany, was subsequently adopted by other German-speaking countries as well as educators based in parts of Scandinavia and Italy (McBurney 2012). In the United Kingdom and Austria, it is believed that a combined system of sign and speech was in use (Dotter and Okorn 2003; Kyle and Woll 1985). Whatever the medium of instruction, sign languages were able to flourish as pupils continued to sign outside of the classroom. The Milan Congress in 1880 marked the widespread adoption of the oral method in deaf schools in many countries (McBurney 2012). As a result, the system of deaf education in the late nineteenth and early to mid twentieth century is typically known as the period where increasing emphasis was placed on the ability to speak. It was not until the mid to late twentieth century when sign languages were argued to be legitimate languages that they again began to occupy a credible role in deaf schools in many parts of the world.

But why should residential deaf schools play an important role in the origin of sign languages? This is because – typically in these macro-communities – only 5–10 per cent of deaf children, born to deaf signing parents, will acquire sign language in the home (Mitchell and Karchmer 2004). Most deaf children are born into hearing, non-signing families who may have never encountered a deaf person in their lifetime. This means that, for many deaf children, the process of language acquisition and transmission is very different to that seen in children learning to speak. Deaf schools therefore typically provide the first point of encounter of widespread sign language use for many deaf children.

In addition to deaf schools, deaf clubs have historically flourished within macro-communities. These clubs have organized political, cultural, and sporting events, providing space for deaf individuals to interact with each other. Together with deaf schools, deaf clubs are considered to play a crucial role in the establishment and maintenance of the concept of a 'deaf community' (Ladd 2003; Padden and Humphries 1988). Deaf individuals choosing to interact within the deaf community frequently pride themselves on being a part of a community which defines them as a member of a linguistic minority as opposed to one that defines them by their level of hearing.

It should not be assumed that all sign language users in macro-communities are deaf. Hearing people are also likely to use a sign language for a variety of reasons. They may be parents or siblings of a deaf child, or hearing children born to deaf parents. They may also be an individual who, later in life, has decided to learn sign language. In the United States, ASL is the fourth most popular language taught in universities (Furman, Goldberg, and Lusin 2010) which suggests a large population of second language hearing signers that may or may not be a part of the American Sign Language community. The degree to which these hearing signers use sign language everyday is likely to vary depending on their background and motivations for doing so (and also the degree to which it is available in colleges and universities throughout the nation). The crucial point here is that formal sign language instruction may be available within the nation states of these macro-communities. Instruction may be aimed simply at teaching a second language or for interpreter-training programmes with the aim of enabling access for deaf people to a variety of educational, legal, and medical services in their countries.

When we consider deaf signers living in macro-communities from the point of view of multilingualism, it is easy to see why all deaf signers can be considered multilingual. A very large proportion of deaf community members are born into homes that use a spoken language. These members may learn to sign at school but, even in school, there is usually some emphasis on the national spoken and written languages. For those individuals born to deaf signing parents, there will still be some degree of interaction with a spoken language from an early stage. In other words, these members contend with the fact they use a minority language that exists alongside a national spoken and written language(s) used by the overwhelming hearing majority. This fundamental fact means that sign language users in these communities are all at least bilingual by default.

To summarize, sign languages in macro-communities are transmitted primarily through peers at schools or are learned later in life. They are minority languages surrounded by majority-spoken languages, consist of both deaf and hearing signers, and are young languages. In the next section, we turn to sign languages arising in micro-communities.

Micro-communities

Sign language micro-communities are characterized as small labour-intensive economy-based communities, with a much higher incidence of deafness than that seen in developed countries and urban communities. These communities can be traced back centuries; for example, one of the earliest known communities was located on Martha's Vineyard off the east coast of the USA during the eighteenth century (Groce 1985). Individual sociocultural characteristics of these micro-communities determine the type of language transmission and their degree of stabilization. These sign languages may also be referred to as minority, indigenous, rural, shared and/or village sign languages (Nyst 2012; Zeshan and de Vos 2012).

It is unclear how many of these communities exist today or may have existed. Sign language research has uncovered many, such as those in Alipur, India (Panda 2012), on the island of Grand Cayman in the Caribbean (Washabaugh 1981), Chican, Mexico (Delgado 2012; Johnson 1994), Bedouin Arab communities in Israel (Kisch 2008; Sandler, Meir, Padden, and Aronoff 2005), Bali, Indonesia (Branson, Miller, and Marsaja 1996; de Vos 2012; Marsaja 2008), Adamorobe, Ghana (Kusters 2012; Nyst 2007), Ban Khor, Thailand (Nonaka 2011), Jewish Algerian immigrant communities in Israel (Lanesman and Meir 2012), Douentza, Mali (Nyst, Sylla, and Magassouba 2012), Konchri Sain, Jamaica (Cumberbatch 2012), Inuit communities in Canada (Schuit 2012), a Mardin village in Turkey (Dikyuva 2012), and the Yolngu community in Australia (Maypilama and Adone 2012). Nyst (2012) notes that no such communities are currently reported in Europe, although they may have existed in the past.

These communities are typically characterized as having a higher incidence of deafness than that observed in macro-communities (an incidence rate of 0.1% is typically reported for macro deaf communities, Martin *et al.* 1981; Woll, Sutton-Spence, and Elton 2001). For example, an incidence rate of 3.2% is observed among Bedouin Arabs in Al-Sayyid, Israel and 2% in the village of Desa Kolok, Indonesia (Nyst 2012). This incidence rate leads to a high number of deaf signers and hearing signers living in close proximity who are related by blood or marriage. This setting means, in contrast to macro-communities, that deaf children are much more likely to acquire a signed language from signing parents or from other extended family members and neighbours who can sign.

Given that these communities are characterized by a high degree of interaction between hearing and deaf signers, it is not surprising that these communities (like macro-communities) can be considered bilingual. However, a unique characteristic of these languages is that they can also be in contact with a more dominant sign language as deaf children in these communities are often taught at a school that uses the national sign language. The collected papers in Zeshan and de Vos (2012) show that minority sign language users are more likely to know another sign language used by the larger population. For example, in the Adamorobe, Ban Khor, Algerian Jewish, Al-Sayyid, Konchri Sain, Mardin, and Yolngu communities, some deaf signers are reported to also know the national sign languages of their respective countries. In rare cases, as in Bengkala, Bali, villagers may be taught using the sign language of the micro-community (de Vos 2012).

Another suggested difference between macro- and micro-communities lies in the notion of the deaf community. Some researchers argue that the construct of a deaf community only applies to macro-communities where deaf people are more marginalized from mainstream society compared to deaf people in micro-communities. It is reported that, in Bengkala, deaf villagers do not frequently encounter people who are unwilling or unable to communicate with them using sign language and are equally as likely to get married or enter into professional occupations as their hearing counterparts (de Vos 2012). In other words, being deaf and using a sign language is not viewed as a disadvantage as is often the case within macro-communities.

Clearly, as is the case for macro-communities, hearing signers constitute a part of the sign language community. Hearing villagers are frequently exposed to sign languages through their families and local community network and outnumber the number of deaf signers within the community. However, the ratio of hearing signers to deaf signers may be much higher within micro-communities (e.g., de Vos 2012) than that observed in macro-communities, although it must be remembered that accurate figures are often lacking for the latter. One crucial difference between the two communities is that there is no formal instruction for these languages (in contrast to macro-communities where formal instruction is provided to train interpreters). These sign languages also appear to be limited to members of the micro-community; except for Yolngu people, few white people who work in community services appear to have learned the signs of these communities (Maypilama and Adone 2012).

Many field linguists who work with indigenous spoken languages receive anecdotal reports about deaf people and/or communities who use sign languages which underscore the potential of a higher number of sign language micro-communities. We cannot know for sure how many of these sign languages exist in the world. However, it is clear they represent a group that differs from the sign languages of macro-communities, and provides an interesting line of enquiry for understanding multilingualism.

In sum, sign language micro-communities are small face-to-face communities characterized by a high incidence of deafness. These sign languages are transmitted primarily through families and may exist alongside other signed and spoken/written languages.

The sociolinguistic lives of sign languages: past and present

In the previous section, the factors that lead to two different types of sign language communities were described. However, our descriptions of sign languages so far have largely implied (particularly for macro-communities) that these languages are quite independent from one another and, as a result, we have not really begun to account for the linguistic diversity that exists in sign language communities. In this section, we describe further the sociolinguistic circumstances of these sign languages and the extent to which the world's sign languages have interacted with one another. Furthermore, we also outline the multilingual environments that can exist *within* these communities.

Sign language and education

Just as we can speak of language families when referring to spoken languages, we can also do so for sign languages. We should not, however, assume that the familial relationship between sign languages closely mirror that of spoken languages. While ASL is used in the USA and English-speaking parts of Canada, it is unrelated to the variety of signing used in other predominantly English-speaking countries such as the United Kingdom, Ireland, New Zealand, and Australia. Few, however, have tried to develop descriptions that outline such relationships on a large scale (although see Woll *et al.* 2001, for a description of one such attempt by Anderson 1979). Our understanding of how the world's sign languages are related stem from lexico-statistical studies (although very few have been conducted) that compare the lexicon of two sign languages to determine the extent to which they overlap. Woodward examined the lexicons of ASL and LSF and found a high similarity score confirming that the two are indeed related (1978). Lexico-statistical studies comparing BSL, Auslan, and New Zealand Sign Language (NZSL) have suggested that the three should be considered dialects of a single language termed BANZSL (Johnston 2003). In some cases, these lexico-statistical studies have led linguists to speculate about the multilingual environments that may have existed. For example, Woodward (1978) suggests that modern ASL was derived by a process of creolization between LSF and the indigenous sign language in use in the USA in the early nineteenth century, although little is known about what this indigenous variety may have looked like.

But why are these sign languages related? Why does LSF relate to modern-day ASL? The answer to this question comes from each country's educational history. The first deaf school in the USA was the American School for the Deaf in Hartford, Connecticut, established in 1817. Thomas Hopkins Gallaudet, a private tutor seeking instruction in how to teach his deaf student to read, travelled to Paris to visit a deaf school and brought back to Hartford a deaf LSF signer, Laurent Clerc, who then had a profound influence on the creation of the curriculum and the training of deaf teachers (Lane 1984). In Australia, two deaf schools were established in Melbourne and Sydney in 1860 by deaf men from London and Edinburgh respectively who brought with them signs used in the United Kingdom. Furthermore, the history of signing in New Zealand schools for the deaf is associated with both the UK and Australia which explains why the three languages are considered to be closely related today (Johnston and Schembri 2007). German Sign Language, Austrian Sign Language, and Hungarian Sign Language are closely related as their respective countries were all once part of the Hapsburg Empire; teachers of the deaf trained in Germany had considerable influence on the sign languages used throughout the empire (McCagg 1993). Modern-day Irish Sign Language (ISL) is considered to be related to LSF following the establishment of Catholic deaf institutions which taught deaf children using an adapted version of the French signing system in the early nineteenth century (Leeson and Saeed 2012; Matthews 1996). This marked a shift away from the sign language used in Protestant schools which is believed to have been similar to BSL (Leeson and Saeed 2012; Matthews 1996).

The impact of a foreign sign language on indigenous languages when introduced via their education system can be seen within developing nations that were in receipt of foreign aid programmes designed to support deaf education. For example, in the mid-twentieth century, Andrew Foster, a deaf African-American, founded a number of deaf schools in French-speaking countries in Africa using ASL as the language of instruction (Lane, Hoffmeister, and Bahan 1996) which subsequently led to the development of an ASL-based creole sign language variety replacing the indigenous variety. Since then, several foreign sign languages have been introduced to sign language communities via foreign aid programmes. Such cases can be perceived as an example of linguistic imperialism involving sign languages (Phillipson 2012). Table 2.1 (from Schmaling 2003) provides an overview of the foreign sign languages that have been imported to six African countries. Although many sign languages of macro-communities (particularly those from Western countries) continue to exert an influence on other sign languages in this way, ASL appears to be the most frequent example.

Table 2.1 *An overview of foreign sign languages introduced to signing communities in Africa*

Country	Sign language
Botswana	American SL, Danish SL, German SL
Ethiopia	Swedish SL, Finnish SL, American SL
Gambia	Dutch SL, British SL
Mali	American SL, French SL
Nigeria	American SL
Tanzania	American SL, Swedish SL, Finnish SL

The impact of a foreign sign language on the indigenous variety can be illustrated using lexico-statistical studies. Woodward (2011) describes two such studies: one comparing three sign language varieties in Costa Rica with ASL and another comparing three sign language varieties in Thailand with ASL. In each study, it is suggested that the modern variety in current use has moved further away from the original sign languages used in each country and is highly cognate with ASL (e.g., 52% of signs in Modern Thai Sign Language' basic vocabulary are cognate with ASL, while only 26–29% are cognate with the original sign languages). Woodward (2011) states that this scenario is likely to be true for other sign languages used in the Philippines, Malaysia, Singapore, Laos, and may well be a general characteristic of sign languages in some Asian and Latin American countries. However, research also shows that these communities will maintain culturally specific vocabulary (e.g., words for food and drink, clothes, plants and trees, crafts, and religious terms) as imported sign languages often do not have signs for them (Schmaling 2003). Even when a foreign sign language is not deliberately introduced into schools in other countries, the presence of a signer from abroad can influence the indigenous variety. For example, in Nicaragua, the presence of foreign deaf and hearing researchers and visitors has resulted in deaf Nicaraguans borrowing signs from other sign languages (Senghas 2003).

Importantly, the education histories of each nation state demonstrate that the use of sign languages in education can be multilingual in nature since deaf children in these communities can experience contact with foreign sign languages when introduced as the medium of instruction. Changes in education policy, such as that witnessed in Ireland, would have led to further multilingual contexts. The sign language in use before the shift towards the education policy of the Catholic institutions would have existed alongside a new emerging variety (see above) and the two would have interacted with one another to a certain extent. It is clear then that deaf schools and their educational histories provide an important insight into how the world's sign languages have inter-acted and the type of multilingual environments that may have existed.

Sign language, geography, and politics

When we consider the world's sign languages, one must also acknowledge geopolitical boundaries and the effect that they have on the categorization and distribution of the world's languages. Politically, we continue to refer to BSL, Auslan, and NZSL as three separate varieties despite claims from lexico-statistical studies suggesting they are in fact dialects of one language. Similarly, the sign language varieties in India and Pakistan have been labelled as Indian Sign Language and Pakistani Sign Language (Vasishta, Woodward, and Wilson 1978; Zeshan 2000) although the variety used in India is very similar to the one in Pakistan (and sometimes called Indo-Pakistani Sign Language as a result). Crucially, the deaf community that resides within each country recognizes that the language that they use forms an important part of their national identity.

However, many countries have not formally recognized sign languages as official and/or minority languages (although it should be noted that not all countries adopt the practice of giving languages an official status, e.g., USA). In 1995, Uganda was the first country to recognize a sign language, Ugandan Sign Language, as an official language (World Federation of the Deaf 2013b); and other countries such as Austria, Brazil, Finland, New Zealand, and Portugal have also conferred constitutional recognition on their sign languages (de Quadros 2012; McKee 2011; Wheatley and Pabsch 2012). Elsewhere, in countries such as Norway, sign languages are recognized as languages used in deaf education (Wheatley and Pabsch 2012). Most countries however (e.g., Bulgaria, Luxembourg, Malta, Italy, and China), continue not to formally recognize sign languages as official national sign languages (Wheatley and Pabsch 2012; Yang 2011). The legal recognition of sign languages often plays an important role in terms of securing governmental funding for deaf education, interpreting, employment, linguistic and cultural resources, and other services. In other words, it can have an impact on the extent to which a sign language is used throughout a nation.

A changing geopolitical landscape can also lead to the creation of new multilingual environments involving sign languages. This is the case with Israeli Sign Language (ISL), which is a hybrid of several sign languages due to immigrants who settled in Palestine from Germany, Hungary, Russia, and other central European countries (Meir and Sandler 2008; Namir, Sella, Rimor, and Schlesinger 1979). Some dialects of Taiwanese Sign Language are said to be very similar to NS as a result of the Japanese occupation of Taiwan, although a high number of Chinese immigrants in later years has led to another variety described to be similar to the sign language used in Shanghai (Ann 1998). The years of the British Empire saw many deaf children from countries such as India, Malta, and South Africa being educated in the United Kingdom and the subsequent influence of BSL within their communities once these children returned home (Woll 2006). These cases all illustrate how, like spoken languages, sign languages can travel considerable distances and are often not confined within a single nation.

So far, this chapter has described the world's sign languages by referring to a single national sign language within each country. However, this idea contradicts the fact presented at the beginning of this chapter: that there is no one-to-one correspondence between the number of recognized nations and the number of languages. Here also, sign languages are no exception. Woodward (2011) lists three sign languages that are used in Vietnam today: Ho Chi Minh

City Sign Language, Ha Noi Sign Language, and Hai Phong Sign Language. In Switzerland, three sign languages are noted to be in use: Swiss German Sign language, Swiss French Sign Language, and Swiss Italian Sign Language (Boyes-Braem and Rathmann 2010). Similarly, there are two distinct sign languages in Belgium that are associated with the Flemish-speaking and French-speaking community (Sáfár *et al*. in press). Countries such as Belgium, Switzerland, and Vietnam highlight that the sign language community is not a homogeneous one. It is possible to see varieties used throughout the community that can be recognized as distinct in some way (although detailed lexico-statistical studies comparing these varieties may yet have to be conducted). In the following section, we describe some of the other varieties that can be observed within a single nation.

Multilingual settings within these communities

The division between sign languages varieties within a single nation may sometimes reflect similar divisions between speech communities in the same nation. However, we can also observe sign languages varieties that are independent of spoken language communities. These varieties can occur on a much smaller scale: they may be observed within an individual household (such as is the case for households using more than one sign language) or within a larger number of individuals (e.g., within a geographical region consisting of a centralized deaf school). In some cases, not much is known about these varieties, as they have yet to be to subject to serious inquiry.

One such variety is a *home sign system*. Home sign systems refer to signed communication used by families within the home. As they are confined to a single family or household, they are thought to be highly variable across groups and are not traditionally considered to be fully-fledged languages (Goldin-Meadow 2012). Deaf children who use home sign systems are likely to replace them with national sign languages if they go on to attend a deaf school. It is often suggested that sign languages in macro-communities are likely descended from home sign systems which combined with other home signs systems as well as the sign language used by deaf schools to form the national languages we see today (Johnston and Schembri 2007). This variety of sign language is typically understudied; researchers are still learning how families maintain their individual systems over time and the extent to which signers may use them in the wider community.

Many of the world's sign languages are reported to have a number of regional varieties such as those in the United Kingdom (Stamp *et al*., accepted), the Netherlands (Schermer 2004) and Australia (Johnston and Schembri 2007). These varieties are thought to be intimately associated with the location of deaf schools. For example, the geographical locations of each of the five regional varieties identified in Sign Language of the Netherlands (NGT, Nederlandse Gebarentaal) also serve as the location of a deaf residential school (Schermer 2004). However, the existence of several deaf schools within a nation does not always presuppose the existence of several regional varieties. The lexicon of ASL is reported to be comparatively more uniform (particularly in key areas of the lexicon, e.g., numbers) which is attributed to a central training program for deaf teachers originating from the first deaf school in Hartford (Lucas, Bayley, and Valli 2001).

The fact that schools play a pivotal role in the creation of these varieties can be seen in countries with a history of educational segregation. In Dublin, Ireland, deaf boys and girls were taught at two separate schools which led to the existence of two gender variants (observed at the lexical level) of ISL situated within the same city (Leeson and Saeed 2012). These varieties were used into adulthood, although the women tended to adopt the male variants upon leaving school. A long period of racial segregation in deaf schools (as well as deaf clubs) in the USA has led to a variety of ASL termed 'Black ASL' which is said to be phonologically, lexically, and syntactically distinct from the ASL variety used by white signers (McCaskill, Lucas, Bayley, and Hill 2011). These varieties may be mutually intelligible but questions remain about the extent to which they should be recognized as distinct from one another.

As sign languages are minority languages surrounded by majority-spoken languages (this is the case for both macro- and micro-communities), they cannot always be said to be completely autonomous from spoken languages. As a consequence, language contact takes place with spoken language being mixed to various extents with sign languages. These varieties of sign language have been described as 'contact signing' in which signers borrow words from the surrounding spoken language through fingerspelling and mouthing (Lucas and Valli 1992) and structure their discourse in a way as to resemble the grammar of the spoken language (see Chapter 3, this volume for a detailed description of contact signing). The use of contact signing is said to exist on a continuum with some signers exhibiting features typical of contact signing to a greater extent than other signers. The extent to which they do so may be underlined by various social factors as well as the degree to which they interact with the hearing speaking community. Although signers vary in how much they display features of contact signing, it is arguably true that it is this aspect of multilingualism that is strongly characteristic of deaf communities worldwide.

Deaf people are also likely to interact with one another on an international scale for a variety of reasons. The deaf community has a long tradition of holding international events for sports (the Deaflympics were established in 1924), leisure, and politics (Haualand 2007; Murray 2009) which are likely to have led to continued interaction between the world's deaf communities. In other cases, deaf adults or families might choose to move to another country for educational, economic, or personal reasons and therefore will be likely to learn a new national sign language together with the surrounding spoken/written languages. Despite no formal studies tracking the movements of deaf people globally, anecdotal reports from the deaf community suggests that there is an international mix of signers in many of the world's major cities and consequently, a range of rich multilingual environments that have yet to be investigated.

One outcome of deaf people meeting one another across borders is a variety of sign language known as *foreigner talk*, which occurs when native signers simplify their language input in order to accommodate others who are not fluent (Ferguson 1981). This type of interaction may also be observed when a deaf person communicates with hearing people learning to sign. Another type of foreigner talk is known as International Sign (IS) which is observed among signers attending international events and is described as a 'flexible and highly context-dependent form of communication' (Hiddinga and Crasborn 2011; Rosenstock 2004) (see Chapter 3, this volume for a description of IS). To date, there are no formal studies examining modifications of linguistic features made by native signers when signing with second language learners and much of the research conducted on IS is in the early stages.

In some cases, the interaction of deaf people across borders may lead to the intermarriage of deaf individuals creating new multilingual environments involving sign languages. Although there is scarce information about multilingual deaf families where more than one sign language is used at home, there is evidence to suggest that they do exist. A recent WFD newsletter (World Federation of the Deaf 2013a) ran a report on a young deaf boy from Belgium whose parents are both deaf. As his father is British, the young boy is exposed to both British Sign Language and Flemish Sign Language (Vlaamse Gebarentaal, VGT) regularly at home. Reports like this indicate that multilingual households may well exist within the deaf community the world over but, as they have yet to be subject to serious inquiry, we can only guess the extent to which they are prevalent.

Deaf schools today in developed nations are also likely to feature a range of signers from different ethnic, cultural, and language backgrounds as a consequence of immigration. Studies in Australia, Germany, Slovakia, the UK, and the USA have reported that at least 20 per cent of children in deaf schools are from migrant/minority language backgrounds (Willoughby 2012). Hispanics (from the Caribbean, Central America, and Mexico) are the fastest growing minority in the American education system for deaf and hard-of-hearing students, representing more than 16 per cent of the national deaf student population (Gerner de Garcia 1995). Deaf children in these cases are likely to be exposed to a variety of languages (spoken, written, and signed) whether at home or at school. In some cases, these deaf children may come from families who do not speak the language of their new environment, and will therefore learn to mediate the differing multilingual environments they find themselves in. We do not yet fully understand this aspect of multilingualism or the varieties of signing that may emerge in such contexts but more research is necessary as studies suggest that this is increasingly becoming the norm (Gallaudet Research Institute 2008).

Multilingual environments involving sign languages may also be thriving due to an explosion in affordable, accessible technology. While older telecommunication devices required deaf people to use written languages to communicate with deaf and hearing people, today, deaf people are using both text-based and visual forms of communication (e.g., texting, emailing, social networking, and videoconferencing). Together with the internet, deaf people's social networks and activity space are rapidly being scaled up to international levels (Valentine and Skelton, 2008) and this, as a consequence, leads to an increase in the number of multilingual environments (perhaps involving more than one sign language). For example, videoconferencing software often allows for an elaborate set-up in which signed and written languages (e.g., PowerPoint slides) are mixed together in a single discourse space. Visual forms of communication, however, are not always favoured over text-based forms; text messaging continues to be a popular form of communication among young deaf people in Japan despite the availability of visual communication devices (Okuyama and Iwai 2011). There have been few studies documenting the type of multilingual environments that can be observed as a consequence of technology and how languages involved in these environments are negotiated. However, its effect on sign production (Keating, Edwards, and Mirus 2008) and its role in the loss of regional variants within a national community (Stamp et al., accepted) have been noted. Technology, therefore, has a clear potential to impact on language use and mediate communication practices across the world's sign languages.

Looking to the future: factors that impact upon multilingualism

We have considered many multilingual situations that exist within deaf communities today. Here, we begin to look to the future and wonder what lies ahead for sign languages. As sign languages used by macro- and micro-communities are described as minority languages surrounded by majority-spoken languages, they are often said to be under threat of endangerment or extinction (Johnston 2004; Nonaka 2004). In this section, we outline the factors that contribute to a sign language's endangered status; these factors can be different for macro- and micro-communities.

Generally, language endangerment is characterized as a reduction in the number of users of a given language and the number of settings where it is used (UNESCO 2003). In turn, this reduction has the effect of interrupting intergenerational transmission so that the language in question is not passed onto children of the next generation. Earlier, we described how sign languages used in macro-communities are different since deaf schools have historically served as sites of transmission for the majority of the signing population. For many countries today, the future of large centralized deaf schools is in doubt with an increasing number of deaf children entering mainstream school following vast improvements in assistive hearing technology. This has been noted in Switzerland (Boyes-Braem and Rathmann 2010), Australia (Johnston 2004), Denmark (Bergman and Engberg-Pederson 2010), the Netherlands (Boyes-Braem and Rathmann 2010) and is likely typical of other macro-communities around the world. This educational trend is likely to lead to language shift (i.e., when speakers of a given language begin to favour another language) where increasing numbers of deaf people begin to use a spoken language instead. Given the role that deaf schools play in intergenerational transmission, and the importance that linguists place on intergenerational transmission as a form of language maintenance (i.e., ensuring the continued use of a language through the community) (Potowski 2013), the decline of deaf schools is likely to disrupt this transmission pattern and lead to a reduction in the number of sign language users in future.

Medical and technological advancements in the last thirty years have led to improvements in hearing aid technology and an increase in the number of deaf children receiving a cochlear implant. For example, in Switzerland, approximately 80 per cent of deaf infants received a cochlear implant in 2006 with many of them being implanted as early as 13 months of age (Boyes-Braem and Rathmann 2010). Families of children receiving a cochlear implant are also likely to be discouraged from using sign language by medical officials. This recent increase in the number of children receiving cochlear implants can be seen in most macro-communities within developed countries (countries are likely to vary according to the wealth of a nation and the extent to which public health care is available). Further advancements in the field of medicine are also likely to have an effect on the rate of childhood deafness. Johnston (2004) tracks a decline in the rate of deafness in the 1980s in Australia following the introduction of a rubella vaccination and similar patterns are likely to be observed in other countries where the MMR (measles, mumps, and rubella) vaccine is routinely administered. Future medical intervention, including advances in genetic screening, are also likely to lead to a reduction in the number of deaf children being born. Within macro-communities, these factors are all likely to further contribute to a declining sign language population.

The factors that are likely to lead to language endangerment in micro-communities can be different. Changes in educational and marital practices and employment opportunities are known to affect the social and linguistic dynamics of these communities. Language contact with national sign languages in schools may lead to language shift in favour of these national sign languages, or, like in macro-communities, spoken languages. Language shift may also emerge when deaf people migrate outside of their communities in search of employment opportunities. In the Al-Sayyid Bedouin community in Israel, Kisch (2012) describes how deaf men who sign ABSL are now using ISL for work. Deaf people may also marry outside of their communities as they seek deaf partners who share similar linguistic and cultural identities instead of hearing partners within their communities. Exogamous marriage (i.e., marrying outside of the community) may not only lead to language contact but a decrease in incidence of deafness within these micro-communities (Kisch 2012) There may also be external pressures from above to adopt other languages. For example, the provision of government funded interpreting services often depends on economical feasibility and practicality; based on these criteria, sign languages of micro-communities are unlikely to be well catered for. Nonaka (2012) describes how the Ban Khor community in Thailand is marginalized as its members are expected to learn other languages in order to function in various activities (e.g., business and education). These factors are all likely to lead to language shift and these languages being classified as endangered.

As hearing signers form a substantial part of the signing community in micro-communities, an interesting case of language maintenance emerges. In these communities, hearing signers may be viewed as the 'gatekeeper' of their sign language as they ensure its continued use for future generations. In other words, they are less likely to be exposed to more dominant sign languages in educational settings (unlike their deaf counterparts) and therefore may not be as subject to the effects of language contact. In contrast, deaf signers in macro-communities demonstrate language maintenance in different ways: through the introduction of standardized language instruction, frequent social events, and providing familial mentoring in sign language (e.g., the New Mexico School for the Deaf in the USA sends deaf role models to visit families at home to provide signing environments for deaf children). Advances in technology may also act as a platform for language maintenance in sign language communities as the internet is described as a forum that invites and promotes linguistic creativity and flexibility (Crystal 2001). One example of this can be seen in the creation of BSL Zone, an online channel offering a wide range of programmes in BSL made by deaf people and for deaf people (British Sign Language Broadcasting Trust 2014). However, there is much to be learnt with regard to language maintenance (e.g., how do sign languages maintain their resiliency during precarious periods in their history?) and the factors surrounding sign language endangerment.

Sign language and multilingualism: future research

This chapter has demonstrated that deaf sign language users can be considered multilingual since they use a variety of signed, spoken, and written languages. Descriptions of deaf communities worldwide have illustrated that multilingualism is prevalent and is driven by socio-cultural, political, occupational, ideological, and educational pressures. However, multilingualism in signing communities (particularly where a signer may know two sign languages) remains poorly examined. There is limited knowledge about how deaf signers manage different linguistic environments and the extent to which these patterns resemble non-signing bilinguals. For example, how might multilingual households mediate between more than one sign language, and to what extent might this parallel multilingual households involving spoken languages? Additionally, how might the impact of a foreign sign language introduced within a developing country's education system differ from similar circumstances involving spoken languages? Is the change we observe here quicker for signed than spoken languages because the number of signers is typically fewer than their hearing counterparts? The variety of multilingual contexts in which we observe sign languages may also provide an interesting point of enquiry that may be unique to sign languages. For example, although the use of two sign languages are associated with two different speech communities in Belgium, they are observed to have overlapping lexicons which are differentiated only by the mouthed components of their surrounding speech community (Sáfár *et al.* in press). Situations like these allow us to investigate the degree to which divisions within a nation may also manifest themselves in the corresponding sign languages. Other lines of enquiries may investigate the extent to which contact signing is distinct from what is considered to be 'the norm' as this has yet to be subjected to rigorous analysis in many sign languages – although communities clearly recognize varieties with a high degree of contact as separate from the language of the deaf community (e.g., Benenz 2003; Schmaling 2003). Technology also provides many avenues for future research. One may wonder what happens when signers of two distinct languages communicate via videoconferencing? If both parties are familiar with both sign languages, then which language do they choose and what are the reasons that drive them to choose the given language? Do we see power imbalance among different types of language dyads?

It is clear that there remains much to be uncovered in order to understand the various multilingual contexts that characterize sign language communities and the extent to which they mirror spoken language communities. It is likely that the current trend of globalization will provide an even more fertile ground for deaf people to engage with linguistic communities near and far. It also remains to be seen the impact that changing educational practices and medical advancements may have on the deaf community and the vitality of these languages. What is important is that our perspective and understanding of multilingualism should always allow for a much broader scope that encompasses all hearing and deaf global citizens.

REFERENCES

Anderson, L. (1979) A comparison of some American, British, Australian and Swedish Signs: Evidence on historical changes in signs and some family relationships of sign languages. Paper presented at the First International Symposium on Sign Language, Stockholm, Sweden.

Ann, J. (1998) Contact between a sign language and a written language: Character signs in Taiwan Sign Language. In C. Lucas (ed.), *Pinky Extension and Eye Gaze: Language Use in Deaf Communities* (pp. 59–99). Washington, DC: Gallaudet University Press.

Benenz, N. (2003) Surdos Veceremos: The rise of the Brazilian Deaf community. In L. Monaghan, C. Schmaling, K. Nakamura, and G. Turner (eds.), *Many Ways to Be Deaf: International Variation in Deaf Communities* (pp. 173–193). Washington, DC: Gallaudet University Press.

Bergman, B. and Engberg-Pederson, E. (2010) Transmission of sign languages in the Nordic countries. In D. Brentari (ed.), *Sign Language*. Cambridge: Cambridge University Press.

Bloomfield, L. (1933) *Language*. London: George Allen and Unwin.

Boyes-Braem, P. and Rathmann, C. (eds.) (2010) *Transmission of Sign Languages in Northern Europe*. Cambridge: Cambridge University Press.

Branson, J., Miller, D., and Marsaja, I. G. (1996) Everyone here speaks sign language too: A deaf village in Bali, Indonesia. In C. Lucas (ed.), *Multicultural Aspects of Sociolinguistics in Deaf Communities* (pp. 39–57). Washington, DC: Gallaudet University Press.

British Sign Language Broadcasting Trust (2014) BSL Zone.

Crystal, D. (2001) *Language and the Internet*. Cambridge: Cambridge University Press.

Cumberbatch, K. (2012) Sociolinguistic sketch of Konchri Sain. In U. Zeshan and C. de Vos (eds.), *Sign Languages in Village Communities: Anthropological and Linguistic Insights* (pp. 387–388). Nijmegen: Ishara Press.

de Quadros, R. M. (2012) Linguistics policies, linguistic planning, and Brazilian Sign Language in Brazil. *Sign Language Studies*, 12(4): 543–564.

de Vos, C. (2012) *Sign–spatiality in Kata Kolok: How a village sign language of Bali inscribes its signing space*, Ph.D. dissertation, Max Planck Institute for Psycholinguistics, Nijmegen.

Delgado, C. E. E. (2012) Chican Sign Language: A sociolinguistic sketch. In U. Zeshan and C. de Vos (eds.), *Sign Languages in Village Communities: Anthropological and Linguistic Insights* (pp. 377–380). Nijmegen: Ishara Press.

Dikyuva, H. (2012) Mardin Sign Language: Signing in a 'deaf family'. In U. Zeshan and C. de Vos (eds.), *Sign Languages in Village Communities: Anthropological and Linguistic Insights* (pp. 395–400). Nijmegen: Ishara Press.

Dotter, F. and Okorn, I. (2003) Austria's hidden conflict: Hearing culture versus deaf culture. In L. Monaghan, C. Schmaling, K. Nakamura, and G. Turner (eds.), *Many Ways to Be Deaf: International Variation in Deaf Communities* (pp. 49–66). Washington, DC: Gallaudet University Press.

Edwards, J. (1994) *Multilingualism*. London: Routledge.

Emmorey, K. (2002) *Language, Cognition, and the Brain: Insights from Sign Language Research*. Mahwah, NJ: Lawrence Erlbaum.

Ferguson, C. (1981) 'Foreigner talk' as the name of a simplified register. *International Journal of the Sociology of Language*, 28: 9–18.

Furman, N., Goldberg, D., and Lusin, N. (2010) *Enrollments in Languages other than English in United States Institutions of Higher Education, Fall 2009*. New York: Modern Language Association of America. www.mla.org/pdf/2009_enrollment_survey.pdf

Gallaudet Research Institute (2008) *Regional and National Summary Report of Data from the 2007–08 Annual Survey of Deaf and Hard of Hearing Children and Youth*. Washington, DC: Gallaudet University Press.

Gerner de Garcia, B. A. (1995) ESL applications for Hispanic deaf students. *Bilingual Research Journal*, 19(3–4): 453–467.

Goldin-Meadow, S. (2012) Homesign: Gesture to language. In R. Pfau, M. Steinbach, and B. Woll (eds.), *Sign Language: An International Handbook* (pp. 601–625). Berlin: De Gruyter Mouton.

Groce, N. (1985) *Everyone Here Spoke Sign Language*. Cambridge, MA: Harvard University Press.

Haualand, H. (2007) The two-week village: The significance of sacred occasions for the Deaf community. In B. Ingstad and S. R. Whyte (eds.), *Disability in Local and Global Worlds* (pp. 33–55). Berkeley, CA: University of California Press.

Hiddinga, A. and Crasborn, O. (2011) Signed languages and globalization. *Language in Society*, 40: 483–505.

Johnson, R. E. (1994) Sign language and the concept of deafness in a traditional Yucatec Mayan village. In C. Erting, R. E. Johnson, D. Smith, and B. Snider (eds.), *The Deaf Way: Perspectives from the International Conference on Deaf Culture* (pp. 102–109). Washington, DC: Gallaudet University Press.

Johnston, T. (2003) BSL, Auslan and NZSL: Three signed languages or one? In A. Baker, B. van den Bogaerde, and O. Crasborn (eds.), *Cross-Linguistic Perspectives in Sign Language Research: Selected papers from TISLR 2000* (pp. 47–69). Hamburg: Signum Verlag.

(2004) W(h)ither the Deaf community? Population, genetics and the future of Australian Sign Language. *American Annals of the Deaf*, 148(5): 358–375.

Johnston, T. and Schembri, A. (2007) *Australian Sign Language: An Introduction to Sign Language Linguistics*. Cambridge: Cambridge University Press.

(2013) Corpus analysis of sign languages. In C. A. Chapelle (ed.), *Encyclopedia of Applied Linguistics* (pp. 1312–1319). Wiley-Blackwell.

Keating, E., Edwards, T., and Mirus, G. (2008) Cybersign: Impacts of new communication technologies on space and language. *Journal of Pragmatics*, 40(6): 1067–1081.

Kendon, A. (1988) *Sign Languages of Aboriginal Australia: Cultural, Semiotic and Communicative Perspectives*. Cambridge: Cambridge University Press.

Kisch, S. (2008) Deaf discourse: The social construction of deafness in a Bedouin community. *Medical Anthropology*, 27(3): 283–313.
  (2012) Demarcating generations of signers in the dynamic sociolinguistic landscape of a shared sign language: The case of the Al-Sayyid Bedouin. In U. Zeshan and C. de Vos (eds.), *Sign Languages in Village Communities: Anthropological and Linguistic Insights* (pp. 87–126). Nijmegen: Ishara Press.
Kusters, A. (2012) *Since time immemorial until the end of days: An ethnographic study of the production of Deaf space in Adamorobe*, Ph.D., University of Bristol, UK.
Kyle, J. and Woll, B. (1985) *Sign Language: The Study of Deaf People and Their Language*. Cambridge University Press.
Ladd, P. (2003) *Understanding Deaf Culture: In Search of Deafhood*. Clevedon, UK: Multilingual Matters.
Lane, H. (1984) *When the Mind Hears: A History of the Deaf*. New York: Random House.
Lane, H., Hoffmeister, R., and Bahan, B. (1996) *A Journey into the Deaf World*. San Diego: Dawn Sign Press.
Lanesman, S. and Meir, I. (2012) The survival of Algerian Jewish Sign Language alongside Israeli Sign Language in Israel. In U. Zeshan and C. de Vos (eds.), *Sign Languages in Village Communities: Anthropological and Linguistic Insights* (pp. 153–180). Nijmegen: Ishara Press.
LaSasso, C. J., Crain, K. L., and Leybaert, J. (eds.) (2010) *Cued Speech and Cued Language for Deaf and Hard of Hearing Children*. San Diego, CA: Plural Publishing.
Leeson, L. and Saeed, J. I. (2012) *Irish Sign Language*. Edinburgh: Edinburgh University Press.
Lewis, P. M., Simons, G. F., and Fennig, C. D. (2013) *Ethnologue: Languages of the World*. www.ethnologue.com
Lucas, C., Bayley, R., and Valli, C. (2001) *Sociolinguistic Variation in American Sign Language* (vol. VII). Washington, DC: Gallaudet University Press.
Lucas, C. and Valli, C. (1992) *Language Contact in the American Deaf Community*. San Diego, CA: Academic Press.
McBurney, S. (2012) History of sign languages and sign language linguistics. In R. Pfau, M. Steinbach, and B. Woll (eds.), *Sign Language: An International Handbook* (pp. 909–948). Berlin: Mouton de Gruyter.
McCagg, W. (1993) Some problems in the history of Deaf Hungarians. In J. V. van Cleve (ed.), *Deaf History Unveiled* (pp. 252–271). Washington, DC: Gallaudet University Press.
McCaskill, C., Lucas, C., Bayley, R., and Hill, J. (2011) *The Hidden Treasure of Black ASL: Its History and Structure*. Washington, DC: Gallaudet University Press.
McKee, R. (2011) Action pending: Four years on from the New Zealand Sign Language Act 2006. *Victoria University of Wellington Law Review*, 42(2): 277–297.
Marsaja, I. G. (2008) *Desa Kolok: A Deaf Village and Its Sign Language in Bali, Indonesia*. Nijmegen: Ishara Press.
Martin, J. A. M., Bentzen, O., Colley, J. R., Hennebert, D., Holm, C., Iurato, S., Morgon, A. (1981) Childhood deafness in the European community. *Scandinavian Audiology*, 10: 165–174.
Matthews, P. (1996) *The Irish Deaf Community: Survey Report, History of Education, Language and Culture* (vol. I). Dublin: Linguistic Institute of Ireland.

Maypilama, E. and Adone, D. (2012) Yolngu Sign Language: A sociolinguistic profile. In U. Zeshan and C. de Vos (eds.), *Sign Languages in Village Communities: Anthropological and Linguistic Insights* (pp. 401–404). Nijmegen: Ishara Press.

Meir, I. and Sandler, W. (2008) *A Language in Space: The Story of Israeli Sign Language*. New York: Lawrence Erlbaum.

Mitchell, R. E. and Karchmer, M. A. (2004) Chasing the mythical ten percent: parental hearing status of deaf and hard of hearing students in the United States. *Sign Language Studies*, 4(2): 138–163.

Murray, J. (2009) Sign languages. In Pierre-Yves (ed.), *The Palgrave Dictionary of Transnational History* (pp. 947–948). Basingstoke, UK: Palgrave Macmillan.

Namir, L., Sella, I., Rimor, M., and Schlesinger, I. M. (1979) *Dictionary of Sign Language of the Deaf in Israel*. Jerusalem: Ministry of Social Welfare.

Nonaka, A. M. (2004) Sign languages – the forgotten endangered languages: lessons on the importance of remembering. *Language in Society*, 33(5): 737–767.

(2011) Interrogatives in Ban Khor Sign Language: A preliminary description. In G. Mathur and D. J. Napoli (eds.), *Deaf Around the World* (pp. 194–220). New York: Oxford University Press.

(2012) Language ecological change in Ban Khor, Thailand: An ethnographic case study of village sign language endangerment. In U. Zeshan and C. de Vos (eds.), *Sign Languages in Village Communities: Anthropological and Linguistic Insights* (pp. 277–312). Nijmegen: Ishara Press.

Nyst, V. (2007) *A Descriptive Analysis of Adamorobe Sign Language (Ghana)*. (Ph.D.), University of Amsterdam, Utrecht.

(2012) Shared sign languages. In R. Pfau, M. Steinbach, and B. Woll (eds.), *Sign Language: An International Handbook* (pp. 552–574). Berlin: Mouton de Gruyter.

Nyst, V., Sylla, K., and Magassouba, M. (2012) Deaf signers in Douentza, a rural area in Mali. In U. Zeshan and C. de Vos (eds.), *Sign Languages in Village Communities: Anthropological and Linguistic Insights* (pp. 277–312). Nijmegen: Ishara Press.

Okuyama, Y. and Iwai, M. (2011) Use of text messaging by deaf adolescents in Japan. *Sign Language Studies*, 11(3): 375–407.

Padden, C. (2011) Sign language geography. In G. Mathur and D. J. Napoli (eds.), *Deaf Around the World* (pp. 19–37). New York: Oxford University Press.

Padden, C. and Humphries, T. (1988) *Deaf in America*. Cambridge, MA: Harvard University Press.

Panda, S. (2012) Alipur Sign Language: A sociolinguistic and cultural profile. In U. Zeshan and C. de Vos (eds.), *Sign Languages in Village Communities: Anthropological and Linguistic Insights* (pp. 353–360). Nijmegen: Ishara Press.

Phillipson, R. (2012) English: From British empire to corporate empire. *Sociolinguistics Studies*, 5(3): 441–464.

Plann, S. (1997) *A Silent Minority: Deaf Education in Spain, 1550–1835*. Berkeley, CA: University of California Press.

Potowski, K. (2013) Language maintenance and shift. In R. Bayley, R. Cameron, and C. Lucas (eds.), *The Oxford Handbook of Sociolinguistics* (pp. 321–339). New York: Oxford University Press.

Rosenstock, R. (2004) *An Investigation of International Sign: Analyzing Structure and Comprehension*. Ann Arbor, MI: University of Michigan Press.

Sáfár, A., Meurant, L., Haesenne, T., Nauta, Y. N., De Weerdt, D., and Ormel, E. (in press). Mutual intelligibility among the sign language of Belgium and the Netherlands. *Linguistics.*

Sandler, W., Meir, I., Padden, C., and Aronoff, M. (2005) The emergence of grammar: Systematic structure in a new language. *Proceedings of the National Academy of Sciences,* 102(7): 2661–2665.

Schembri, A. (2010) Documenting sign languages. In P. Austin (ed.), *Language Documentation and Description* (vol. VII, pp. 105–143). London: School of African and Oriental Studies.

Schembri, A., Cormier, K., Johnston, T., McKee, D., McKee, R., and Woll, B. (2010) Sociolinguistic variation in British, Australian and New Zealand Sign Languages. In D. Brentari (ed.), *Sign Languages* (pp. 476–498). Cambridge: Cambridge University Press.

Schermer, T. (2004) Lexical variation in Sign Language of the Netherlands. In M. Van Herreweghe and M. Vermeerbergen (eds.), *To the Lexicon and beyond: Sociolinguistics in European Deaf Communities* (pp. 91–110). Washington, DC: Gallaudet University Press.

Schmaling, C. (2003) The impact of ASL on the Deaf community in Kano state. In L. Monaghan, K. Nakamura, C. Schmaling, and G. Turner (eds.), *Many Ways to be Deaf: International Variation in Deaf Communities* (pp. 302–310). Washington, DC: Gallaudet University Press.

Schuit, J. (2012) Signing in the Arctic: External influences on Inuit Sign Language. In U. Zeshan and C. de Vos (eds.), *Sign Languages in Village Communities: Anthropological and Linguistic Insights* (pp. 181–208). Nijmegen: Ishara Press.

Senghas, R. J. (2003) New ways to be Deaf in Nicaragua: Changes in language, personhood, and community. In L. Monaghan, K. Nakamura, C. Schmaling, and G. H. Turner (eds.), *Many Ways to be Deaf: International, Linguistic, and Sociocultural Variation* (pp. 260–282). Washington, DC: Gallaudet University Press.

Stamp, R., Schembri, A., Fenlon, J., Rentelis, R., Woll, B., and Cormier, K. (accepted). Lexical variation and change in British Sign Language. *PLoS ONE.*

Stokoe, W. (1960) Sign language structure: An outline of the visual communication system of the American Deaf. Paper presented at the Studies in Linguistics Occasional Paper 8, University of Buffalo.

Sutton-Spence, R. and Woll, B. (1999) *The Linguistics of British Sign Language: An Introduction.* Cambridge: Cambridge University Press.

UNESCO (2003) *Language Vitality and Endangerment.* Document adopted by the International Expert meeting on UNESCO Programme Safeguarding of Endangered Languages. Paris, 10–12 March 2003: UNESCO.

Valentine, G. and Skelton, T. (2008) Changing spaces: The role of the internet in shaping Deaf geographies. *Social and Cultural Geography,* 9(5), 469–485.

Vasishta, M., Woodward, J. C., and Wilson, K. (1978) Sign language in India: Regional variation within the deaf population. *Indian Journal of Applied Linguistics,* 2: 66–74.

Washabaugh, W. (1981) The Deaf of Grand Cayman, British West Indies. *Sign Language Studies,* 31: 117–133.

Wheatley, M. and Pabsch, A. (2012) *Sign Language Legislation in the European Union.* Brussels: European Union of the Deaf.

Willoughby, L. (2012) Language maintenance and the deaf child. *Journal of Multilingual and Multicultural Development*, 33(6): 605–618.

Woll, B. (2006) Sign language: History. In K. Brown (ed.), *The Encyclodpedia of Language and Linguistics* (pp. 307–310). Amsterdam: Elsevier.

Woll, B., Sutton-Spence, R., and Elton, F. (2001) Multilingualism: The global approach to sign languages. In C. Lucas (ed.), *The Sociolinguistics of Sign Languages*. New York: Cambridge University Press.

Woodward, J. C. (1978) Historical bases of American Sign Language. In P. Siple (ed.), *Understanding Language through Sign Language Research* (pp. 333–348). New York: Academic Press.

(2011) Research methodology in lexicostatistical studies of sign languages. In G. Mathur and D. J. Napoli (eds.), *Deaf Around the World* (pp. 38–53). New York: Oxford University Press.

World Federation of the Deaf (2013a) WFD Newsletter, September 2013.

(2013b) Frequently asked questions, retrieved September.

Yang, J. H. (2011) Social situations and the education of deaf children in China. In G. Mathur and D. J. Napoli (eds.), *Deaf Around the World* (pp. 339–351). New York: Oxford University Press.

Zeshan, U. (2000) *Sign Language in Indo-Pakistan*. Amsterdam: John Benjamins.

(2004) Hand, head, and face: Negative constructions in sign languages. *Linguistic Typology*, 8: 1–58.

Zeshan, U. and de Vos, C. (eds.) (2012) *Sign Languages in Village Communities: Anthropological and Linguistic Insights*. Nijmegen: Ishara Press.

3   Sign languages in contact

David Quinto-Pozos and Robert Adam

Introduction

In some regions of the world, the regular use of more than one language within a single geographical area is commonplace in everyday life. This is true from the hills and valleys of the American Southwest, where English and Spanish can be heard in everyday conversations in restaurants, shopping areas, and other public places, to the campus of Gallaudet University in Washington, DC, where American Sign Language (ASL), English, and other signed and spoken languages pepper the auditory and visual landscape of that historical institution. Evidence of language contact can be found in everyday conversations (e.g., with bits of one language surfacing in the other) and also in various linguistic features of languages that have been in sustained contact over a period of time (e.g., fully integrated words that originated in another language). One can find features of an ambient spoken or written language within a signed language just as one can find words, sounds, and grammatical constructions from one spoken language within another. Language contact is part of the evolutionary history of languages in the world, and in this chapter we focus on various aspects of contact that surface when considering communities of language users that are bilingual and bimodal (i.e., they use languages that are perceived either visually, auditorally, or both).[1]

Language contact is the norm in Deaf communities, and Deaf people are typically multilingual and multicultural (e.g., see Grosjean 2010; Plaza-Pust and Morales-López 2008 for detailed discussions). They use signed, written, and, in some cases, spoken languages for daily communication, which means that aspects of the spoken and/or written languages of the larger communities

The support of the Economic and Social Research Council (ESRC) is gratefully acknowledged. Robert Adam was supported by the ESRC Deafness Cognition and Language Research Centre (DCAL) Grant RES-620-28-0002.
[1] See Chapter 2 for a discussion of different examples of societal bilingualism and multilingualism.

are in constant interaction with the signed languages.[2] In some cases, the contact has resulted in spoken language structures that have become incorporated into the sign languages – having been modified over time to conform to the linguistic processes of a sign language. In other cases, the contact may not be influencing structural changes to either language. Interestingly, language contact processes are at work whether interaction occurs between deaf and hearing signers or solely among deaf signers, and they have played a very important role in the creation and evolution of signed languages.

It is also true that contact phenomena in Deaf communities could stem from the use of two (or more) signed languages. Such a scenario is especially true in international border areas and in transnational gatherings of Deaf people, although such contact might also occur within a single country when communities of Deaf signers from different signed language backgrounds interact. Two different signed languages can coexist within a single city (e.g., Langue de Signes Québécoise and American Sign Language in Montreal, Canada) or within a country (Yucatec Maya Sign Language and Mexican Sign Language in Mexico; Johnson 1991).

This chapter is designed to provide the reader with an overview of language contact topics and a selection of examples of language contact in signed languages. This field of linguistic inquiry is rather broad – ranging from work on code-switching within a conversation to contact-induced change that occurs when languages are in sustained contact with each other. The prevalence of language contact within Deaf communities throughout the world provides a rich web of linguistic phenomena to be investigated. If one considers the contact that results from users of two different signed languages interacting, various comparisons can be made to contact that occurs across two or more spoken languages. The term *unimodal contact*, or that which comes about because of interaction between two languages within the same modality (whether the modality be visual–gestural or auditory–oral) can be used to characterize such contact. However, if one considers the contact that results from interaction between a signed and a spoken or written language, the term *bimodal* (or even *multimodal*) *contact* is more appropriate. It should be noted that even in cases where unimodal contact occurs between two signed languages, bimodal or multimodal contact phenomena surface as well.

It has been argued that particular aspects of the visual-gestural modality create outcomes of language contact that do not typically characterize spoken

---

[2] We use the term "sign language(s)" to refer to specific sign languages (e.g., Mexican Sign Language or Irish Sign Language) or nonspecific languages within an intended delimited set (e.g. sign languages with one-handed finger spelling), and we use "signed language(s)" to contrast with the term "spoken language" or else to refer more generally to visual–gestural language(s). See Wilcox and Wilcox (1997) for a similar discussion.

language contact situations (Lucas and Valli 1992; Quinto-Pozos 2007; Quinto-Pozos and Adam 2013). Specifically, the prevalence of visual iconicity and the utilization of gestural resources create language contact phenomena that are rather unique to signed language. In addition, the cross-linguistic structure similarity of signed languages likely has an effect on contact between sign languages (see Adam 2012; Quinto-Pozos 2007, for additional discussion). This topic is taken up in the last section of this chapter.

The majority of the chapter is organized by common outcomes of language contact that occur based on languages and communication systems within and across communication modalities (sign, speech, and writing). It may be the case that the categories of contact outcomes that we propose are not mutually exclusive (i.e., an example of contact that is described in one classification could also appear within another, related category). The reader will also notice that, at least with respect to sign-speech contact and sign-writing contact, the effects of contact on each language are clearly not equal. It is most often the case that the spoken and written languages have an influence on the structure and daily use of signed languages, though it appears that signed languages have much less influence on the structure and usage of spoken and written languages. This section covers borrowings and loan phenomena, interference, code-switching/code-mixing, pidgins and creoles, and language shift/death. For each topic, a basic introduction based on spoken language work is provided for the reader, which is followed by examples of signed language contact phenomena.

Borrowings and loans

Among the most recognized products of contact between two or more languages over a period of time are borrowings from one language to the other, referred to commonly as *loans* (including loan shifts, loan translations or calques, and loanwords). Loan shift, as defined by Lehiste (1988, 20) is "the extension of a morpheme in Language A to include the meaning of the same morpheme in Language B." Grosjean (1992: 317) notes that, for example, Portuguese speakers in the USA have taken the Portuguese word *grosseria* ("a rude remark") and also used it to refer to a grocery store (note: this takes the first syllable *gros* from "a rude remark" and reinterprets it to match the first syllable of the English word; then the typical morpheme for "type of business," *-eria*, completes the word). A loan translation or calque is the direct translation of the meaning of a morpheme in Language A with the meaning of a morpheme in Language B. The English word "skyscraper" has a loan translation or calque equivalent in multiple languages, including Spanish *rascacielo* (*rasca* = to scratch, *cielo* = sky) and Indonesian/Malay *pencakar langit* (*pencakar* = scraper, *langit* = sky). Alternatively, a borrowing or loanword is a word that originated in Language A but that has been partially or wholly integrated – phonologically and morphologically – into Language B. One example is the English word corral (kəˈɹæl), which can be contrasted with the Spanish pronunciation (koˈrɑl). This word, meaning a "pen or yard," is used commonly in English (in fact a well-known gunfight in the American Southwest occurred in 1881, which is famously known as the gunfight at the O.K. Corral).

Ann (2001) provided several examples of borrowings. When some English words are borrowed into Japanese, consonant clusters tend to be broken up with vowels to conform to Japanese syllable structure – since Japanese does not allow for the vast array of consonant clusters that are available in English. English words like *strike* and *Christmas* are rendered as Japanese loanwords as *sutoraiku* and *kurisimasu*, respectively.

Signed language–signed language contact

Borrowings are challenging to analyze in signed language. The issue is that borrowings, in spoken language work, have been traditionally characterized by partial or complete phonological integration of the borrowed word into the phonology of the host language. However, this phonological integration may not be as evident in signed languages because signed language phonologies share many basic components with one another, a claim that was suggested in early writings of language contact in the signed modality (Lucas and Valli 1992). Thus, in an environment in which two signed languages are frequently used, it might be difficult to determine definitively, in some instances, which phonology (e.g., that of Language A or Language B) the signer may be accessing and producing. As one example, ASL and BSL, which are typically not considered to be related historically, share most of the elements of their handshape inventories, and a sign such as THANK-YOU, which is articulated similarly across both languages, would be difficult to attribute to one language versus the other, although historically it is known that BSL is the older language.

One way to consider borrowings in signed languages is to conduct studies of lexical similarity across signed languages that have been in contact with each other – as well as those that have not. Several studies that have compared lexical items across signed languages generally agree that signed languages are lexically more similar to each other than spoken languages are (e.g., see Guerra Currie *et al.* 2002; Parkhurst and Parkhurst 2003; Woll *et al.* 2001). While this may not be a result of contact between sign languages, some researchers have investigated the likelihood of historical contact (e.g., Davis 2007, 2010; McKee and Kennedy 2000). Higher degrees of lexical similarity clearly hold even for languages that are unrelated and whose users live in very disparate parts of the world. As a result, these works raise questions about the role of visual iconicity in the development of signed languages and in the comparison of signed language lexicons (see Quinto-Pozos 2007, for a discussion of the role of iconicity with respect to lexical similarity across signed languages).

Some authors have also examined current lexicons of different languages in order to test theories of historical contact. In a comparison of the sign languages of the UK, Australia, New Zealand, and the USA, McKee and Kennedy (2000) demonstrated that ASL is very different, at least lexically, from the varieties that have connections to nineteenth-century British Sign Language. This is true in spite of the claim that ASL may have been influenced somewhat by BSL of the late-eighteenth and early-nineteenth centuries (Groce 1985). To date, no detailed analyses have provided historical evidence for this claim.

Another type of analysis that concerns historical contact is presented by Davis (2007, 2010), in which the author investigates signs used by Native Americans during the early development of ASL (1880s and early 1900s). His analysis found that language contact and lexical borrowings took place between the two languages in the early history of the United States. For example, signs such as COME-OUT, TRUE, SUN, and STEAL from illustrations of Indian signs dated 1880 were analyzed by Davis as being similar to ASL signs used at that time (2010: 111).

Discussions of signed languages in Asia and Africa have also appeared in literature descriptions of lexical borrowing across signed languages. Sasaki (2007) addresses lexical contact between Japanese Sign Language (NS, or Nihon Shuwa) and Taiwan Sign Language (TSL). Historical accounts of the development of TSL cite JSL as one of the sign languages that influenced the development of TSL (Ann *et al.* 2007). Schmaling (2001) suggests that ASL in contact with Hausa Sign Language (HSL) in northern Nigeria has resulted in the appearance of some ASL forms in HSL (e.g., loan signs and the use of the manual alphabet for the creation of initialized signs).

Signers also take advantage of commonly used gestures from the ambient hearing communities. Whereas this is not technically contact between two signed languages, it does represent influence on a signed language from manual and nonmanual communication that occurs in the larger ambient community. For this reason, we include this topic within this section. Some of those gestures may become part of the lexicon or grammar of the signed languages as evidenced, in part, by changes in their articulation compared to the way in which hearing people use those gestures. However, Deaf signers also produce gestures that do not differ from those that hearing people use (e.g., emblems such as "thumbs-up" to mean "good/OK"). As with iconic devices, such gestural resources present challenges for the researcher of signed language contact. One challenge for some analyses (e.g., a syntactic account of code switching) is to determine whether a meaningful form is, in some cases, a sign or a gesture.

Various authors have suggested ways in which the gestures – both manual and nonmanual – of hearing people can now be considered as part of a sign language. For example, Janzen and Shaffer (2002) maintain that some hand gestures have been grammaticalized as modals in ASL and that some facial gestures (specifically brow raise) have been incorporated as nonmanual signals that provide syntactic information (e.g., topic markers). Among other influences on signed languages that have been claimed to come from hearing gestures are head shifts for direct quotes (McClave 2001, for ASL), and head movements and negation (Antzakas and Woll 2002, for Greek Sign Language). It is likely that there are many more examples that are not mentioned here. Casey (2003) has shown that directional gestures and torso movements of non-signers are similar to verb directionality and torso movement for role shift in signed language. She suggests that directionality in ASL (and other sign languages) originated from nonlinguistic gestures.

The roles of other gestures within the signed stream have been addressed by various researchers. Pietrosemoli (2001) writes about the emblems (see McNeill 1992, for a discussion of categories of gesture) that hearing Venezuelans commonly use and that signers of Venezuelan Sign Language (LSV) also produce. She reports that the emblematic signs appear to reflect a code-switching of emblems with linguistic items or a borrowing of the emblems into LSV. Various other works have addressed emblems in signed language data: Quinto-Pozos (2002) noted that emblematic gestures alternate with lexical signs of LSM and ASL in the discourse of deaf signers who live along the US–Mexico border, Hoyer (2007) reported on the lexicalization of hearing Albanians' emblematic gestures into Albanian Sign Language, and Hou and Mesh (2013) described five manual negators in Chatino Sign Language, all of which were used as emblems in the co-speech gestures of hearing Chatino-speaking non-signers in Mexico.

Signed language–spoken language contact

Sign-speech contact seems to have generated the most scholarly interest throughout the years. We begin by highlighting some seminal work that has influenced the field for decades and include more recent studies that have allowed us to push the boundaries of what we know about signed language contact.

Mouthings   A notable characteristic of contact between a signed and a spoken language is the signer's voiceless articulation of spoken words while producing signs, known as *mouthings*. In such cases, the signer articulates aspects of the *visual* signal that is perceived when looking at the mouth of the spoken language user.[3] Sometimes the visual signal seems to capture aspects of the entire spoken word, whereas other times there are only parts of that word visible (e.g., the onset of the word or certain syllables with other parts of the spoken word not represented in the visual signal). Mouthings tend to occur most often when signers are manually articulating nouns, open-class items, and morphologically simpler signs (see Crasborn *et al.* 2008). These mouthings have generally been considered to differ from *mouth gestures*, which are often used for adjectival or adverbial functions and typically assumed to originate within a sign language. Some mouth gestures, however, may appear very similar in form (and in some cases, in meaning) across unrelated signed languages, which raises other questions about their origins.

Several authors have addressed the phenomenon of mouthings with data from various signed and spoken languages (ASL/English: Davis 1989; Swiss German Sign Language/German: Boyes Braem 2001; New Zealand Sign Language (NZSL) and Maori-influenced English: McKee *et al.* 2007; Chinese Sign Language/Chinese: Yang 2008; and Italian Sign Language/Italian: Ajello *et al.* 2001; see Ann 2001 for other examples). For many authors this type of contact reflects instances of borrowing, and the mouthings are often viewed as integrated into the morphosyntactic structures of signed languages (see Crasborn *et al.* 2008 for references). Whereas, another point of view is that the mouthings, while still coming about because of language contact, are examples of code-mixing and not integrated into the linguistic structure of the signed language (e.g., see Ebbinghaus and Hessmann 2001; Hohenberger and Happ 2001). Vinson, Thompson, Skinner, Fox, and Vigliocco (2010), based on their study that included BSL signs and English mouthings, largely support this latter view. They argue for separate representations of mouthings and manual components of lexical signs, which they suggest resembles accounts of code blends in sign (e.g., Emmorey *et al.* 2008).

Signed languages also exist within regions where more than one spoken language is used regularly, and that can result in mouthings that reflect contact with either or both of the spoken languages. Quinto-Pozos (2002, 2009) reports that in a transnational border region where English and Spanish are used regularly, mouthings of Spanish words can accompany ASL signs and mouthings of English words can accompany Mexican Sign Language (LSM) signs. In one example from the border data, the Spanish word *igual* ("same") appeared as a mouthing while the signer simultaneously signed the ASL sign SAME.

---

[3] In many cases, Deaf and hard-of-hearing people, like those with typical hearing, are also users of spoken language. This likely depends on various factors such as the level of hearing that a deaf or hard-of-hearing person possesses, their own personal beliefs, and in which setting they were educated.

Vocabulary creation   Some vocabulary items in signed languages appear to be borrowed from spoken and written language words. For example, Johnston and Schembri (2007) note that, in Auslan, compounds such as SPORT+CAR are created through contact with English. In some cases, the English-influenced compound coexists with a sign that is native to the signed language, such as the loan translation BREAK+DOWN and the native sign BREAKDOWN, the latter of which was not borrowed from English. For the most part, the semantics of the spoken language are used in the borrowed form. Brentari and Padden (2001) discuss similar examples in ASL such as DEAD+LINE and BABY+SIT. Some compounds contain fingerspelled components such as SUGAR+F-R-E-E. In all of these cases, lexical items from the ambient spoken language have influenced the signs (and sign plus fingerspelling combinations) that are used in the particular sign language.

Signed language–written language contact

Plaza-Pust (2008) provides a detailed account of literacy development for deaf children who sign German Sign Language (DGS) and are learning written German. She argues that the variation and errors that are demonstrated by the children in their written German is representative of L2 acquisition of literacy – rather than from primary contact with DGS. However, the author also notes some types of influence that DGS seems to be exerting on the children's written German. As one example, various written German sentences produced by the children did not contain overt verbs (as in (1) below), a feature of DGS (and other sign languages), which can use other means to create predication.

(1)   Taken from Plaza-Pust (2008: 122)
      Written German: der   Junge   Angst
      English: the   boy   fear
      Translation: "The boy is frightened."

Fingerspelling   Manual systems for representing entire words of written language are commonly known as *fingerspelling*, and it is the case that many (if not most) sign languages possess fingerspelling systems. Some of the systems are articulated with one hand (e.g., French Sign Language and Mexican Sign Language) and others require the use of two hands for production (e.g., British Sign Language and Czech Sign Language; see Sutton-Spence 2003). In one-handed systems, certain handshapes and movements represent letters of the written alphabet, while two-handed systems employ combinations of two handshapes interacting in specific ways to create manual letters. Duarte (2010) found that fingerspelling in Ethiopian Sign Language employs a system which represents Amharic orthography – particularly consonant–vowel sound pairs. Handshape is used to encode a base consonant, and other features such as timing, placement, and orientation play important roles, in encoding paired vowels.

Various researchers have highlighted ways in which fingerspelling can adapt to the natural processes of a signed language. In an early work on the linguistic processes that operate on fingerspelling, Battison (1978) addressed the manner in which some one-handed fingerspelled words become lexicalized over time. For example, the fingerspelled letters J-O-B were the source material for a sign that developed in ASL (often transcribed as #JOB) with the same meaning and only some features of the original fingerspelled item. Only the handshapes that represent the first and last letters of the word are visible in the lexicalized form, and the B-handshape changes orientation so that the palm faces toward the signer at completion of the sign.

Similar types of lexicalization processes can occur in sign languages that utilize a two-handed system, such as British Sign Language. As with one-handed systems, BSL fingerspelling can demonstrate processes of nativization (Cormier *et al.* 2008: 3; Kyle and Woll 1985; Sutton-Spence 1994, 1998) where a fingerspelled event is considered a lexical sign, for example, S-O-N (Johnston and Schembri 2007:163)

Fingerspelling has also been considered within a model that divides elements of signed languages into native and non-native items (Brentari and Padden 2001; Padden 1998). In that analysis, fingerspelling is viewed as a non-native subset of the lexicon, a part that is "borrowed" from English through contact though the non-native items can undergo processes that allow them to appear more ASL like (i.e., native like), a suggestion that was also made earlier (Battison 1978). In some cases, the fingerspelled items can form compounds with ASL signs – as was mentioned earlier.

As evidence that contact phenomena can become nativized within a language, a recent study has shown that the processing of fingerspelling has become incorporated into a signed language to the extent that it is processed by the brain like other aspects of sign for deaf language users – rather than as written language, which it represents (Waters *et al.* 2007).

Other works have suggested that fingerspelling can be viewed as code-switching between ASL and written English (Kuntze 2000), and it can also be considered a form of borrowing (Miller 2001).

Initialization   In signed languages with one-handed fingerspelling systems, initialized signs are those whose handshape(s) correspond to the manual representations of letters of the written alphabet (see Padden 1998 for a discussion of such signs and various examples from ASL). For example, the ASL sign WATER is articulated with an ASL W-handshape, and the ASL sign TEAM is produced with an ASL T-handshape. In some cases, there are initialized and non-initialized variants of signs in ASL – the latter of which might be more semantically general in nature. For example, in the case of the two-handed sign T̲EAM, there are non-initialized variants (produced with other handshapes) that contain the same movement and place of articulation values, but different handshapes. So, the signs C̲LASS and G̲ROUP are also initialized, though there is a general sign for the concept of 'group' that is articulated with the ASL clawed-5 handshape. However, in the case of some initialized signs (e.g., ASL WATER), there exist no non-initialized variants in current ASL.

Padden (1998) also writes about abbreviation signs in ASL, or those that also demonstrate some influence from letters of English words. Examples of such signs in ASL are W̲ORKS̲HOP, F̲EEDB̲ACK, and W̲ITHD̲RAW. Such signs are like the initialized signs described above, yet they display the manual handshapes that correspond with two letters of the written word rather than just the initial letter of the word. So, for WORKSHOP, the letters "W" and "S" are found within the handshapes that comprise the sign, though the movement, place of articulation, and orientation values adhere to native phonological constraints of word formation for the language.

Initialization of signs in languages with two-handed fingerspelling systems is also possible, but it is perhaps less common. The reason for this difference is that the one-handed systems usually support the identification of the alphabetic item with solely a handshape (in most cases), and that allows for the movement and place of articulation parameters to either mirror non-initialized variants or else to engage in their own sanctioned combinations in order to create a sign. Since two-handed systems require place of articulation values (and also movements, in some cases), there are fewer parameters that are free for sign formation. However, some authors (Cormier *et al.* 2008; Sutton-Spence 1994; Sutton-Spence and Woll 1999) have described particular signs in two-handed systems referred to as *single manual letter signs* (SMLS), which are signs that are produced by articulating the fingerspelled letter that corresponds with a letter (usually the first, as in initialized signs in one-handed systems) of a semantically equivalent written word from the ambient spoken language. An example of an SMLS is the BSL sign FATHER. These signs generally allow for limited movements from the non-dominant hand and are usually articulated in neutral space (Cormier *et al.* 2008).

We have noted that initialized signs of signed languages represent contact between the signed and the written version of the spoken language. Certainly, initialized signs attest to long-standing contact between signed languages and the ambient spoken/written languages of their communities. Much of this contact begins early in the history of a signed language, with the establishment of schools for deaf children and teaching methods that focus on the learning of spoken and/or written language.

Initialized signs exist in many sign languages. For example, they have been attested for Mexican Sign Language, which represents contact between LSM and Spanish (Guerra Currie 1999), Thai Sign Language, for contact with Thai (Nonaka 2004), and Quebec Sign Language, which reflects contact with French (Machabée 1995). Johnston and Schembri (2007) also report that some initialized signs in Australian Sign Language, a language with a two-handed fingerspelling system, are actually produced as one-handed signs because of contact with Irish Sign Language initialized signs. The Irish Sign Language (ISL) fingerspelling system is one-handed, and an example of such contact is the ISL sign GARDEN.

The advent of electronic communication has also seen borrowings into signed language from written language. Schneider *et al.* (2011) report this for ASL and English. They found that internet messaging and short messaging service (SMS), characterized by abbreviations and acronyms, have become so widespread that some abbreviations such as LOL ("laugh out loud"/"laughing out loud") and WTF ("what the fuck") have become a part of the ASL lexicon, among earlier signs such as ASAP ("as soon as possible") and FYI ("for your information"). In this study, Schneider *et al.* also found age- and gender-based variation and this work indicates the centrality of electronic communication in the modern evolution of language.

The tracing of written forms – either in the palm of the hand or in the air – by the signer within signed language discourse is another phenomenon relating to the influence of spoken languages on signed languages. Older signers of New Zealand Sign Language (NZSL) use this strategy (Forman 2003, though also see Dugdale, Kennedy, McKee, and McKee 2003 for noteworthy commentary on Forman's writings) where the signer uses an index finger to trace the shape of the written alphabetic letter or logographic character that is being referenced. This tracing alternates with signs and other aspects of the signed language. However, there often also exist signs that represent certain logographic characters. Yang (2008) provides an example of a Chinese Sign Language user tracing a character sign on the palm of his hand during sign discourse. Ann (2001) provides examples of Taiwan Sign Language signs that represent Chinese characters. Figure 3.1, taken from Ann's writings, shows the Taiwan Sign Language sign for JIE ("*introduce*").

Because Taiwan Sign Language does not have a fingerspelling system, the written Chinese character for JIE (which means "introduce") has been restructured into a sign, although the sign version does not represent any tonal information. Such character signs are not numerous in TSL, and they conform to some linguistic constraints of TSL while also violating phonological rules in some cases (for example, the use of a handshape for a character sign that does not appear in native TSL signs).

Figure 3.1 Taiwan Sign Language JIE

Interference

Language interference has been described as the "deviations from the norms of either language that occur in the speech of bilinguals as a result of their familiarity with more than one language" (Lehiste 1988: 1–2). Such deviations are typically considered to be involuntary, and they can occur at various levels of language structure, such as the phonological, lexical, and syntactic levels (Grosjean 1989; Lehiste 1988). For example, two languages that are in contact may share a phoneme, but their phonetic realizations of that phoneme may be different. Thus, in a contact situation, the pronunciation of a word that contains that phoneme may be influenced by the phonetic realization of the phoneme from the other language. Lehiste explains that this type of interference is often referred to as sound substitution. Lehiste (1988: 2–3) presents the following example:

The phoneme /t/ is found in Slavic languages as well as in English, but in Slavic languages /t/ is normally dental (articulated with the tip of the tongue against the inner surface of the upper front teeth), whereas in English /t/ is normally alveolar (articulated with the tip of the tongue against the alveolar ridge). In Slavic languages the phoneme /r/ is realized as a tongue-tip trill, whereas in American English /ɹ/ is a retroflex continuant.

This means that a person who natively speaks a Slavic language and who acquired English as an adult may systematically pronounce instances of /t/ in English words as dental consonants rather than alveolar consonants. Likewise, instantiations of /r/ for a native speaker of a Slavic language who learns English as an adult may tend to surface as tongue-tip trills instead of retroflex continuants.

Exploring the effects of language interference between very distinct, albeit historically related languages such as English and various Slavic languages, as in the example from Lehiste (1988), may be quite different from determining what occurs with two languages that are more closely related. Portuguese and Spanish, both Romance languages, provide the linguistic content from which to investigate interference between closely related languages; the border between Uruguay and Brazil in South America provides the context for the study of such contact. A description of various contact phenomena that were demonstrated by speakers of Portuguese and Spanish along that border can be found in Hensey (1993). As part of the data, he describes instances of phonological interference from Portuguese in the Spanish spoken by school-children. In particular, the children reduced standard Spanish diphthongs to monophthongs and articulated standard Spanish simple vowels as diphthongs. In essence, features from one language were found in articulations of the other language.

Interference is also a possible outcome of contact between two signed languages, and this phenomenon can be described as the surfacing of the articulatory norms of one sign language in the production of another. Some instances of interference may be evident in the phonological parameters of sign formation. Lucas and Valli (1992: 35) refer to this type of interference as: "the lack of phonological integration that might signal interference – for example, the involuntary use of a handshape, location, palm orientation, movement, or facial expression from one sign language in the discourse of the other." Interference may also be evident at other levels of language structure, such as the morphology or syntax of one or both of the signed languages.

Interference is also discussed in Quinto-Pozos (2002, 2009). The analyses focus primarily on the phonological parameter of handshape and the LSM and ASL nonmanual signals that are used for *wh*-question formation. The data indicate that signers, like users of spoken language, exhibit features of interference when they articulate items from their nonnative language. For example, a signer who grew up in Mexico signing LSM might sign ASL FAMILY with an LSM F handshape rather than an ASL F handshape. The two handshapes are similar, but they differ in the contact between thumb and index finger and also in the degree to which the non-selected fingers (i.e., the middle and ring fingers and the pinky) are spread apart. Johnston and Schembri (2007) describe a similar, albeit slightly different, situation for a few initialized signs in Auslan. Even though Auslan is normally produced with a two-handed fingerspelling system, the language shows evidence of contact with Irish Sign Language (ISL), which utilizes a one-handed system. The ISL T-handshape is similar to the ASL T-handshape, although there are differences (the thumb tip protrudes between the index and middle fingers in the ASL T-handshape, whereas it is in contact with the index finger – at the most distal joint of the finger – in the ISL T-handshape). Johnston and Schembri report that Auslan signers articulate ASL-initialized signs (e.g., TEAM and THEORY) with the ISL T-handshape rather than the ASL handshape, and this language use reflects borrowings from ASL that have been adapted phonologically to Auslan. It could also be the case that initialized signs that enter into the Auslan lexicon come from ISL. For example, the sign TEAM appears to be articulated similarly in ISL and ASL (Leeson, personal communication), although this is not the case for the sign THEORY, which differs between ISL and ASL. Questions about initialized signs and contact reflect an area that is ripe for research in the world's sign languages.

Code-switching and code-mixing

Code-switching and code-mixing have been discussed in the spoken language literature for decades, and there has been much disagreement about what constitutes *switching*, *mixing*, or even the *code* to or from which the shift occurs (see Bullock and Toribio 2009). The definitions of code-switching versus code-mixing also vary, though the former is often used as a cover term for the phenomenon. Furthermore, there is not full agreement about the difference between loans/borrowed items and code-switches, with some researchers seeing the two phenomena lying along a continuum (or code-switching subsuming borrowing) rather than as categorically different concepts (e.g., see Clyne 2003; Bullock and Toribio 2009 for in-depth discussion of these points).

Some researchers would suggest that various types of code-switching exist. For example, one type of code-switch has been described by Muysken (2000) as an *insertion*, which is the embedding of a constituent (this could be one word or a multiple-word constituent) in the middle of material from a different code or language. An example of this would be the Spanish–English–Spanish sequence seen in (2) below:

(2)   Vamos a caminar *to the store* en la mañana
        "We will walk to the store in the morning."

In the example in (2), the prepositional phrase "to the store" was embedded within a larger sentence that comprises Spanish lexical items and grammar. In addition to insertions, Muysken noted that other code-switching patterns included alternations and congruent lexicalization. These patterns vary depending on the linguistic and social relationships between two languages. Insertion is found most commonly where there is typological distance between the two languages, and is characteristic of colonial settings, recent migrant communities, and asymmetry in a speaker's proficiency in two languages.

Alternation is found in stable bilingual communities where there is typological distance and where there is a tradition of language separation. Congruent lexicalization is found where there is typological similarity, where the two languages in contact have roughly equal prestige and where there is no tradition of overt language separation. The linguistic and social relationships between two signed languages has been hitherto unstudied, and the dynamics between two signed languages can be examined using this typology.

Signed language–signed language contact

As can be expected, code-switching is also a feature of contact between two sign languages.[4] In a study of US–Mexico border signers, Quinto-Pozos (2002, 2009) found evidence that signers of Mexican Sign Language (LSM) and ASL engage in *reiterative code-switching*, the sequential use of synonymous signs for the purposes of reiteration – much like certain switches described in spoken languages. One example (taken from Quinto-Pozos 2008: 230) is provided in (3).

(3)   point: middle finger (for listing)   TOMATO **TOMATE (LSM sign)**
        ADD-INGREDIENTS   MIX   gesture: "thumbs-up"
        "(and then you take) tomatoes and you add them to the other ingredients and mix everything together. It's great."

It is worthwhile pointing out that reiterative code-switches resemble signed language discourse strategies referred to commonly as *chaining* (Kelly 1991; Humphries and MacDougall 1999/2000; Quinto-Pozos and Reynolds 2012). In chaining, a signer typically references an object or concept by employing more than one mechanism (e.g., sign, fingerspelled word, point) in succession. This strategy has been claimed to be important for language teaching with children (Humphries and MacDougall 1999/2000), but it often appears in adult-directed language use, too (Quinto-Pozos and Mehta 2010). A similar strategy has been reported by Schembri and Johnston (2007) for Auslan, and they provide the example of a signer signing TENNIS followed by the fingerspelled T-E-N-N-I-S.

Other studies of code-switching between two sign languages have also discovered examples of non-reiterative code-switching (Nonaka 2004; Quinto-Pozos 2008). Nonaka describes instances of code-switching between Ban Khor Sign Language and Thai Sign Language, where inventories of color terms are not similar across the two languages. The code-switching, occurs when a particular item does not exist within one language.

Other issues must be considered when analyzing data from two signed languages (Quinto-Pozos 2008), where some items may be articulated similarly

---

[4] See Quinto-Pozos (2007, 2008) for reviews of code-switching phenomena in signed languages.

in both sign languages, and that makes it difficult to determine which language is being produced. Examples are various types of points, so-called classifier constructions, commonly used gestures, and enactments that involve upper body parts (known in the literature as *constructed action*, Metzger 1995). It is sometimes not clear how to categorize a particular utterance (e.g., a so-called classifier construction from Language A or Language B, an emblem from the ambient hearing community versus a sign, or the use of constructed action versus a language-specific lexical item).

In a study of code-switching between Australian Irish Sign Language (AISL) and Auslan, Adam (2012) found that insertion was the predominant type of code-switching in the conversation data that he collected. An insertion (AISL in bold text, Auslan in plain text) can occur as shown in (4):

(4)   PRO-1 GO T-O **WARATAH** AGE **WHEN** FIVE-YEARS-OLD
       "I started school at Waratah when I was 5 years old."

or as an inserted clause as shown in (5) which also shows an example of reiterative code-switching:

(5)   DOOR-OPEN STRIDE G:wow NUN LOVE PRO-3 **NUN LOVE**
       H-E-R GOOD T-O REMEMBER PRO-3
       "the door would burst open and [she] would come striding in the room, she was amazing and the nuns loved her. It is nice to remember her."

The reiterative switches presented in Quinto-Pozos (2002, 2009) appeared primarily in the form of single lexical items, whereas the example in (5) shows that an entire phrase could be reiterated.

As noted above, Muysken (2000) describes insertion as being characteristically found in colonial settings and where there is an asymmetry in proficiency in the two languages. The conversational data in Adam (2012) revealed individuals are more fluent in the dominant sign language than the minority sign language. The finding from the sociolinguistic interviews that the bilingual situation between the two languages is not stable, is confirmed. The minority sign language has not been taught as a language of instruction in schools for Deaf children since the 1950s, and many families do not use the language in the home. Additionally, both sign languages have a colonial history, the majority sign language having arrived in Australia much earlier than the minority sign language.

Signed language–spoken language contact

Bimodal bilinguals   Studies of the simultaneous use of a spoken and a signed language have focused on the language use of hearing individuals who are fluent in a signed and a spoken language, but this could also appear in the language use of deaf individuals who choose to use speech in addition to sign – such as with their hearing children. These signers are known as *bimodal bilinguals*[5] (Bishop 2006; Bishop and Hicks 2008; Emmorey, Borinstein, and Thompson 2005; Emmorey, Borinstein, Thompson, and Gollan 2008), and the language mixing is called *code-blending* because of the simultaneous expression of features of both languages.

An example of code-blending is shown in (6), which is taken from Emmorey *et al.* (2008: 48). In this example, the signs and English words are produced simultaneously.

(6)   English: I don't think he would really live.
        ASL: NOT THINK REALLY LIVE

The word orders of the two sentences are similar in this case, but aspects of one language are sometimes not represented, and the interlocutor must understand both languages to fully comprehend a message. This phenomenon has also been referred to as "Coda talk" (Bishop and Hicks 2008) by some authors ("Coda" is an acronym referring to hearing "children of deaf adults").

Code-blending has been distinguished from signing while speaking, or what is referred to as Simultaneous Communication or SimCom. Essentially, Sim-Com is claimed to engender speech dysfluencies because of the dual-task properties of that mode of communication that are not apparent during natural bilingual communication (Emmorey *et al.* 2005: 670). Emmorey and colleagues suggest that code-blending is one of the characteristics of natural language use by those bilinguals who acquire a signed and a spoken language as children.

Some analyses have examined variation within the types of language mixing that are produced by bimodal bilinguals (Baker and van den Bogaerde 2008; Bishop and Hicks 2008; van den Bogaerde and Baker 2005). In such analyses, the researchers examine code-blended segments in order to determine a *base language*, a designation based on the meaning generated by each language. For example, Baker and van den Bogaerde report on variation in code-blending strategies in Dutch and Sign Language of the Netherlands (NGT) in families with Deaf and hearing members. The researchers noted that code-blends were found both in mothers' input to their children and in the children's output.

---

[5] Although not generally the practice, the term bimodal bilingual could, in theory, also be used to refer to Deaf signers who engage in reading and writing. However, many Deaf and hearing people use signed, written, and spoken language for communication, which would suggest that the term *multimodal* may also be appropriate.

Pidgins and creoles

The study of *pidgins* and *creoles* is a notable part of language contact research. Typically, pidgins are described as contact languages between speakers of different languages who are trying to communicate despite not sharing a common language (Thomason and Kaufman 1988). Historically, they have arisen in cases of slavery, migration, conquest, trade, etc., and they are usually characterized as having no native speakers and being less complex than full-fledged languages. Creoles, on the other hand, are often described as being more stable (grammatically and lexically) and also having native speakers whose parents were usually speakers of the related pidgin. There are many details of the study of pidgins and creoles, such as which features of the languages provide grammatical and lexical material, the processes of lexicalization and grammaticalization of items, and the complex sociolinguistic situations in which they form.

Contact between ASL and English in the US Deaf community was hypothesized to result in a signed pidgin, and such an analysis was adopted by many people (perhaps more by laypersons than by linguists); this resulted in common use of the term Pidgin Sign(ed) English, or PSE.[6] That label was used for years, even though the initial analysis was not without debate. Woodward (1973b: 40) was an early proponent of the pidgin analysis, and he noted that PSE is characterized by "reduction and mixture of grammatical structures of both languages as well as some new structures that are common to neither of the languages." Among the structures referred to by Woodward were articles, plural markers, and the copula – none of which are common to both English and ASL.[7] However, over the years various authors have pointed out that, in several ways, PSE does not seem to resemble spoken language pidgins. Cokely (1983) argued in favor of an analysis that considered interactions between deaf and hearing signers as instances of foreigner talk, judgments of proficiency, and ASL learners' attempts to master the target language. Lucas and Valli

---

[6] See Chapter 7 in this volume for a discussion on attitudes toward these different forms of signing.

[7] Woodward was also a proponent of an analysis that suggested that ASL and English coexisted in a *diglossic* situation for signers (1973a), a point that Stokoe (1970) also advanced. Two varieties of a language can exist within a diglossic relationship if there exists a superposed – more prestigious – variety (an "H," or high variety) and a regional dialect (an "L," or low variety) and if they are typically used in contrastive situations (see Ferguson 1959 for a definitional account). Some writers disagree with the diglossia analysis for signed languages (e.g., Tervoort 1973: 378) with the argument that, for diglossia to be present, the H and L forms have to be varieties of the same language. Since ASL and English are two different languages, Tervoort suggested that signed language use in Deaf communities could be better characterized as a form of bilingualism. We do not challenge Tervoort's claim about bilingualism in these communities, but he was likely not taking into account bilingual diglossic situations (see Fishman 1967). The concept of diglossia in Deaf communities has generally not been discussed in the recent signed language literature.

(1992) and Fischer (1996) pointed out that the alleged pidgin, PSE, is the opposite of what is typically found in spoken language pidgins since its vocabulary comes from the substrate (ASL), whereas its grammar comes from the superstrate (English). We revisit the idea of pidgin creation through contact in our discussion of International Sign.

ASL has also been claimed to resemble various aspects of a young creole (e.g., Fischer, 1978). Part of the evidence comes from the fact that several linguistic features of ASL are also commonly found in young creole languages. Among the features discussed by Fischer are the following: content words are used for grammatical purposes, very little tense marking, and rich aspectual marking. Recent writings have also discussed the creole analysis with respect to signed languages (e.g., Aronoff, Meier, and Sandler 2005; Adone, 2012), and the debate continues. Aronoff and colleagues propose that signed languages differ from young creole languages in an important way: signed language morphologies are particularly rich and complex. Additionally, they suggest that signed languages demonstrate iconically motivated representations that allow morphological processes to be notably complex, and this is true for many signed languages that have been studied. Adone (2012) also provides an argument for supporting a creole analysis, and she highlights patterns of language acquisition in deaf children who are in impoverished linguistic environments (e.g., no or limited signed language models) and their ability to regularize fragmented input in order to create a more robust linguistic system.

Perhaps the most in-depth analyses of contact between ASL and English appeared in a series of published works by Ceil Lucas and Clayton Valli; the work was important for various reasons, including providing detailed descriptions of contact phenomena that had previously not appeared, and showing that contact phenomena are commonplace in ASL – even in the conversations between fluent Deaf signers of the language. Several works are synthesized in Lucas and Valli (1992), which argued in favor of a different analysis of the contact between English and ASL. In short, the authors suggested that the term *contact signing* was a more suitable label than "PSE (Pidgin Sign English)" for varieties of signed language that combine features of ASL and English and exhibit significant individual variation in terms of the occurrence of features. They also pointed out that, despite the individual variation, some linguistic features from ASL and English seldom occur in contact signing, such as ASL nonmanual syntactic markers that occur with topicalization and various bound morphemes from English (e.g., plural -*s*, third person singular -*s*, possessive *'s*, past tense -*ed*, or comparative -*er*).

In terms of the creation of mixed systems as a result of contact, it is vital to include discussion of *International Sign*, a "type of signing used when deaf signers communicate across mutually unintelligible language boundaries"

(Supalla and Webb 1995: 334). Segments of the international Deaf community are highly mobile and regularly attend international and regional events (e.g., meetings of the World Federation of the Deaf Congress and the Deaflympic Games) that occur throughout parts of the world. Deaf individuals who interact with each other in these types of international gatherings use International Sign for communication. As a result, International Sign may function as a type of "foreigner talk." There do not appear to be native users of International Sign, which is employed only for restricted purposes. Based on these social phenomena, some may wonder if International Sign resembles spoken language pidgins, though various structural and social patterns of International Sign suggest otherwise. In terms of grammatical devices, various researchers claim that International Sign is structurally more complex than spoken language pidgins are (McKee and Napier 2002; Rosenstock 2004; Supalla and Webb 1995). Supalla and Webb discuss the rule-governed nature of the syntactic structure of International Sign and various features of its vocabulary. In particular, they claim that verb agreement, word order, and negation in International Sign are systematic and rule governed. They also report that verbs are frequently inflected in complex ways. The word order of International Sign is usually SVO, but it can also be described in terms of other regular structures. With regard to negation, Supalla and Webb (1995: 346–347) claim that a signer of International Sign appears to use "a limited number of negative devices similar in structure and form to those used in full signed languages." Rosenstock (2004) reports that International Sign contains highly iconic signs, as well as more arbitrary ones that may be loans from full sign languages. By describing a number of grammatical and otherwise communicative devices used in International Sign, Rosenstock shows that International Sign contains an "extremely complex grammatical system with a rather limited lexicon" (2004: 212). This is possibly due to the great similarity of the grammatical and morphological structures of the languages in contact – to the extent that International Sign has been suggested to possibly represent a koine (Supalla and Webb 1995).

Regarding lexical matters, International Sign does not have its own lexicon like a full-fledged sign language (Allsop, Woll, and Brauti 1995), though there do exist a core set of signs that are commonly recognized as conventional within International Sign. A signer who is using International Sign normally incorporates a myriad of meaningful devices within their signing (e.g., signs from their own native sign language, signs from another sign language, signs recognized as conventional in International Sign, mimetic enactments, or so-called classifier signs). The lexicon of conventional signs is also "highly situational, shifting from event to event according to the participants' multilingual ability in various national sign languages" (Murray 2009: 947). As can be noted, signers of International Sign combine what appears to be "a relatively rich and structured grammar with a severely impoverished lexicon" (Allsop *et al.* 1995: 197).

Language shift and language death

Language shift occurs when speakers in a community give up speaking their language and take up the use of another in its place (Fishman 1991). Language shift has clear (and often devastating) implications for many minority communities, such as Native Americans and Indigenous Australians, many of whose languages are slowly dying as the number of speakers diminishes and native speakers grow old and die and younger generations have shifted to speaking another language; such a situation is often referred to as *language death* (Crystal 2000). Simons and Lewis (2013) estimate that approximately 19 percent of the world's languages are no longer being learned by children.

However, it is not necessarily true that language death results from the passing of its last native speaker, such as with the recent example of Klallam, a Native American language from the Salishan (Salish) family (www.reuters.com/article/2014/02/07/us-usa-klallam-death-idUSBREA1605W20140207). Hazel Sampson passed away in Washington state (United States) early in 2014 at the age of 103. In some cases, community and government efforts to keep languages alive result in resources for language revitalization, such as the creation of dictionaries and study materials for those who wish to learn the endangered language as a second language. In the case of Klallam, it is estimated that 3,000 second language speakers remain, which provides some hope for the survival of the language.

Language shift occurs in both immigrant and non-immigrant communities. Regarding the former, immigrants arrive in a new country speaking their language. They may find that the number of reasons to speak their language grows fewer and fewer, and the number of reasons to speak the dominant language grows greater. On the other hand, in non-immigrant communities, language shift may happen very slowly over hundreds of years, but can still result in the eventual cessation of using a particular language and the replacement with another. Language shift has thus been characterized as the return of a bilingual state of affairs to a monolingual one (Grosjean 1982: 38).

Yoel (2007) reported on the decline in use of an immigrant community's language due to replacement of that language by the host country's language. She focused on the attrition of Russian Sign Language (RSL) in several individuals who immigrated to Israel and subsequently learned Israeli Sign Language (ISL). Whereas, some of the signs of RSL were remembered and correctly articulated by the immigrants years after arriving in Israel, there were multiple examples in Yoel's data of incorrectly articulated RSL signs or else signs that were fully forgotten.

Language death has also been suggested, albeit minimally, to result from contact between signed languages. Much of this contact is a result of the work of foreign missionaries, foreign instructors, and even deaf people from those countries who have learned ASL and other Western sign languages and returned to their own country. Woodward (2000) claims that indigenous sign languages of Southeast Asia seem to be dying out and are apparently being replaced by signed languages influenced by ASL or French Sign Language (LSF).

Yoel (2009) reports on the rapid decline in the use of Maritime Sign Language (MSL), which is used by elderly Deaf people in Canada's Maritime provinces. The majority of Deaf Canadians use American Sign Language (ASL) though there is also a population of Langue de Signes Québécoise (LSQ) in the province of Quebec. Yoel suggests that there are fewer than 100 users of MSL, and contact with ASL may be at the heart of the decline. MSL is reported to have its roots in British Sign Language (BSL), but contact with ASL has resulted in the addition of many lexical items from that language. Unfortunately, her analysis suggests that MSL is "moribund; it is beyond revival and survival. It will die out within its last remaining users" (2009: iii).

Likewise, Nonaka (2004), in her account of indigenous signed languages of Thailand, writes of the need to remember sign languages in discussions of language endangerment and in language preservation efforts. Nonaka discusses indigenous varieties of signed language in Thailand such as Ban Khor Sign Language and those referred to as Old Bangkok and Old Chiangmai sign varieties. Whereas the national sign language, Thai Sign Language, seems to be thriving, according to Nonaka, the future of the indigenous varieties is uncertain. It is clear that language contact can result not only in the creation of new varieties but also in the drastic alteration or destruction of others.

Characteristics of signed language that likely influence contact in the visual–gestural modality

Thus far, we have shown that signed languages provide evidence of contact phenomena that can readily be compared to contact between spoken languages, but there are also some unique considerations for sign–sign contact. Quinto-Pozos (2007) proposed that three prominent characteristics of signed languages influence the outcomes of contact in that modality: (1) the prevalence of iconicity; (2) the utilization of gestural (i.e., nonlinguistic) resources; and (3) the interlingual structural similarity of signed languages. Earlier in the chapter we provided details about gestural resources, and here we provide an argument for the role of iconicity and the degree of similarity across signed languages.

The prevalence of iconicity

One of the most commonly discussed topics in the field of sign linguistics is the iconic characteristics of signed languages and the various implications of that iconicity. For the study of signed language contact (either with another signed language or with users of spoken language), iconicity is particularly important because it likely allows people who do not use the same language to comprehend each other more easily than if they relied exclusively on spoken and/or written language. This could have a noticeable effect on the outcome of such contact.

Iconicity is present in various signed language devices. It appears in some lexical signs (e.g., the sign TREE in various sign languages, even though properties of a tree are selectively represented across the various signs), in the signs of so-called classifier constructions (e.g., Klima and Bellugi 1979; Quinto-Pozos 2007; Taub 2001), and it is also present in metaphorical constructions (Taub 2001; Wilcox 2004). Aspects of iconicity are also evident in the ways in which signers use their bodies to portray postures and movements of an animate referent (Liddell and Metzger 1998; Metzger 1995; Quinto-Pozos 2007; Taub 2001).

The degree of iconicity in signed language can be considered a true modality difference between sign and speech: both have iconicity, but signed languages are much more characterized by visual iconicity than spoken languages are by auditory iconicity (Liddell 2003; Perniss, Thompson, Vigliocco 2010). In some cases, iconicity can make certain signs and gestures transparent (to varying degrees) to a non-signer of a particular sign language. For example, Pizzuto and Volterra (2000) examined the comprehension of Italian Sign Language (LIS) signs by (deaf) signers and (hearing) non-signers in various parts of Europe. Interestingly, the deaf signers consistently guessed the meanings of signs even though they were not LIS signers. As a result, the authors suggest that the data point to "the existence of potential universals across sign languages" (283). The "universals" that they refer to are mostly due to the prevalence of iconicity in the visual–gestural modality. The Pizzuto and Volterra study seems to echo some of the comments made by early writers on the topic of the cross-linguistic intelligibility of signed languages (Battison and Jordan 1976; Jordan and Battison 1976; Mayberry 1978); specifically, it suggests that there are ways in which the viewer of an unknown signed language might be able to understand at least a portion of what is being communicated.

The interlingual structural similarity of signed languages

Based on the sign languages that have been studied thus far, it seems that many (or perhaps, most) share various structural features. Lucas and Valli (1992) suggest that signed language phonologies are more similar to each other than spoken language phonologies, and Newport and Supalla (2000) point out that signed languages show more typological similarity to each other than spoken languages do, at least in terms of their morphological structure. If one uses an agreement analysis for signed language verbs, signed languages seem to favor object agreement over subject agreement, and verbs can be classified into two or three general categories based on the inflectional morphology they may accept (Padden 1983). Another major similarity between signed languages is the use of the signing space and so-called classifiers for spatial descriptions. Such constructions allow the signer to communicate various types of information such as figure, ground, motion, location, orientation, direction, manner, aspect, extant, shape, and distribution (Schembri 2003).

There are, of course, some differences across signed languages. For example, differences in phonetic inventories and phonological processes exist, but, compared to phonetic and phonological variations across spoken languages, they seem to be relatively few. Some sign languages have auxiliary verbs that aid in the use of the signing space to depict grammatical relationships, while many do not (Rathmann 2000). Basic word order across signed languages is not as uniform as the use of space for showing grammatical relationships in conjunction with the verb (Newport and Supalla 2000). Moreover, signers certainly use nonmanual signals (e.g., head tilt, eyebrow raise, and furrow) in different ways for grammatical and prosodic functions. As an example, a *wh*-question in ASL requires a brow furrow, whereas the same type of question in LSM requires a backward head thrust.

Some writers have suggested that the similarities among signed languages may be partly due to the fact that they are relatively young (it is believed that most of the oldest signed languages currently in use date to approximately the eighteenth and nineteenth centuries and that the youngest have been created within the last twenty to thirty years). Their histories are thus not long enough to show evidence of significant divergence (Aronoff, Meir, and Sandler 2005; Meier 2002; Newport and Supalla 2000). The similarity across signed languages is true for those that are genetically related, as well as those that are purported to have developed with little or no historical or genetic relationship to other signed languages.

Concluding remarks

Most work on signed language contact has focused on the interaction of signed and spoken and/or written languages. This multimodal contact may be due to the fact that signed languages most often exist within larger communities where spoken and written languages are used daily. These oral and written modalities of language exert much linguistic (and cultural) influence on signed languages. This has been true as long as deaf children have been educated and guided through the acquisition of literacy. This has also been true because of the interactions between deaf and hearing users of signed languages. Deaf people and signed languages do not exist in a vacuum; they are surrounded by many non-native signers and languages (both spoken and written) that are structured differently. We suggest that the fact that Deaf signers are multi-modal bilinguals/multilinguals creates a fertile landscape for the creation of contact phenomena.

There are also cases of signed languages coming into contact with each other – either in transnational border communities or through international travel experiences. Such cases of unimodal contact are particularly interesting because they allow the investigator of language contact an opportunity to examine how language contact may have unique characteristics if considered solely within the visual–gestural modality (see Quinto-Pozos 2007 for discussions of common characteristics of such contact).

It has been suggested that Deaf learners of a spoken/written language demonstrate learning strategies consistent with a L2 learner of a spoken/written language (Plaza-Pust 2008). Additionally, the multilingual development that most Deaf individuals experience likely leads to very specific language mixing. As Plaza-Pust (2008: 127) notes, "This is an important conclusion given the myths that surround the acquisition of a written language by deaf students." Language mixing and contact are the norm in Deaf communities.

The study of contact in the visual–gestural modality is a fascinating area of research. It can tell us much about language structure, the influence of society on language, and the role of modality on language. By considering the ways in which bimodal bilinguals/multilinguals shape their languages, the general study of the human language capacity is advanced.

REFERENCES

Adam, R. (2012) Language contact and borrowing. In R. Pfau, M. Steinbach, and B. Woll (eds.), *Sign Language: An International Handbook* (pp. 841–862). Berlin: Mouton de Gruyter.

Adam, Robert (2012) Unimodal bilingualism in the Deaf community: Contact between dialects of BSL and ISL in Australia and the United Kingdom, dissertation submitted for Ph.D., University College London, London.

Adone, D. (2012) Language emergence and creolisation. In *Handbücher zur Sprach- und Kommunikationswissenschaft/Handbooks of Linguistics and Communication Science: Sign Language: An International Handbook* (pp. 862–889). Berlin: Walter de Gruyter.

Ajello, R., Mazzoni, L., and Nicolai, F. (2001) Linguistic gestures: Mouthing in Italian Sign Language (LIS). In P. Boyes Braem and R. Sutton-Spence (eds.), *The hands are the head of the mouth: The mouth as articulator in sign language* (pp. 231–246). Hamburg: Signum.

Allsop, L., Woll, B., and Brauti, J. M. (1995) International sign: The creation of an international Deaf community and sign language. In H. F. Bos, and G. M. Schermer (eds.), *Sign Language Research 1994: Proceedings of the Fourth European Congress on Sign Language Research, Munich, September 1–3, 1994* (pp. 171–188). Hamburg: Signum.

Ann, J. (2001). Bilingualism and language contact. In C. Lucas (ed.), *The sociolinguistics of sign language* (pp. 33–60). New York: Cambridge University Press.

Ann, J., Smith, W. H., and Yu, C. (2007) The sign language of mainland China at the Ch'iying School in Taiwan. In D. Quinto-Pozos (ed.), *Sign Language Contact* (pp. 235–258). Washington, DC: Gallaudet University Press.

Antzakas, K. and Woll, B. (2002) Head movements and negation in Greek Sign Language. In I. Wachsmuth and T. Sowa (eds.), *Gesture and Sign Language in Human–Computer Interaction* (pp. 193–196). Berlin: Springer.

Aronoff, M., Irit M., and Wendy S. (2005) The paradox of sign language morphology. *Language* 81(2): 301–344.

Baker A. E. and van den Bogaerde, B. (2008) Codemixing in signs and words in input to and output from children. In C. Plaza-Pust and E. Morales-López (eds.), *Sign Bilingualism: Language Development, Interaction, and Maintenance in Sign Language Contact Situations* (pp. 1–27). Amsterdam: John Benjamins.

Battison, R. (1978) *Lexical Borrowing in American Sign Language.* Silver Spring, MD: Linstok.

Battison, R. and Jordan, I. K. (1976) Cross-cultural communication with foreign signers: Fact and fancy. *Sign Language Studies* 10.

Bishop, M. (2006) Bimodal bilingualism in hearing, native users of American Sign Language, unpublished doctoral dissertation, Gallaudet University.

Bishop, M. and Hicks, S. (2008) Coda talk: Bimodal discourse among hearing, native signers. In M. Bishop and S. Hicks (eds.), *Hearing, Mother Father Deaf: Hearing People in Deaf Families* (pp. 54–96). Washington, DC: Gallaudet University Press.

Bogaerde, B. van den and Baker, A. (2005) Code mixing in mother–child interaction in deaf families. *Sign Language and Linguistics* 8: 155–178.

Boyes Braem, P. (2001) Functions of the mouthing component in the signing of deaf early and late learners of Swiss German Sign Language. In D. Brentari (ed.), *Foreign Vocabulary in Sign Languages: A Cross-Linguistic Investigation of Word Formation* (pp. 1–47). Mahwah, NJ: Lawrence Erlbaum.

Brentari, D. and Padden, C. A. (2001) Native and foreign vocabulary in American Sign Language: A lexicon with multiple origins. In D. Brentari (ed.), *Foreign Vocabulary in Sign Languages: A Cross-Linguistic Investigation of Word Formation* (pp. 87–119). Mahwah, NJ: Lawrence Erlbaum.

Bullock, B. and Toribio, J. (2009) *The Handbook of Code-Switching.* Cambridge: Cambridge University Press.

Casey, S. (2003) "Agreement" in gestures and signed languages: The use of directionality to indicate referents involved in actions, Ph.D. dissertation, University of California, San Diego.

Clyne, M. (2003) *Dynamics of Language Contact.* Cambridge: Cambridge University Press.

Cokely, D. (1983) When is a pidgin not a pidgin? *Sign Language Studies* 38: 1–24.

Cormier, K., Tyrone, M., and Schembri, A. (2008) One hand or two? Nativisation of fingerspelling in ASL and BANZSL. *Sign Language and Linguistics* 11: 3–44.

Crasborn, O., van der Kooij, E., Waters, D., Woll, B., and Mesch, J. (2008) Frequency distribution and spreading of different types of mouth actions in three sign languages. *Sign Language and Linguistics* 11: 45–67.

Crystal, D. (2000) *Language Death*. Cambridge, UK: Cambridge University Press.

Davis, J. (1989) Distinguishing language contact phenomena in ASL interpretation. In C. Lucas (ed.), *The Sociolinguistics of the Deaf Community* (pp. 85–102). San Diego, CA: Academic Press.

(2007) North American Indian signed language varieties: A comparative historical linguistic assessment. In D. Quinto-Pozos (ed.), *Sign Languages in Contact* (pp. 85–122). Washington, DC: Gallaudet University Press.

(2010) *Hand Talk: Sign Language among Indian Nations of North America*. Cambridge: Cambridge University Press.

Duarte, K. (2010) The mechanics of fingerspelling: Analyzing Ethiopian Sign Language. *Sign Language Studies* 11(1): 5–21.

Dugdale, P., Kennedy, G., McKee, D., and McKee, R. (2003) Aerial spelling and NZSL: A response to Forman (2003). *Journal of Deaf Studies and Deaf Education* 8: 494–497.

Ebbinghaus, H. and Hessmann, J. (2001) Sign language as multidimensional communication: Why manual signs, mouthings, and mouth gestures are three different things. In P. Boyes Braem and R. Sutton-Spence (eds.), *The Hands Are the Head of the Mouth: The Mouth as Articulator in Sign Language* (pp. 133–151). Hamburg: Signum.

Emmorey, K., Borinstein, H., and Thompson, R. (2005) Bimodal bilingualism: Code-blending between spoken English and American Sign Language. In J. Cohen, K. T. McAlister, K. Rolstad, and J. MacSwan (eds.), *ISB4: Proceedings of the 4th International Symposium on Bilingualism* (pp. 663–673). Somerville, MA: Cascadilla Press.

Emmorey, K., Borinstein, H., Thompson, R., and Gollan, T. (2008) Bimodal bilingualism. *Bilingualism: Language and Cognition* 11: 43–61.

Ferguson, C. (1959) Diglossia. *Word* 15: 325–340.

Fischer, S. D. (1978) Sign language and creoles. In P. Siple (ed.), *Understanding Language through Sign Language Research* (pp. 309–331). New York: Academic Press.

(1996) By the numbers: Language-internal evidence for creolization. *International Review of Sign Linguistics* 1: 1–22.

Fishman, J. A. (1967) Bilingualism with and without diglossia; Diglossia with and without bilingualism. *Journal of Social Issues* 23: 29–38.

(1991) *Reversing Language Shift*. Clevedon, UK: Multilingual Matters.

Forman, W. (2003) The ABCs of New Zealand Sign Language: Aerial spelling. *Journal of Deaf Studies and Deaf Education* 8: 92–96.

Groce, N. E. (1985) *Everyone Here Spoke Sign Language*. Cambridge, MA: Harvard University Press.

Grosjean, F. (1982) *Life with Two Languages*. Cambridge, MA: Harvard University Press.

(1989) Neurolinguists, beware! The bilingual is not two monolinguals in one person. *Brain and Language* 36: 3–15.

(1992) Another view of bilingualism. In R. Harris (ed.), *Cognitive Processing in Bilinguals* (pp. 51–62). Amsterdam/New York: North Holland.

(2010) Bilingualism, biculturalism, and deafness. *International Journal of Bilingual Education and Bilingualism* 13: 133–145.

Guerra Currie, A.-M. (1999) A Mexican Sign Language lexicon: Internal and cross-linguistic similarities and variation, Ph.D. dissertation, University of Texas, Austin.

Guerra Currie, A.-M. P., Meier, R. P., and Walters, K. (2002) A cross-linguistic examination of the lexicons of four sign languages. In R. P. Meier, K. Cormier, and D. Quinto-Pozos (eds.), *Modality and Structure in Signed and Spoken Languages* (pp. 224–236). New York: Cambridge University Press.

Hensey, F. G. (1993) Portuguese and/or 'Fronterizo' in northern Uruguay. In Rebecca Posner and John N. Green (eds.), *Trends in Romance Linguistics and Philology. Volume 5: Bilingualism and Linguistic Conflict in Romance* (pp. 433–452). Berlin: Mouton de Gruyter.

Hohenberger, A. and Happ, D. (2001) The linguistic primacy of signs and mouth gestures over mouthing: Evidence from language production in German Sign Language (DGS). In P. Boyes Braem and R. Sutton-Spence (eds.), *The Hands Are the Head of the Mouth: The Mouth as Articulator in Sign Language* (pp. 159–189). Hamburg: Signum.

Hou, L. and Mesh, K. (2013) Negation in Chatino sign, poster presentation. Theoretical Issues in Sign Language Research Conference 11. London, England.

Hoyer, Karin (2007) Albanian Sign Language: Language contact, international sign and gesture. In D. Quinto-Pozos (ed.), *Sign Languages in Contact* (pp. 195–234). Washington, DC: Gallaudet University Press.

Humphries, T. and F. MacDougall (1999/2000) "Chaining" and other links: Making connections between American Sign Language and English in two types of school settings. *Visual Anthropology Review* 15(2): 84–94.

Janzen, T. and Shaffer, B. (2002) Gesture as the substrate in the process of ASL grammaticization. In R. P. Meier, K. Cormier, and D. Quinto-Pozos (eds.), *Modality and Structure in Signed and Spoken Languages* (pp. 199–223). New York: Cambridge University Press.

Johnson, R. (1991) Sign language, culture, and community in a traditional Yucatec Maya village. *Sign Language Studies* 73: 461–474.

Johnston, T. and Schembri, A. (2007) *Australian Sign Language (Auslan): An Introduction to Sign Language Linguistics.* Cambridge: Cambridge University Press.

Jordan, I. K. and Battison, R. (1976) A referential communication experiment with foreign sign languages. *Sign Language Studies* 5(10): 69–80.

Kelly, A. B. (1991) Fingerspelling use among the Deaf senior citizens of Baltimore. In E. A. Winston (ed.), *Communication Forum 1991* (pp. 90–98). Washington, DC: Gallaudet University School of Communication.

Klima, E. and Bellugi, U. (1979) *The Signs of Language.* Cambridge, MA: Harvard University Press.

Kuntze, M. (2000) Codeswitching in ASL and written English language contact. In K. Emmorey and H. Lane (eds.), *The Signs of Language Revisited: An Anthology to Honor Ursula Bellugi and Edward Klima* (pp. 287–302). Mahwah, NJ: Lawrence Erlbaum.

Kyle, J. and Woll, B. (1985) *Sign Language: The Study of Deaf People and Their Language.* New York: Cambridge University Press.

Lehiste, I. (1988) *Lectures on Language Contact.* Cambridge, MA: MIT Press.

Liddell, S.K. (2003) *Grammar, Gesture, and Meaning in American Sign Language.* Cambridge: Cambridge University Press.

Liddell, Scott K. and Metzger, M. (1998) Gesture in Sign Language Discourse. *Journal of Pragmatics* 30: 657–697.

Lucas, C. and Valli, C. (1992) *Language Contact in the American Deaf Community.* San Diego, CA: Academic Press.

Machabée, D. (1995) Description and status of initialized signs in Quebec Sign Language. In C. Lucas (ed.), *Sociolinguistics in Deaf Communities* (pp. 29–61). Washington, DC: Gallaudet University Press.

McClave, E. Z. (2001) The relationship between spontaneous gestures of the hearing and American Sign Language. *Gesture* 11: 51–72.

McKee, D. and Kennedy, G. (2000) Lexical comparison of signs from American, Australian, British, and New Zealand sign languages. In K. Emmorey and H. Lane (eds.), *The Signs of Language Revisited: An Anthology to Honor Ursula Bellugi and Edward Klima* (pp. 49–76). Mahwah, NJ: Lawrence Erlbaum.

McKee, R. and Napier, J. (2002) Interpreting into International Sign Pidgin. *Sign Language and Linguistics* 51: 27–54.

McKee, R. L., McKee, D., Smiler, K., and Pointon, K. (2007) Māori signs: The construction of indigenous Deaf identity in New Zealand Sign Language. In D. Quinto-Pozos (ed.), *Sign Languages in Contact* (pp. 31–81). Washington, DC: Gallaudet University Press.

McNeill, D. (1992) *Hand and Mind.* Chicago, IL: University of Chicago Press.

Mayberry, R. (1978) French Canadian Sign Language: A study of inter-sign-language comprehension. In P. Siple (ed.), *Understanding Language through Sign Language Research* (pp. 349–372). New York: Academic Press.

Meier, Richard P. (2002) The acquisition of verb agreement in ASL. In Morgan, G. and Woll, B. (eds.), *Directions in Sign Language Acquisition* (pp. 115–141). Amsterdam: John Benjamins.

Metzger, M. (1995) Constructed dialogue and constructed action in American Sign Language. In C. Lucas (ed.), *Sociolinguistics in Deaf Communities* (pp. 255–271). Washington, DC: Gallaudet University Press.

Miller, C. (2001) The adaptation of loan words in Quebec Sign Language: Multiple sources, multiple processes. In D. Brentari (ed.), *Foreign Vocabulary in Sign Language: A Cross-Linguistic Investigation of Word Formation* (pp. 139–173). Mahwah, NJ: Lawrence Erlbaum.

Murray, J. (2009) Sign languages. In A. Iriye and P. Y. Saunier (eds.), *The Palgrave Dictionary of Transnational History* (pp. 947–948). Basingstoke, UK: Palgrave Macmillan.

Muysken, P. (2000). *Bilingual speech. A typology of code-mixing.* Cambridge: Cambridge University Press.

Newport, E. L. and Supalla, T. (2000). Sign language research at the millennium. In K. Emmorey and H. Lane (eds.), *The Signs of Language Revisited: An Anthology in Honor of Ursula Bellugi and Edward Klima.* Mahwah, NJ: Lawrence Erlbaum Associates.

Nonaka, A. M. (2004) The forgotten endangered languages: Lessons on the importance of remembering from Thailand's Ban Khor Sign Language. *Language in Society* 33: 737–767.

Padden, C. (1983) Interaction of morphology and syntax in American Sign Language. Ph.D. dissertation, University of California, San Diego.

(1998) The ASL lexicon. *Sign Language and Linguistics* 1: 39–60.

Parkhurst, D. and Parkhurst, S. (2003) Lexical comparisons of sign languages and the effects of iconicity. *Work Papers of the Summer Institute of Linguistics, University of North Dakota Session* 47: 1–17.

Perniss, P., Thompson, R., and Vigliocco, G. (2010) Iconicity as a general property of language: Evidence from spoken and signed languages. *Frontiers in Psychology* 1: 227. Retrieved from: www.frontiersin.org/Journal/Abstract.aspx? ART_DOI=10.3389/fpsyg.2010.00227&name=language_sciences

Pietrosemoli, L. (2001) Politeness in Venezuelan Sign Language. In V. Dively, M. Metzger, S. Taub, and A. M. Baer (eds.), *Signed Languages: Discoveries from International Research* (pp. 163–179). Washington, DC: Gallaudet University Press.

Pizzuto, E., and Volterra, V. (2000) Iconicity and transparency in sign languages: A cross-linguistic cross-cultural view. In K. Emmorey and H. Lane (eds.), *The Signs of Language Revisited: An Anthology to Honor Ursula Bellugi and Edward Klima*. Mahwah, NJ: Lawrence Erlbaum Associates.

Plaza-Pust, C. (2008) Why variation matters. In C. Plaza-Pust and E. Morales-López (eds.), *Sign Bilingualism: Language Development, Interaction, and Maintenance in Sign Language Contact Situations* (pp. 73–135). Amsterdam: John Benjamins.

Plaza-Pust, C. and Morales-López, E. (2008) Sign bilingualism. In C. Plaza-Pust and E. Morales-López (eds.), *Sign Bilingualism: Language Development, Interaction, and Maintenance in Sign Language Contact Situations* (pp. 333–379). Amsterdam: John Benjamins.

Quinto-Pozos, D. (2002) Contact between Mexican Sign Language and American Sign Language in two Texas border areas, Ph.D. dissertation, University of Texas at Austin.

(2007) Outlining considerations for the study of sign language contact. In D. Quinto-Pozos (ed.), *Sign Languages in Contact* (pp. 1–28). Washington, DC: Gallaudet University Press.

(2008) Sign language contact and interference: ASL and LSM. *Language in Society* 37: 161–189.

(2009) Code-switching between sign languages. In B. Bullock and J. Toribio (eds.), *The Handbook of Code-Switching* (pp. 221–237). Cambridge: Cambridge University Press.

Quinto-Pozos, D and Adam, R. (2013) Sign language contact. In R. Bayley, R. Cameron and C. Lucas *The Oxford Handbook of Sociolinguistics* (pp. 379–400). New York: Oxford University Press.

Quinto-Pozos, D. and Mehta, S. (2010) Register variation in mimetic gestural complements to signed language. *Journal of Pragmatics* 42: 557–584.

Quinto-Pozos, D. and Reynolds, W. (2012) ASL discourse strategies: Chaining and connecting–explaining across audiences. *Sign Language Studies* 12(2): 41–65.

Rathmann, C. (2000) Does the presence of a person agreement marker predict word order in SLs? Paper presented at the Seventh International Conference on Theoretical Issues in Sign Language Research, July 23–27, Amsterdam, the Netherlands.

Rosenstock, R. (2004) An investigation of international sign: Analyzing structure and comprehension, Ph.D. dissertation, Gallaudet University.

Sasaki, D. (2007) Comparing lexicons of Japanese Sign Language and Taiwan Sign Language: A preliminary study focusing on the differences in the handshape parameter. In D. Quinto-Pozos (ed.), *Sign Languages in Contact* (pp. 123–150). Washington, DC: Gallaudet University Press.

Schembri, A. (2003) Rethinking "classifiers" in signed languages. In K. Emmorey (ed.), *Perspectives on Classifier Constructions in Sign Languages* (pp. 3–34). Mahwah, NJ: Lawrence Erlbaum Associates.

Schembri, A. and Johnston, T. (2007) Sociolinguistic variation in the use of fingerspelling in Australian Sign Language: A pilot study. *Sign Language Studies* 7(3): 319–347.

Schmaling, C. (2001) ASL in northern Nigeria: Will Hausa Sign Language survive? In V. Dively, M. Metzger, S. Taub, and A. M. Baer (eds.), *Signed Languages: Discoveries from International Research* (pp. 180–193). Washington, DC: Gallaudet University Press.

Schneider, E., Kozak, L. Viola, and Santiago, R. (2011) *The Effects of Electronic Communication on American Sign Language.* Georgetown University Roundtable on Languages and Linguistics.

Simons, G. F. and Lewis, M. P. (2013) The world's languages in crisis. In E. Mihas, B. Perley, G. Rei-Doval, and K. Wheatley (eds.), *Responses to Language Endangerment: In Honor of Mickey Noonan. New Directions in Language Documentation and Language Revitalization* (pp. 3–20). Amsterdam: John Benjamins.

Stokoe, W. (1970) Sign language diglossia. *Studies in Linguistics* 21: 27–41.

Supalla, T. and Webb, R. (1995) The grammar of International Sign: A new look at pidgin languages. In K. Emmorey and J. Reilly, (eds.), *Language, Gesture, and Space* (pp. 333–352). Mahwah, NJ: Lawrence Erlbaum.

Sutton-Spence, R. (1994) The role of the manual alphabet and fingerspelling in British Sign Language, Ph.D. dissertation, University of Bristol.

(1998) English verb loans in BSL. In C. Lucas (ed.), *Pinky Extension and Eye Gaze: Language Use in Deaf Communities.* Washington, DC: Gallaudet University Press.

(2003) British manual alphabets in the education of Deaf people since the 17th century. In L. Monaghan, C. Schmaling, K. Nakamura, and G. T. Turner (eds.), *Many Ways to Be Deaf: International Variation in Deaf Communities* (pp. 25–48). Washington, DC: Gallaudet University Press.

Sutton-Spence, R. and Woll, B. (1999) *The Linguistics of British Sign Language: An Introduction.* Cambridge: Cambridge University Press.

Taub, S. F. (2001) *Language from the Body: Iconicity and Conceptual Metaphor in American Sign Language.* Cambridge: Cambridge University Press.

Tervoort, B. (1973) Could there be a human sign language? *Semiotica* 9: 347–382.

Thomason, S. G. and Kaufman, T. (1988) *Language Contact, Creolization, and Genetic Linguistics.* Berkeley, CA: University of California Press

Vinson, D., Thompson, R., Vigliocco, G., Skinner, R., Woolfe, T., and Fox, N. (2010) The hands and mouth do not always slip together in British Sign Language: Dissociating articulatory channels in the lexicon. *Psychological Science*, 22(8).

Waters, D, Campbell, R., Capek, Cheryl M., Woll, B., David, Anthony S., McGuire, Phillip K., Brammer, Michael J., and MacSweeney, M. (2007) Fingerspelling, signed language, text and picture processing in deaf native signers: The role of the mid-fusiform gyrus. *Neuroimage* 35: 1287–1302.

Wilcox, P. (2004) A cognitive key: Metonymic and metaphorical mappings in ASL. *Cognitive Linguistics*, 15: 197–222.

Wilcox, S. and Wilcox, P. (1997) *Learning to See: Teaching American Sign Language as a Second Language.* Washington, DC: Gallaudet University Press.

Woll, B., Sutton-Spence R., and Elton, F. (2001) Multilingualism: The global approach to sign languages. In C. Lucas (ed.), *The Sociolinguistics of Sign Languages* (pp. 8–32). Cambridge: Cambridge University Press.

Woodward, J. (1973a) Implicational lects on the deaf diglossic continuum, Ph.D. dissertation, Georgetown University.

(1973b) Some characteristics of Pidgin Sign English. *Sign Language Studies* 3: 39–46.

(2000) Sign languages and sign language families in Thailand and Viet Nam. In K. Emmorey and H. Lane (eds.), *The Signs of Language Revisited: An Anthology to Honor Ursula Bellugi and Edward Klima* (pp. 23–47). Mahwah, NJ: Lawrence Erlbaum.

Yang, Jun Hui (2008) Sign language and oral/written language in deaf education in China. In C. Plaza-Pust and E. Morales-López (eds.), *Sign Bilingualism: Language Development, Interaction, and Maintenance in Sign Language Contact Situations* (pp. 297–331). Amsterdam: John Benjamins.

Yoel, J. (2007) Evidence for first-language attrition of Russian Sign Language among immigrants to Israel. In D. Quinto-Pozos (ed.), *Sign Languages in Contact* (pp. 153–191). Washington, DC: Gallaudet University Press.

(2009) Canada's Maritime Sign Language, Ph.D. dissertation, University of Manitoba.

4   Variation and change in sign languages

Robert Bayley, Adam C. Schembri, and Ceil Lucas

All human languages vary in both time and space as well as according to the linguistic environment in which a particular form is used. For example, the ASL sign DEAF has three main forms. It can be produced with a movement from ear to chin (the citation or dictionary form), from chin to ear or by contacting the check once (both non-citation forms). Even though the form of DEAF varies from signer to signer, and even within the signing of the same signer, the variation we observe is not random. Rather, signers' choices among the three forms of DEAF are systematically constrained by a range of linguistic and social influences, or factors. For example, compared to signers in other parts of the United States, signers in Boston, Massachusetts use the citation form of DEAF more often. In contrast, signers in Kansas, Missouri, and Virginia tend to prefer non-citation forms. Indeed, a study of variation in the sign DEAF showed that signers in these states used non-citation forms of DEAF 85 percent of the time, more than twice the rate of signers in Boston (Bayley, Lucas, and Rose 2000: 92).

The region of the country where a signer lives is not the only influence on the choice of a form of DEAF. For example, although ASL signers in Boston generally used more citation forms of DEAF than signers in other areas of the United States, Boston signers aged 55 and older are far less likely to choose a non-citation form of DEAF than are younger signers. Bayley *et al.* (2000) reported that Boston signers aged 55 and older used the citation form of DEAF 76 percent of the time. In contrast, signers between the ages of 26 and 55 used the citation form 54 percent of the time, and signers between the ages of 14 and 26 used the citation form only 46 percent of the time. In addition, variation can be affected by linguistic factors. To continue with the example of DEAF, Lucas (1995) and Bayley *et al.* (2000) found that signers were very likely to use a non-citation form of DEAF when it was part of a compound, as in DEAF^CULTURE or DEAF^WORLD. However, when DEAF was a predicate adjective, as in PRO.1 DEAF ('I am deaf'), signers were more likely to choose the citation form.

We gratefully acknowledge Joseph Hill for his work on the figures in this chapter.

As the example of variation in the form of DEAF shows, signers' choices among variable linguistic forms are affected both by *social* (e.g., region, age) and by *linguistic* (e.g., grammatical class) factors. In this chapter, we review the study of language variation. We pay special attention to the many intersecting social factors that can influence variation and to the kinds of linguistic units and processes that vary in signed and spoken languages. We include examples from recent work on variation in Australian Sign Language (Auslan), British Sign Language (BSL), New Zealand Sign Language (NZSL), and Italian Sign Language (LIS, Lingua dei Segni Italiana), as well as from ASL.

Variation in spoken languages

The 1960s was a period of rapid development in linguistics. During the same period that Stokoe (1960) and Croneberg (1965) were showing that sign languages could be studied in the same way as any other human language, a number of scholars began to demonstrate that much of the variation in spoken languages that had previously been thought to be random is highly systematic. Thus, the study of variation in the modern sense, which began with Labov's work on Martha's Vineyard and in New York City (1963, 1966, 1969) and similar work by Shuy, Wolfram, and Riley (1968) and Wolfram (1969) in Detroit, was contemporaneous with the rapid increase in linguists' understanding of sign languages that developed as a consequence of the work of Stokoe and his colleagues. In this section, we outline the main tenets of the variationist approach.

The sociolinguistic variable

Several researchers have explained the concept of a *sociolinguistic variable*. Drawing upon the work of Labov (1972), Fasold characterized the sociolinguistic variable as "a set of alternative ways of saying the same thing, although the alternatives will have social significance" (1990: 223–224). Milroy defined a sociolinguistic variable as "a linguistic element . . . which co-varies not only with other linguistic elements, but also with a number of extra-linguistic independent social variables such as social class, age, sex, ethnic group or contextual style" (1987: 10). Wolfram viewed a linguistic variable as a "convenient construct employed to unite a class of fluctuating variants within some specified language set" (1991: 23). He drew the distinction between a linguistic variable, which has to do with variation within a language, and a sociolinguistic variable, a construct that unifies the correlation of internal variables and external constraints. Internal constraints are the features of a linguistic nature – a sound, a handshape, a syntactic structure – that vary. External constraints are the factors of a social nature that may correlate with the behavior of the linguistic variable.

Variable units in spoken languages

Linguists generally accept that spoken languages are composed of segments of sound produced by the vocal apparatus and that these segments are themselves composed of a variety of features. In spoken languages, whole segments or features of segments may be variable. For example, a word-final voiced consonant may be devoiced, a non-nasal vowel may acquire the feature of nasalization, and vowels may vary from their canonical position and be raised or lowered within the vowel space.

A new segment may also be created from the features of other segments, as often happens in palatalization. Individual segments may be variably added or deleted, and syllables (that is, groups of segments) can be added or deleted. Parts of segments, whole segments, or groups of segments can also be variably rearranged, as we see with metathesis in English, in the variable pronunciations *hundred* and *hunderd*.

Variation may also be seen in word-sized combinations of segments or in combinations of words. In lexical variation, we find separate morphemes for the same concept, and use of these separate morphemes correlates with non-linguistic categories such as region, ethnicity, and gender. But we may also see syntactic variation characterized by the deletion of whole morphemes or by the variable position of whole morphemes.

Variation also is present in units of discourse (i.e., units consisting of many words), as in variation in text type or in lists used in narratives (Schiffrin 1994). What varies in spoken languages ranges from the features of a segment to a discourse unit that consists of many segments, from the very smallest unit that we can identify to the largest.

It is evident even to a casual observer that people vary in their use of linguistic forms. At the level of phonology, speakers of English sometimes pronounce the progressive morpheme ING with the apical variant /n/, as in *workin'*, and sometimes with the velar nasal /ŋ/ (Trudgill 1974). Speakers of all dialects of English also sometimes delete the final /t/ in words such as *mist by the lake* and sometimes pronounce it, as in *miss/t/ my bus* (Guy 1980; Labov 1989). Note that what is being deleted may be a morpheme, i.e., a segment with independent meaning, as in *missed*, where the past tense marker -ed is pronounced as [t]. Numerous studies have shown that language varies at the level of morphology. For example, speakers of many English dialects variably use third person singular verbal -s, as in *he want/he wants* (see, e.g., Godfrey and Tagliamonte 1999).

Language also varies at the level of syntax. For example, speakers of Spanish, Chinese, and many other languages as well as signers of ASL, Auslan, and NZSL sometimes use an overt subject pronoun and sometimes omit it (Jia and Bayley 2002; McKee *et al.* 2011; Otheguy and Zentella 2012;

Wulf *et al.* 2002), as shown in example 1, from Spanish, and example 2, from ASL:

(1)   *yo/Ø quiero ir a la playa.* (I want to go to the beach.)
(2)   PRO.1/Ø WANT MEET PRO.3 (I want to meet him/her.)

In addition, in English, the alternation between pied-piped relative pronouns and stranded prepositions provides a convenient example of syntactic variation (Guy and Bayley 1995), e.g.

(3a)   To whom did you give the money?
(3b)   Who(m) did you give the money to?

Furthermore, as Lucas and Valli (1992), Quinto-Pozos (2009), Poplack (1980), Zentella (1997), and many others have shown, language users vary in their choice of code. Thus, ASL signers will sometimes alternate between ASL and Signed English and many bilingual speakers alternate between two (or more) languages in the same discourse and often even within the same sentence, for example:

(4a)   *La* security *viene pa' chequear el* building.
          ("Security comes to check the building.")
(4b)   PRO.1 NOT SAYING 100% SUPPORT, NO...
          ("I'm not saying 100% support, no...," with a sign for the suffix -ing produced and continuous English mouthing)

Variable processes in spoken languages

These examples lead us to ask what kinds of *processes* are involved in spoken language variation. Our discussion here takes its departure from Wolfram's (1993; Wolfram and Schilling-Estes 2006) work on variation in spoken languages. One set of processes involved in variation involves the phonological component of a language. For example, variation may be the result of the process of assimilation, such as vowel nasalization or consonant gemination. Variation may result from weakening, as in vowel or consonant deletion. We may see variation resulting from the processes of substitution or addition of elements, as with coalescence (the creation of a new segment from two other segments), metathesis (the rearranging of the order of segments or features of segments), or epenthesis (the addition of a segment). Variation may result from analogy, as in the generalization of third person singular -s to all present tense forms of a verb in English or conversely, the deletion of third person singular -s by analogy with all other verb forms in a given paradigm.

Other processes involved with variation have to do with the morphosyntactic structure of a language. For example, variation may have to do with the process of the co-occurrence of items in syntactic structure. In English, for example, some varieties allow the co-occurrence of more than one negative element while other varieties disallow such co-occurrence. Another process involved in variation at the syntactic level concerns permutation of items within sentences. The variable placement of adverbs in English provides a convenient example.

(5a)   *Quickly*, John ran to the door.
(5b)   John *quickly* ran to the door.
(5c)   John ran *quickly* to the door.
(5d)   John ran to the door *quickly*.

Constraints on variation in spoken languages

Internal constraints on variation are features within the immediate linguistic environment that may influence variation. Wolfram (personal communication, 1994) has stated that the internal constraints on variables may be compositional, sequential, functional, or having to do with structural incorporation. Compositional constraints are those that have to do with the linguistic nature of the variable itself. For example, Wolfram (1989) studied final nasal absence in the speech of 3-year-old African-American children. He found that final /n/ was much more likely to be absent than either /ŋ/ or /m/. A sequential constraint has to do with the role of an element occurring in the same sequence as the variable, either preceding or following it. For example, the final consonant in a word-final consonant cluster is more likely to be deleted if the following segment is another consonant than if it is a vowel. Functional constraints relate to the function of the variable. For example, as explained above, the final consonant in a word-final consonant cluster may function as the past tense morpheme -ed, and this may influence the frequency of deletion of this consonant. Finally, the constraint of structural incorporation concerns the syntactic environment in which a variable finds itself. For example, deletion of *to be* in African American English (AAE) is more likely in a construction with *gonna* (e.g., *He is gonna do it/He gonna do it*) than in one in which the copula is followed by a noun phrase (e.g., *He is my brother/He my brother*).

External constraints on variation include demographic factors such as region, age, race, gender, sexual orientation, and socioeconomic class – all factors that have been shown to co-vary with linguistic factors. Co-variance here means that there is a correlation between the behavior of a linguistic factor and social factors, so that working-class speakers use more of a variant than middle-class speakers, or African-American speakers use a particular variant less than white speakers, and so forth. These correlations make the variation sociolinguistic. Earlier studies of both spoken and sign languages focused on a fairly limited inventory of demographic factors such as those listed above, but more recent studies have focused on the nature of communication networks (Milroy 1987), the dynamics of situational context (Biber and Finegan 1993), and the projection of social identity (Eckert 2000), "in an effort to describe more authentically the social reality of dialect in society" (Wolfram 1997: 116). That is, researchers have realized that the external constraints on variation are more complex than previously thought. They may certainly include the more discrete factors such as region and socioeconomic level, but other factors such as the people that a person interacts with on a daily basis and a person's desire to project a particular identity to others may also play a central role in constraining variation.

For students of language variation, the examples given above, as well as the many other examples that could be given, raise important questions. Is the variation that we observe in all human languages systematic? If the observed variation is indeed systematic, what are the linguistic and social factors that condition a signer's or a speaker's choice among variable linguistic forms? How can we model these choices quantitatively? What does the patterning of linguistic and social factors reveal about the underlying grammar of the language under investigation? Are the patterns that we observe stable or are they the result of ongoing linguistic change? What does linguistic variation reveal about the social structure of the community to which users of the language belong? Finally, what can the study of variation reveal about the similarities and differences in sign and spoken languages? Is variation in sign languages subject to the same kinds of processes as variation in spoken languages? Are there processes that are unique to sign languages? Are there processes that operate only in spoken languages? Although many outstanding questions remain, particularly with respect to sign languages, after five decades of research on linguistic variation we are in a position to answer the questions posed in this paragraph with considerable confidence, as we illustrate in the following discussion of several variables in different sign languages.

Variation in sign languages

Since William C. Stokoe's (1960) pioneering work, there has been widespread recognition that, as natural sign languages are full-fledged linguistic systems shared by communities of users, the sociolinguistics of sign languages can be described in ways that parallel the description of spoken languages. It follows that sign languages must exhibit sociolinguistic variation similar to the variation seen in spoken languages. In the following sections, we review a broadly representative sample of research on variation in several different sign languages.

Prior to the large-scale project documented in Lucas, Bayley, and Valli (2001), a number of scholars had investigated sociolinguistic variation in ASL and to a lesser extent in other sign languages, but for the most part their investigations were limited to small numbers of signers, based on data collected with a wide variety of methods, and focused on a disparate collection of linguistic features. Much of this early work was reviewed by Patrick and Metzger (1996), who examined fifty sociolinguistic studies of sign languages conducted between 1971 and 1994. They found that more than half of the studies involved ten or fewer signers, and that one third included only one or two signers. Only nine studies involved fifty or more signers, and a number of these drew on the same data set. As a result, only during the twenty-first century have we begun to have a reasonably broad picture of what kinds of units may be variable in sign languages and of what kinds of internal and external constraints might be operating on those variable units.

With respect to linguistic structure, many early studies focused on lexical variation. Recent years, however, have seen an increase in studies of phonological and morphosyntactic variation. Among social factors, regional variation has continued to be a major focus, as it was in the work reported in Lucas, Bayley, Valli, Wulf, and Rose (2001). However, studies have increasingly examined factors such as ethnicity, gender, and age, as well as factors particular to Deaf communities, such as whether signers grew up in a Deaf family and hence acquired sign language from birth or whether signers acquired the language during early childhood from Deaf peers at school. Space precludes a full discussion of the many sociolinguistic studies that have been undertaken in recent years. For reviews of work in ASL, interested readers may refer to Lucas (2007), and Lucas and Bayley (2010). Reviews of variation in other sign languages in addition to ASL include Fischer and Gong (2010), Lucas and Bayley (2011), Schembri et al. (2010), Schembri and Johnston (2013), and Schembri et al. (2013). In the remaining sections of this chapter, we first compare variation in spoken and sign languages. We then discuss methodological issues in studying variation in sign languages and then illustrate the findings from recent research on lexical variation in black and white ASL and BSL; phonological variation in Auslan, NZSL, and black and white ASL; subject personal pronoun (SPP) variation in Auslan, NZSL, and ASL; and variation in the position of wh- signs in LIS.

Sign languages vs. spoken languages

Variable units in sign and spoken languages

Sign languages, like spoken languages, exhibit both regional and social variation. This variation has been described mainly at the phonological and lexical levels, and to a much lesser extent at the morphological and syntactic levels.[1]

---

[1] The term *phonology* is used in sign linguistics to describe the same area of linguistics that it refers to in spoken language studies, i.e. the study of the basic units of the language, in this case the handshape, location, orientation, movement, and nonmanual features.

Table 4.1 *Variability in spoken and sign languages*

Variable unit	Example	
	Spoken languages	Sign languages
Features of individual segments	final consonant devoicing, vowel nasalization, vowel raising and lowering	change in location, movement, orientation, handshape in one or more segments of a sign
Individual segments deleted or added	*-t, d* deletion, *-s* deletion, epenthetic vowels and consonants	hold deletion, movement epenthesis, hold epenthesis
Syllables (i.e., groups of segments) added or deleted	aphesis, apocope, syncope	first or second element of a compound deleted
Part of segment, segments, or syllables rearranged	metathesis	metathesis
Variation in word-sized morphemes or combinations of word-sized morphemes (i.e., syntactic variation)	copula deletion, negative concord, *avoir/être* alternation, lexical variation	null pronoun variation, lexical variation
Variation in discourse units	text types, lists	repetition, expectancy chains, deaf/blind discourse, turn-taking, back-channeling, questions

Table 4.1 compares spoken and sign language variability and shows that the same kinds of variation found in spoken languages can also be found in sign languages. Specifically, the features of individual segments of signs can vary, individual segments and whole syllables can be deleted or added, and parts of segments or syllables can be rearranged. There can be variation in word-sized morphemes (i.e., lexical variation) or in combinations of word-sized morphemes (i.e., syntactic variation). Finally, there can be variation in discourse units. Phonological variation can be seen in the production of the component parts of signs such as handshape, location, orientation, number of articulators, nonmanual features, and segmental structure. For example, the ASL signs FUNNY, BLACK, and CUTE might be produced with the thumb extended or with the thumb closed; the ASL signs BORED and DEAF might be produced with the little finger extended or with the little finger closed; the ASL sign WEEK might be produced with the palm of the dominant hand facing upward or the palm facing downward; the ASL sign KNOW might be produced on the forehead or on the cheek.[2]

---

[2] English glosses of signs are typically written in upper case. KNOW, for example, refers to the ASL sign rather than the English word.

Sign languages, then, demonstrate many of the same kinds of variation found in spoken languages. However, two kinds of variation in sign languages seem to be artifacts of a language produced with two identical articulators (i.e., two hands as opposed to one tongue). That is, sign languages allow the deletion, addition, or substitution of one of the two articulators. Two-handed signs become one-handed (e.g., ASL CAT, COW), one-handed signs become two-handed (DIE), and a table, chair arm, or the signer's thigh may be substituted for the base hand in a two-handed sign (RIGHT, SCHOOL). In addition, one-handed signs that the signer normally produces with the dominant hand (i.e., the right hand, if the signer is right-handed) can be signed with the non-dominant hand. Research has shown that signers in different regions tend to favor different variants. For example, in Boston, signers tend to favor the one-handed variant of signs that are traditionally produced with two hands, like DEER or WANT. Signers in California, Kansas, and Louisiana, however, tend to favor the two-handed variants (Lucas, Goeke, Briesacher, and Bayley 2007). Variation is also allowed in the relationship between articulators, as in HELP, produced with an ASL A handshape (fist with thumb on the side of the index finger) placed in the upward-turned palm of the base hand. Both hands can move forward as a unit, or the base hand can lightly tap the bottom of the A handshape.

In addition, although many of the same factors constrain variation in spoken and sign languages, we do see effects that may be modality specific. In particular, as shown in studies of a number of variables in ASL including different forms of the sign DEAF, variation in the location of signs like KNOW, and signs produced with a one handshape, grammatical function appears to play a stronger role in conditioning phonological variation in sign than in spoken languages (Lucas, Bayley, and Valli 2001). The question is why this might be so. Lucas (2007) suggests that one answer is that, as in spoken languages, phonological variation in sign languages is not constrained only by features of the preceding and following segments. In fact, there are basic differences between spoken and sign languages in how morphology functions and these differences show up in the factors that influence variation. In contrast to spoken languages, morphology in sign languages is not normally a boundary phenomenon, unlike, for example, regular past tense -ed or inflectional -s in English. There exist few affixes and "morphological distinctions are accomplished by altering one or more features in the articulatory bundle that makes up a sign" (Lucas 2007: 159). For example, the location feature of a segment indicates person and movement between locations indicates subject and object of the verb. Because the variables are not affixes, the immediate phonological environment plays a less prominent role in conditioning phonological variation in sign languages than in many spoken languages.

Variable processes in spoken and sign languages

Also important are the processes that pertain to variation, which can be either linguistic or social. Table 4.2 shows that the same kinds of processes obtain in variation in both spoken and sign languages. For example, when the one-handshape of the BSL sign PRO.1 ("I/me") becomes a flat B handshape in the phrase PRO.1 DON'T-KNOW ("I don't know"), we see an example of assimilation (Fenlon *et al.* 2013). We also see assimilation in the BSL compound sign THINK^TRUE ("believe"), in which the palm orientation of the sign THINK assimilates to the palm orientation of the sign TRUE. The process of weakening is illustrated when holds are deleted or when a two-handed sign becomes one-handed, as in ASL CAT or COW. Substitution can be seen when a table top or the signer's knee is substituted for the base hand of a two-handed sign or in the version of the ASL sign DEAF that begins at the chin and moves to the ear, as opposed to beginning at the ear and moving to the chin. Finally, the process of analogy is seen when a one-handed sign becomes two-handed.

With respect to morphosyntactic variation, we may expect to find variation in co-occurrence relations, as is the case in spoken languages. We are not sure yet what variable co-occurrence relations might look like in sign languages, but a possible candidate for investigation is the co-occurrence of nonmanual features with lexical signs or with morphological or syntactic units. For example, in ASL must a given non-manual feature (such as the mouth configuration in the sign NOT-YET) co-occur with the manual sign? Is there any

Table 4.2 *Variable processes in spoken and sign languages*

Process	Examples	
	Spoken	Signed
Assimilation	vowel harmony, consonant harmony, gemination, nasalization	assimilation in handshape, location, orientation
Weakening	deletion: CC reduction, haplology aphesis, syncope, apocope; vowel reduction	hold deletion; deletion of one articulator; first or second element of a compound deleted
Substitution, Addition	coalescence, metathesis, epenthesis	metathesis; epenthetic movement; substitute hand base
Analogy	3rd person sing. -*s*	add second hand to 1-handed sign
Concerning morphosyntactic structures:		
Co-occurrence relations	negative concord	possibly non-manual features
Item permutation	adverb placement	possibly placement of interrogative words

variation in the morphological and syntactic nonmanual features that co-occur with manual adverbs and sentences? Another kind of morphosyntactic variation concerns the fact that certain items – e.g., adverb placement in spoken English – can occur in different positions in a sentence. One possible candidate in ASL is the placement of interrogative signs (WHO, WHERE, WHAT, WHEN, WHY, WHAT-FOR) in sentences and also their repetition.

Internal constraints on spoken and sign languages

Table 4.3 summarizes the internal constraints on variable units. Constraints may be compositional, having to do with some feature of the variable sign itself, such as movement of the fingers or the number of fingers extended. For example, the ASL sign FUNNY may allow the thumb to be extended but the fact that the fingers oscillate and that both the index and middle fingers are extended may influence whether the thumb gets extended. *Sequential* constraints are those that have to do with the immediate linguistic environment surrounding the variable sign, such as the handshape, location or orientation of the sign immediately preceding or following the variable sign. Sequential constraints have always been very important in explaining variation in spoken languages and have been assumed to be as important in sign language variation as well. Many examples of handshape, location and orientation assimilation are seen, such that the 1 handshape in the first person pronoun PRO.1 ("I") in BSL, with the thumb and all fingers except the index finger closed, may become a B handshape (all fingers extended but held together) in the phrase PRO.1 DON'T-KNOW ("I don't know") or an L handshape (the thumb and index finger extended from the first) in the phrase PRO.1 LUCKY ("I'm

Table 4.3 *Internal constraints on variable units in spoken and sign languages*

Constraint	Example	
	Spoken	Signed
Compositional	phonetic features in nasal absence in child language	other parts of sign in question, e.g., hand shape, location, orientation
Sequential	following consonant, vowel, or feature thereof	preceding or following sign or feature thereof
Functional	morphological status of -s in Spanish -s deletion	function of sign as noun, predicate, or adjective
Structural incorporation	preceding or following syntactic environment for copula deletion	syntactic environment for pronoun variation?
Pragmatic	emphasis	emphasis (e.g., pinky extension)

lucky"), by assimilation with the preceding handshapes of the predicates DON'T-KNOW and LUCKY (Fenlon *et al.* 2013). The same appears to be true with the variation in number of articulators described above, whereby the variable sign may be two-handed or one-handed depending on the number of hands in the preceding and following signs (McCaskill *et al.* 2011).

Functional constraints pertain to the role that the grammatical category of the sign plays in the variation. These functional constraints are being found to have a very strong role in sign language variation (Lucas and Bayley 2005). For example, the ASL sign DEAF varies in its location, such that it can be produced starting at the ear and ending near the chin, starting at the chin and ending at the ear, or as a single contact on the cheek. Earlier analyses explained this variation simply in terms of assimilation, i.e., the location of the preceding or following sign conditioned whether the sign DEAF would start at the ear or at the chin or contact the cheek. More recent research (e.g., Bayley *et al.* 2000) has found that the grammatical category of the sign DEAF itself plays a central role in the variation, such that DEAF as a predicate ("I am deaf") tends to take the ear to chin form, while DEAF as a noun or adjective ("Deaf [people] understand," "deaf cat") can be either the ear to chin or chin to ear form. Finally, structural incorporation has to do with the preceding or following syntactic environment surrounding the variable and *pragmatic* features such as emphasis may help explain the variation being observed.

Social constraints particular to Deaf communities

Social constraints like gender, age, and ethnicity have been examined in numerous studies of sociolinguistic variation. However, many of these constraints need to be articulated more fully when they are put into research practice in a particular community. This is especially true for studies of linguistic variation in Deaf communities. Notions like socioeconomic status or even age cannot simply be borrowed whole from studies of variation in spoken language communities. The differences in social constraints when applied to Deaf communities are of two types. First, there are constraints such as age whose labels have a common application, but which might have a different meaning considering the history of Deaf communities. Second, there are constraints such as language background, which have a unique meaning in Deaf communities.

Considering constraints of the first type, definitions of gender, age, regional background, and ethnicity need to be reevaluated in studies of Deaf communities. For Deaf people, regional background, or where they grew up, may be less significant than where they attended school, if this was a residential school, if it was oral or used a sign language as a medium of instruction, or where their language models acquired a natural sign language. Age as a sociolinguistic variable may have different effects on linguistic variation, because of the differences in language policies in Deaf schools the last century. Thus, while differences in the signing of older and younger people may appear to be due either to age group differences or to natural language change such as occurs in all languages, these differences may also be the result of changes in educational policies, like the shift from oralism to Total Communication that occurred in the United States, or from Total Communication to a bilingual–bicultural approach. These language policies affected not only what language was used in the classroom, but also teacher hiring practices (Deaf signers of ASL, or hearing teachers who knew no ASL). These language policies affected deaf children's access to appropriate language models, and this access may have varied across time to such an extent as to affect the kind of variation we see in sign languages today.

With respect to ethnicity, demographics and oppression may work doubly against our understanding of language use in minority Deaf communities. The linguistic and social diversity in the Deaf community is just beginning to be explored by researchers (Lucas 1996; McCaskill *et al.* 2011; Parasnis 1997), and many questions remain about how ethnic minority Deaf people self-identify and how they use language. Are the boundaries of these groups such that they form coherent groups whose ethnic identity is stronger than their Deaf identity? Or do the members of these groups construct a separate minority, Deaf identity? Is it reasonable to acknowledge multiple potential language influences? Is the use of a particular variant related to a person's identity as a Deaf person, or as an African-American Deaf person, for example? Through the social network technique of contacting potential informants, Lucas, Bayley, and Valli (2001), uncovered one way in which ethnicity and age have intersected to create a situation of oppression multi-plied. They were unable to find any African-American Deaf people over age 55 who were members of the middle class, that is, who had a college education and were working in professional occupations. This finding suggests political, social, and economic factors intersect with race and ethnicity in ways that have profound effects on minority language communities like the Deaf community.

With respect to gender, several questions emerge that are also related to the minority language community status of the Deaf people. Those yet to be answered include: Is there a solidarity in language use between men and women in a language minority group because of oppression from the outside and shared experiences rooted in being Deaf? Or are usage differences as pronounced as in other communities?

Other differences in social constraints arise from the unique characteristics of Deaf communities. The question of the language background of signers who participate in studies is one such characteristic. Most participants in variation studies acquired the language under study as a native language from native-speaking parents, as well as from exposure in their everyday environment. In Deaf communities, some participants had neither of these kinds of exposure to the language at the earliest stages of their development. Even Deaf parents may not be native signers. It may seem that this problem conflicts with the goal of describing use of a particular language. However, if all signers who learned a natural sign language from people other than their parents were excluded from sociolinguistic studies, such studies would be invalidated, because they would not be representative of the community. Researchers should simply take account of the language background of their participants while drawing conclusions from the data. If the analysis is qualitative, the language background of the participants should be expressly stated in the report, and taken account of in the analysis. If the analysis is quantitative, the influence of language background differences on the variables being investigated may be included as a factor in the statistical model.

A related constraint is the school background of study participants. Whether the signers attended a residential or mainstream school may influence their signing. Some questions related to this issue are: Did the signers acquire a natural sign language at a very early age from signing adults, or did they learn it at a later age, having entered the community later? At what age did they acquire the sign language in use in their community? Did their language models use an artificial system such as Signed English or the natural sign language of the community?

Methods for studying variation in sign languages

Participant selection

Selection of participants is a major component of data collection. Studies of sociolinguistic variation seek to determine the correlations between language variation and the language use, e.g., do black and white signers of ASL use the same proportion of two handed and one handed signs or do men and women differ in the extent to which they use citation, or standard forms? Other commonly studied social characteristics include age, educational background, national origin, regional origin, social class, and sexual orientation. In recent work, researchers have also investigated the influence of discourse genre, topic, lexical frequency, and differences between individuals (see e.g., Bybee 2002; Schilling-Estes 2004; Travis 2007). While many characteristics are commonly considered in most large-scale sociolinguistic studies, other characteristics are particular to Deaf communities. Moreover, as we have seen, some commonly studied factors like social class or age cannot simply be taken over from studies of spoken language communities. As Lucas (2013) notes, social characteristics apply differently to Deaf communities in two respects. First, as we have seen, characteristics such as age and region may have a different meaning when we consider the history of Deaf communities. For example, in a recent study of Black ASL, the dialect developed by Deaf African-Americans in the southern United States during the era of segregation, McCaskill *et al.* (2011) divided speakers into two age groups: 55 and over and 35 and younger. The older signers had all attended school before integration and had little contact with white signers, while the younger signers had all attended integrated schools. Second, because most deaf children are born to hearing parents who do not know a sign language, a signer's language background is also clearly relevant because it determines whether the signer had the opportunity to acquire language from birth from signing parents or whether the signer was not exposed to a signed language until later in childhood, perhaps through a school for deaf children.

Describing natural language

The second issue concerns the type of data analyzed. Studies of sociolinguistic variation differ in a fundamental way from formal studies of abstract linguistic competence: studies of variation are committed to studying language in context. Directly eliciting different variants of a sociolinguistic variable would defeat the purpose of studying how the social and linguistic environments of language use condition variation. The sociolinguistic interview, although it has been used in many studies as a way in which linguists could record conversational language use, has been criticized as not being conducive to "natural speech" (Briggs 1986). The ideal would be to document the full range of the community's styles of language use, from formal lectures given to an audience of strangers to casual daily encounters with friends and acquaintances. In reality, this is impossible. First, few people, if any, sit around waiting for linguists to come and record their conversations. Also, the video recorder would be distracting.

Despite these fundamental limitations on linguists' access to "natural language use," all of the studies reported on here made methodological accommodations to gather conversations that were as natural as possible. The conversation types that were recorded differed on many dimensions: how well the participants knew one another, the degree to which the conversations were about language itself, the length of the conversations, and the presence or absence of the researchers during the videotaping. Each of these dimensions might have provided an environment that would affect variation. Therefore, the conclusions take into account these aspects of the conversations.

In Schembri *et al.*'s (2009) studies, for example, groups of signers were videotaped during one- to two-hour data collection sessions. These sessions were divided into three parts. The first consisted of 30 to 50 minutes of free conversation among groups of participants, without the researchers present. In the second part, participants were interviewed in depth by deaf researchers about their educational and linguistic backgrounds, social networks, and patterns of language use. The final part involved eliciting lexical variants from the participants who had been interviewed.

Defining variables and constraints

The third issue is a concern that what is being investigated is, in fact, a sociolinguistic variable. The hope is that we now know enough about the structure of a number of sign languages to identify what varies, to describe this variation and to quantify it. The first steps in variation analysis are to define the variable and the envelope of variation. That is, what forms count as instances of the variable? Are the forms that vary indeed two ways of saying the same thing?

The studies described here required, first, a consideration of what features were noticeably variable. These variables might be found at any level of linguistic structure, from phonology to discourse. For a quantitative study such as Schembri *et al.* (2009), the goal is to determine whether and to what extent variation in sign location correlates with both linguistic and social factors.

An additional issue that arises early in a variation study concerns specifying the factors that may potentially influence a signer's choice of a variant. Lucas (1995), for example, investigated the potential effects of eight separate linguistic factors on the choice of a variant of DEAF. As it turned out, most of these factors proved not to be statistically significant. However, the labor of coding for many factors was not in vain. The study demonstrated that Liddell and Johnson's (1989) hypothesis that variation in the form of DEAF is influenced primarily by the location of the preceding sign is, at best, incomplete.

Another central theoretical issue for variation studies is the identification of internal constraints on the variables. As Labov states, the issue "is to discover whatever constraints may exist on the form, direction or structural character of linguistic change" (1994: 115). Phonological constraints on the variables considered by Lucas, Bayley, and Valli (2001) could include the segmental phonological environment or suprasegmental, or prosodic, environment. Other linguistic constraints could be morphological, syntactic or related to discourse topic or type of discourse.

As for social constraints, the researcher's knowledge of the community should inform what factors are considered in the model of variation. In McCaskill *et al.* (2011), for example, information about the history of black deaf education in the United States was crucial both to the design of the study and to make sense of the findings.

Data collection itself presents a methodological problem. While one goal of sociolinguistic research is to base conclusions on conversation that is as "natural" as possible, one aspect of the basic method required for the careful study of natural language use impinges on this goal. That is, the conversation being studied needs to be recorded, and yet the fact that the conversation is being recorded makes it less likely to be close to everyday language. Labov (1972) called this problem the "Observer's Paradox." In Deaf communities, this problem may be magnified (Schembri *et al.* 2013). Video recording is more intrusive than audio recording. Equally important is the issue of anonymity. While spoken voices cannot easily be connected to a face or a name, except by the researchers, faces on a video are not anonymous. The Deaf community is small, and signers may be concerned that what they say on videotape will be seen by others in the community and understood out of context. On video, complete anonymity is impossible.

The actual tools used to gather data on linguistic variation can include interviews, structured elicitation, and questionnaires as well as free conversation sessions. The first three must be designed with issues specific to Deaf communities in mind. Who is conducting the interviews and the elicitation? Is the interviewer hearing or Deaf? Are questionnaires written in the dominant spoken language of the country entirely accessible to all Deaf signers or does the researcher need to go over the questionnaire with the signer? Recent advances in communication technology have directly affected the collection of sign language data. For example, researchers can now administer survey questions virtually and study participants can respond to them virtually. That is, participants can see the researchers asking them the questions in sign language on a computer and can respond to the researchers in sign language on the same computer. Researchers no longer have to recruit signers to come to a physical location for data collection. This has naturally led to adjustments in the traditional signed consent form and to considerations of the effects of providing virtual responses on the nature of the resulting data. In addition, there now exists a whole new source of publicly available data, in the form of YouTube and vlogs (video logs). Finally, the video relay service (VRS) is now being used widely for interpreting, wherein a Deaf person and a sign interpreter can actually see each other. An interpreter may be interpreting for a Deaf person from anywhere in the country, not just in their immediate area, and issues of how to handle lexical variation have frequently arisen and are being researched (Lucas *et al.* 2013; Palmer, Reynolds, and Minor 2012).

Methods for analysis

The final issue in analyzing the data in studies of sociolinguistic variation concerns methods of quantitative analysis. As suggested by the section on variables and constraints, sociolinguistic variables are usually subject to numerous influences at the linguistic and social levels. For example, Bayley *et al.* (2000) found that variation in the ASL sign DEAF was influenced by the grammatical function of the sign, the location of the following sign, the discourse genre (narrative or interview), and the region where the signer lived. Other studies, such as the studies of the location of signs like KNOW and variation between null and overt pronouns discussed in the following sections, have revealed more complicated patterns. To facilitate analysis, sign language sociolinguists have pioneered the use of coding for multiple factors in digital video annotation software such as ELAN (e.g., Fenlon *et al.* 2013; McCaskill *et al.* 2011), taking advantage of the use of multiple tiers in the ELAN file, which can be time aligned to a variable captured in the accompanying video. The multiplicity of possible influences across possible constraints that characterizes language collected in the community necessitates that we use multivariate analysis.

A detailed discussion of the quantitative methods used in studies of sociolinguistic variation is beyond the scope of this chapter. Readers who wish to investigate further should consult Bayley (2013), Guy (1993), and Tagliamonte (2006). Traditionally, sociolinguists have relied on one or another version of the Varbrul computer program, a specialized application of the statistical procedure known as logistic regression, originally developed by Cedergren and Sankoff (1974). Varbrul provides a measure of the influence of individual factors within a group on the signers' choice of a variant as well as an overall measure of the likelihood of the use of a variant in the data set. Provided that the data are indeed representative of language use in the population and the results are statistically significant, we may expect similar patterns of use in comparable groups of signers.

Recently, mixed effects models of logistic regression have become common in sociolinguistics, particularly with the development of the program known as Rbrul (Johnson 2009). Rbrul allows the user to model not only the fixed effects (e.g., grammatical category or signer gender) that Varbrul is limited to, but also random effects including lexical item and individual signer. Given recent discussions about the role of lexical frequency in variation and change (e.g., Bybee 2010) as well as the increased focus in sociolinguistics on individual agency, the advantages of mixed models seem clear (Gorman and Johnson 2013), and have been adopted by some sign language researchers (Fenlon *et al.* 2013). Nevertheless, as Roy (2014) observes, provided we have sufficient data and we are interested primarily in the grammar, traditional methods of sociolinguistic analysis will serve as well as mixed effects models.

Representative studies

Lexical variation

Lexical variation was the earliest type of sign language variation to be systematically studied. In an appendix to the *Dictionary of American Sign Language*, Croneberg (1965), for example, on the basis of a 134-item sign vocabulary test, reported "a radical dialect difference between the signs" of a young African-American woman from North Carolina and those of white signers in the same city (315). He attributed the dialect difference to the segregation of deaf schools in the southern United States. Other early studies included Woodward (1976), who examined differences between African-American and white signing. His data, based on a small number of signers, included both direct elicitation and spontaneous language production. He suggested that African-Americans tended to use older forms of signs, a suggestion later confirmed by McCaskill *et al.* (2011).

In 1984, Shroyer and Shroyer published their influential work on lexical variation, which drew on signers across the United States. They collected data on 130 words from 38 white signers in 25 states. They collected a total of 1,200 signs for the 130 words, which included nouns, verbs, and some adverbs.

More recent work has included studies of lexical differences in Black and White ASL and regional differences in BSL. In the following section, we examine several recent studies.

Lexical variation in Black and White ASL

As the studies of Croneberg (1965) and Woodward (1976) suggest, lexical differences between African-American and white signing have long been an area of interest. Recent work in this area includes Lucas, Bayley, Reed, and Wulf (2001), McCaskill *et al.* (2011), and Lucas, Bayley, McCaskill, and Hill (2013), which we discuss below.

Lucas, Bayley, Reed, and Wulf, based on the corpus reported on in Lucas, Bayley, and Valli (2001), sought to answer three questions: "(1) Are there lexical differences between African American and white signing? (2) What are the processes of change reflected in the varieties of ASL used by African American and white signers? (3) How does lexical innovation differ from phonological variation in the lexicon?" (339). To answer these questions, they analyzed the responses of 140 signers from various regions and of varying social characteristics to thirty-four pictures and fingerspelled stimuli designed to elicit lexical items. Stimuli included a variety of common nouns and verbs, e.g., RABBIT, DEER, PIZZA, RUN, SNOW, STEAL, as well as the geographical names AFRICA and JAPAN. As a result of the increasing international contact of Deaf people, new forms of AFRICA and JAPAN are replacing the older forms that, because they point to physical characteristics, are regarded by many as offensive.

The results showed that for twenty-eight of the thirty-four signs sampled, African-Americans used signs that none of the white signers used. Lucas, Bayley, Reed, and Wulf (2001) note that the only six signs for which the African-American participants did not have unique variants were CAKE,

MICROWAVE, JAPAN, SANDWICH THIEF, and STEAL. The authors conclude that there are clear differences between African-American and white signing and, although African-American and white signers share a great deal of the lexicon, there are areas that do not overlap. Moreover, there is evidence that African-Americans and white signers participate in phonological variation in the lexicon. Finally, the authors point to the need to distinguish phonological variation in the lexicon from lexical innovation.

Recent research has focused on the incorporation of African American English into Black ASL. McCaskill *et al.* (2011; Lucas, Bayley, McCaskill, and Hill 2013) studied a number of features in the signing of ninety-six African-American Deaf people in seven states in the southern part of the USA. During interviews, participants were asked whether they thought that black people signed differently than white people. In response, signers offered a number of signs that illustrated the results of contact between African-American English and Black ASL and that differed from the signs used by white signers. These included several versions of the sign TRIPPING as well as WHASSUP?, GIRL, PLEASE, and MY BAD, meaning "my mistake." These are illustrated in Figures 4.1–4.4.

Lexical variation in BSL

In 2008, Adam C. Schembri and colleagues set out to investigate variation in British Sign Language (BSL). Working in a manner similar to Lucas, Bayley, and Valli (2001), they collected data from 249 Deaf signers in eight cities

Figure 4.1a TRIPPING, forehead with movement out

Figure 4.1b TRIPPING, forehead, short repeated movement, no movement out

Figure 4.2 WHASSUP?

across the four countries of the United Kingdom (Schembri *et al.* 2013). They focused on lexical and phonological variation (Stamp *et al.* 2011). In this section, we summarize results from their study of lexical variation.

To investigate lexical variation, Schembri *et al.* (2013) presented signers with pictures to elicit 102 signs, all of which have been reported to show variability. Stamp *et al.* (2011) analyzed data from 41 of the 102 signs in the BSL corpus, with a focus on signs for numbers, colors, countries, and British

Figure 4.3 GIRL PLEASE

Figure 4.4 MY BAD

place-names. Variants were divided into 'traditional' variants, believed to be older signs unique to each region, and newer 'non-traditional' variants. Overall, signers produced a far higher percentage of traditional variants than non-traditional variants, but the shift away from traditional signs was faster in some semantic domains (e.g., country signs) than others (e.g., color signs).

Interestingly, multivariate analysis indicated that signers who were older, educated in the same region in which they currently live, and had deaf parents were more likely to produce traditional variants.

Phonological variation: location in Auslan, NZSL, and ASL

A number of studies have examined phonological variation in signed languages. These include Lucas' (1995) study of variation in the form of the ASL sign DEAF, McCaskill *et al.*'s (2011) examination of the size of the signing space in Black and White ASL, their study of variation in the location of ASL signs like KNOW in Black ASL, and their study of two-handed signs that can also be produced with one hand. Other studies include Lucas, Bayley, and Valli's (2001) and Fenlon *et al.*'s (2013) work on variation in signs made with a 1 handshape in ASL and BSL respectively, as well as variation in the location of signs in ASL, a variable also examined in detail in Auslan and NZSL (Schembri *et al.* 2009). Indeed, as a result of the increasing attention to variation in sign languages, far too many studies have been completed for us to review in detail. Therefore, we will illustrate the nature of phonological variation in sign languages by examining variation in the location of signs like ASL KNOW, which are normally produced at the level of the forehead, but which may also be produced at a lower level. Variation in the location of this class of signs has been studied in three languages and thus enables us to compare patterns of variation cross-linguistically in unrelated and related sign languages. Table 4.4 summarizes the results of multivariate analysis of sign lowering in Auslan, NZSL, and ASL. Figure 4.5 shows the forehead variant of three Auslan signs and one lowered variant. The quantitative results in Table 4.4 are from GoldvarbX (Sankoff, Tagliamonte, and Smith 2005), a current implementation of the Varbrul statistical program, a specialized application of the statistical procedure known as logistic regression. To interpret the quantitative results, note that a factor weight between .5 and 1 is said to favor the use of the variant that has been selected as the application value (in this case the lowered, or non-citation form) relative to the other factors in the group. A weight, or value, between 0 and .5 is said to disfavor the application value. The input value (e.g., .427) is the overall likelihood that a signer will choose the application value, or lowered variant, regardless of the presence or absence of any other factor in the environment.

The comparative perspective offered by relatively large-scale studies conducted in three different countries provides a number of worthwhile insights. First, signers in all three countries use the non-citation, or lowered form in more than 40 percent of the examples coded. Second, where age has a significant effect, as it does in Auslan and ASL, younger signers are more likely to choose the lowered form than older signers. This provides evidence in

Table 4.4 *Location variation in Auslan, NZSL, and ASL (application value = –cf)*

	Auslan (n = 2667)	NZSL (n = 2096)	ASL (n = 2594)
Linguistic constraints			
Grammatical category X frequency	Highly frequent verbs (.577) > others (.388)	Highly frequent verbs (.566) > low frequency verbs (.499) > low frequency nouns/adj. (.433) > highly frequent nouns/adj. (.291)	Preposition, interrogative (.581) > noun/verb (.486) > adjective (.316)
Preceding location	Body (.543) > head (.369)	Body (.518) > head (.390)	Body (.514) > head (.463)
Following location	Body (.526) > head (.441)	Body (.534) > head (.393)	ns
Following sign or pause	Pause (.644) > sign (.480)	Pause (.684) > sign (.483)	ns
Preceding contact with head, hands, or body	Head or hands (.537) > no contact (.509) > body (.448)	No contact (.516) > contact (.481)	
Following contact with head, hands, or body	ns	ns	No contact (.525) > contact (.466)
Social constraints			
Age	51 or younger (.565) > 51+ (.411)	ns	15–25 (.602) > 26–54 (.517) > 55+ (.416)
Region	Sydney/Melbourne (0.544) > Adelaide/Brisbane/Perth (0.456)	South (.604) > North (.544) Central (.417)	California, Louisiana, Maryland Massachusetts, Kansas, Missouri (.529) > Washington (.461) > Virginia (.334)
Gender	Female (.536) > Male (.460)	Female (.536) > male (.460)	Male (.544) > female (.451)
Ethnicity	na	Pakeha (European) (.513) > Maori (.423)	White (.555) > African-American middle class (.445) > African-American working class (.314)
Language background	ns	Native NZSL (.630) > middle childhood acquisition (.532) > early acquisition (.491)	Hearing parents > (.519) Deaf parents (.444)
Percentage –cf	45	43	53
Input (corrected mean)	.427	.412	.518

Sources: Lucas, Bayley, and Valli (2001); Schembri *et al.* (2009).
Note: Lexical frequency was not tested in Lucas, Bayley, and Valli (2001).

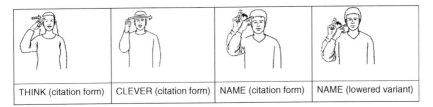

| THINK (citation form) | CLEVER (citation form) | NAME (citation form) | NAME (lowered variant) |

Figure 4.5 Three Auslan/NZSL forehead location signs and one lowered variant

support of Frishberg's (1975) view that a change is in progress, with signs becoming restricted to the central signing space.

Syntactic variation

Variable SPP expression in Auslan, NZSL, and ASL   As we have seen, in many of the world's languages, subject personal pronouns (SPP) may be expressed overtly or omitted without a change in meaning. Numerous studies conducted in a wide range of Spanish dialects as well as in Chinese, Portuguese, and other languages have shown that this alternation is systematic and subject to similar constraints across languages (e.g., Flores-Ferrán 2007; Jia & Bayley 2002; Otheguy and Zentella 2012; Travis 2007). For example, a pronoun is more likely to be expressed when the grammatical subject of a verb differs from the subject of the preceding verb than when the subject is the same as the subject of the preceding verb. In addition, research on spoken languages has consistently shown that singular pronouns are more likely to be realized overtly than plural pronouns.

Research on variation in SPPs has recently been extended to several sign languages. The earliest study, reported in Wulf, Dudis, Bayley, and Lucas (2002), examined SPP variation in a sample of narratives that signers told in sociolinguistic interviews. The researchers examined only plain verbs (Padden 1988) such as THINK, KNOW, and FEEL that do not incorporate indications of subject or object into their structure. Although the fairly small number of narratives that occurred in sociolinguistic interviews yielded only 429 tokens of the variable, the researchers were nevertheless able to identify a number of factors that contributed significantly to a signer's choice between a null and an overt subject. These included English influence in the immediate environment, the person/number of the subject, a switch in reference from the subject of the preceding clause, and whether the token appeared in a passage of constructed action or dialogue.

Several years later, McKee *et al.* (2011) examined SPP variation in Auslan and NZSL, with a much larger data set. Table 4.5 compares results for this

Table 4.5 *SPP variation in ASL, Auslan, and NZSL (application value = null)*

Factor group	ASL (n = 429)	Auslan (n = 977)	NZSL (n = 2145)
Linguistic constraints			
Coreference with previous clause	Different referent (.63) > same referent (.41)	Different referent (.61) > same referent (.36)	Different referent (.66) > same referent (.40)
Person/number of subject	1sg (.61) > 2/3pl (.47) ≈ 2sg (.46) > 3sg (.28) > 1pl (.21)	1 sg (.67) > 3sg/pl (.43) > 1pl (.27) ≈ 2sg/pl (.25)	ns
English influence in the clause	Present (.76) > absent (.46)	Present (.69) > absent (.47)	na
Constructed action	Absent (.57) > present (.42)	Absent (.53) > present (.43)	Absent (.52) > present (.43)
Verb type	na	Plain (.55) > spatial (.43)	Plain (.53) ≈ other predicate (.52) > spatial (.41)
Structural priming: match with preceding subject type	na	Pro subj prior clause (.59) > null subj prior clause (.43)	Noun subj prior clause (.68) ≈ pro subj prior clause (.66) > null subj prior clause (.37)
Social constraints			
Age	55+ (.60) > 15–54 (.45)	ns	65+ (.57) > 15–39 (,51) > 40–64 (.42)
Gender	F (.59) > M (.41)	ns	ns
Ethnicity	Na	na	Maori (.55) > Pakeha (European) (.47)
Percent null	35	55	67

Sources: ASL, Lucas, Bayley, and Valli (2001: 170); Auslan and NZSL, McKee *et al.* (2011: 388). *Notes:* na, factor group was not tested; ns, not significant. ASL, χ^2/ cell = 9857; Auslan, χ^2/ cell = 1.0829NZSL, χ^2/ cell = 1.1709. For Auslan and NZSL, structural priming and corefererence interacted. Hence, the structural priming results come from a separate run without the coreference factor group.

variable from three signed languages. As in Table 4.4, the results were obtained through use of GoldvarbX.

As Table 4.5 shows, overall, Auslan and NZSL have a much higher rate of null subjects than in ASL. However, a number of constraints operate the same way in ASL, Auslan, and NZSL. For example, in all three languages, an overt pronoun is much more likely to be used when there is a switch in reference from the subject of the preceding clause, just as is the case in spoken languages. Moreover, pronouns are less likely to be used in constructed action in all three languages. Not surprisingly, English influence, which was not tested for the NZSL corpus, promotes use of the overt option, which is congruent with English, in both ASL and Auslan.

Although Table 4.5 illustrates a number of differences in patterns of SPP use in ASL, Auslan, and NZSL, comparative studies of patterns of variation provide a means to examine questions such as:

- What constraints occur across all languages, whether spoken or signed?
- What constraints are common to all signed languages?
- What constraints are limited to particular languages or language varieties?

Variation in wh-signs in LIS

Recently a team lead by Caterina Donati, Anna Cardinaletti, Carlo Cecchetto, and Carlo Geraci set out to investigate variation in LIS. Like Schembri and his colleagues in the United Kingdom, they worked in a manner similar to Lucas, Bayley, and Valli (2001). They collected data from 165 Deaf signers in ten Italian cities from Turin and Milan in the north to Bari in the south. Among other variables, researchers on the LIS project examined syntactic variation, particularly the position of wh-signs (Geraci and Bayley 2011; Geraci *et al.* 2015). Previous work, based on grammaticality judgments by native signers, indicated that there is considerable variability in the position of wh- signs (Cecchetto, Geraci, and Zucchi 2009). These signs may come before the predicate, after the predicate, or may be reduplicated. For example, 7a, b, c were produced by a single signer during the course of an elicitation task concerning an auto accident report:

(7a)   HAPPEN WHERE
        "Where did that happen?"
(7b)   IX-2 WHERE BUMP
        "Which part of the car did you bump?"
(7c)   IX-2 WHERE CRASH WHERE
        "Where did the accident happen?"

Wh-signs are rare in sociolinguistic interviews because the interviewer is normally the person asking the questions. Therefore, to elicit a sufficient number of tokens for quantitative analysis, the researchers developed two tasks with information gaps. Each signer was paired with another signer with similar social characteristics. In one task, involving an accident in the home, one signer had to ask the questions necessary to complete an information form. In the second task, involving a report of an auto accident, the other signer became the questioner. The second task is illustrated in Figures 4.6a and 4.6b.

Geraci and Bayley (2011) performed multivariate analysis of 646 signs elicited in two tasks that required the use of numerous questions. Overall, they found that slightly more than 60 percent of the wh- signs analyzed came after the

Figure 4.6a Car accident scene

predicate. The position of wh-signs was significantly constrained by both clause-type (with direct questions more likely to come after the predicate) and grammatical roles (with objects more likely than subjects or adjuncts to come after the predicate). Interestingly, results for age and education, which showed evidence of interaction, suggest that we may be looking at a late stage of a change in progress. Signers over 55 with relatively low levels of education were most likely to place the wh-sign before the predicate, the position that is congruent with Italian, while signers under age 55 with relatively high levels of education were less likely to place the wh- sign before the predicate. The results, then, suggest that in at least one respect, LIS is becoming less like spoken Italian, a development that may be partially attributed to the increasing awareness among younger educated signers of the distinctiveness of LIS and Deaf culture.

Conclusion

Over the past two decades, researchers have examined variation in a number of different sign languages. As the examples discussed in this chapter suggest, many of the influences on variation in sign languages parallel variation in

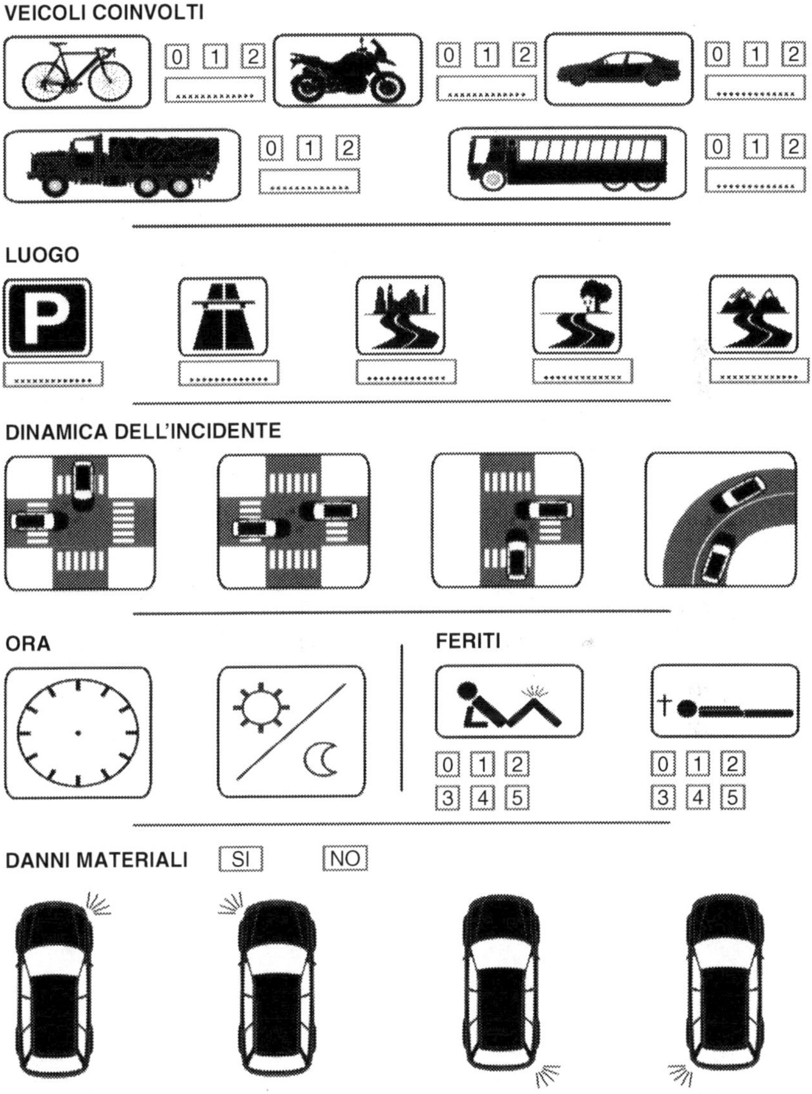
VEICOLI COINVOLTI
0 1 2
LUOGO
P
DINAMICA DELL'INCIDENTE
ORA
FERITI
0 1 2
3 4 5
DANNI MATERIALI
SI
NO

Figure 4.6b Insurance form

spoken languages, although differences in modality certainly affect some of the patterns that we have observed. For example, ASL exhibits variation between one-handed and two-handed versions of signs like DEER. Since the variation involves the deletion of an articulator (one hand), this is clearly a type of variation that is restricted to sign languages. And, as we have observed, a number of social factors, for example, whether the signer comes from a Deaf or hearing family and the type of school the signer attended, are particular to Deaf communities.

In an earlier review of sociolinguistic variation in sign languages, Lucas, Bayley, and colleagues focused on ASL and included nearly all of the variationist studies that had been completed at the time (Lucas *et al.* 2001). Thanks to the increase in studies of variation in a number of the world's sign languages, that type of inclusiveness is no longer possible and we have had to be quite selective. Despite the increase in variationist studies of sign language, however, much remains to be done on the languages that have received attention such as ASL, Auslan, BSL, LIS, and NZSL, as well as on languages that have yet to be investigated from a sociolinguistic perspective. Recent work has enabled us to understand a great deal about how sociolinguistic variation works in sign languages and how variable processes in sign languages are both similar to and differ from variable processes in spoken languages. We are confident that future work on other variables and other languages will provide even more insights into the nature of one of the two main modalities of human language.

REFERENCES

Battison, Robbin M., Markowicz, Harry, and Woodward, James C. (1975) A good rule of thumb: Variable phonology in American Sign Language. In Ralph W. Fasold and Roger Shuy (eds.), *Analyzing Variation in Language*. Washington, DC: Georgetown University Press.

Bayley, Robert (2013) The quantitative paradigm. In J. K. Chambers and Natalie Schilling (eds.), *The Handbook of Language Variation and Change*, 2nd edn (pp. 85–107). Oxford: Wiley-Blackwell.

Bayley, Robert, Lucas, Ceil, and Rose, Mary (2000) Variation in American Sign Language: The case of DEAF. *Journal of Sociolinguistics* 4: 81–107.

Biber, Douglas and Finegan, Edward (eds.) (1993) *Sociolinguistic Perspectives on Register*. Oxford: Oxford University Press.

Briggs, Charles (1986) *Learning How to Ask: A Sociolinguistic Appraisal of the Role of the Interview in Social Science Research*. Cambridge: Cambridge University Press.

Bybee, Joan (2002) Word frequency and context of use in the lexical diffusion of phonetically conditioned sound change. *Language Variation and Change* 14: 261–290.

(2010) *Language, Usage and Cognition*. Cambridge: Cambridge University Press.

Cecchetto, Carlo, Geraci, Carlo, and Zucchi, Sandro (2009) Another way to mark syntactic dependencies: The case for right-peripheral specifiers in sign languages. *Language* 85: 278–320.

Cedergren, Henrietta and Sankoff, David (1974) Performance as a statistical reflection of competence. *Language* 50: 333–355.

Croneberg, Carl. G. (1965) Appendix D: Sign language dialects. In William C. Stokoe, Dorothy C. Casterline, and Carl G. Croneberg, *A Dictionary of American Sign Language* (pp. 313–319). Silver Spring, MD: Linstok.

Eckert, Penelope (2000) *Linguistic Variation as Social Practice: The Linguistic Construction of Identity at Belten High*. Oxford: Blackwell.

Fasold, Ralph (1990) *The Sociolinguistics of Language*. Oxford: Blackwell.

Fenlon, Jordan, Schembri, Adam, Rentelis, Ramas, and Cormier, Kearsy (2013) Variation in handshape and orientation in British Sign Language: The case of the "1" hand configuration. *Language and Communication* 33: 69–91.

Fischer, Susan and Gong, Qunhu (2010) Variation in East Asian sign language structures. In Diane Brentari (ed.), *Sign Languages* (pp. 499–518). Cambridge: Cambridge University Press.

Flores-Ferrán, Nydia (2007) A bend in the road: Subject personal pronoun expression in Spanish after 30 years of sociolinguistic research. *Language and Linguistics Compass* 1: 624–652.

Frishberg, Nancy (1975) Arbitrariness and iconicity: Historical change in American Sign Language. *Language* 51: 696–719.

Geraci, Carlo, Battaglia, Katia, Cardinaletti, Anna, Cecchetto, Carlo, Donati, Caterina, Guiduce, Serena, and Mereghetti, Emiliano (2011) The LIS corpus project: A discussion of sociolinguistic variation in the lexicon. *Sign Language Studies* 11: 328–374.

Geraci, Carlo and Bayley, Robert (2011) Chi, cosa, dove, perché e quando: la distribuzione dei segni wh- in LIS. In Anna Cardinaletti, Carlo Cecchetto, and Caterina Donati (eds.), *Grammatica, lessico e deimensioni di variazione nella LIS* (pp. 127–144). Milan: Franco Angeli.

Geraci, Carlo, Bayley, Robert, Cardinaletti, Anna, Cecchetto, Carlo, and Donati, Caterina (2015) Variation in Italian Sign Language (LIS): The case of wh-signs. *Linguistics* 53: 125–151.

Godfrey, Elizabeth and Tagliamonte, Sali (1999) Another piece for the verbal -*s* story: Evidence from Devon in southwest England. *Language Variation and Change* 11: 87–121.

Gorman, Kyle and Johnson, Daniel Ezra (2013) Quantitative analysis. In Robert Bayley, Richard Cameron, and Ceil Lucas (eds.), *The Oxford Handbook of Sociolinguistics*. Oxford: Oxford University Press.

Guy, Gregory R. (1980) Variation in the group and in the individual: The case of final stop deletion. In William Labov (ed.), *Locating Language in Time and Space* (pp. 1–36). New York: Academic. Press.

(1993) Quantitative analysis. In Dennis R. Preston (ed.), *American Dialect Research* (pp. 223–249). Amsterdam: John Benjamins.

Guy, Gregory R. and Bayley, Robert (1995) On the choice of relative pronouns in English. *American Speech* 70: 148–162.

Hoopes, Rob (1998) A preliminary examination of pink extension: Suggestions regarding its constraints, occurrence and function. In Ceil Lucas (ed.), *Pinky Extension and Eye Gaze: Language Use in Deaf Communities* (pp. 3–17). Washington, DC: Gallaudet University Press.

Jia, Li and Bayley, Robert (2002) Null pronoun variation in Mandarin Chinese. *University of Pennsylvania Working Papers in Linguistics* 8(3): 103–116.

Johnson, Daniel Ezra (2009) Getting off the Goldvarb standard: Introducing Rbrul for mixed-effect variable rule analysis. *Language and Linguistics Compass* 3: 359–383.

Labov, William (1963) The social motivation of a sound change. *Word* 19: 273–309.

(1966) *The Social Stratification of English in New York City*. Washington, DC: Center for Applied Linguistics.

(1969) Contraction, deletion, and inherent variability of the English copula. *Language* 45: 715–762.

(1972) *Sociolinguistic Patterns*. Philadelphia, PA: University of Pennsylvania Press.

(1989) The child as linguistic historian. *Language Variation and Change* 1: 85–97.

(1994) *Principles of Linguistic Change, Vol. 1: Internal Factors*. Oxford: Blackwell.

(2006) *The Social Stratification of English in New York City*, 2nd edn. Cambridge: Cambridge University Press.

Liddell, Scott and Johnson, Robert (1989) American Sign Language: The phonological base. *Sign Language Studies* 64: 195–278.

Lucas, Ceil (1995) Sociolinguistic variation in ASL: The case of DEAF. In Ceil Lucas (ed.), *Sociolinguistics in Deaf Communities* (vol. I, pp. 3–25). Washington, DC: Gallaudet University Press.

(ed.) (1996) *Multicultural Aspects of Sociolinguistics in Deaf Communities*. Washington, DC: Gallaudet University Press.

(2007) Variation and modality. In Robert Bayley and Ceil Lucas (eds.), *Sociolinguistic Variation: Theories, Methods, and Applications* (pp. 145–161). Cambridge: Cambridge University Press.

(2013) Methods for studying sign languages. In Robert Bayley, Richard Cameron, and Ceil Lucas (eds.), *The Oxford Handbook of Sociolinguistics* (pp. 280–298). Oxford: Oxford University Press.

Lucas, Ceil and Bayley, Robert (2005) Variation in ASL: The role of grammatical function. *Sign Language Studies* 6: 38–75.

(2010) Variation in ASL. In Diane Brentari (ed.), *Sign Languages* (pp. 451–475). Cambridge: Cambridge University Press.

(2011) Variation in sign languages: Recent research on ASL and beyond. *Language and Linguistics Compass* 5: 677–690.

Lucas, Ceil, Bayley, Robert, McCaskill, Carolyn, and Hill, Joseph (2013) The incorporation of African American English into Black ASL. *International Journal of Bilingualism*.

Lucas, Ceil, Bayley, Robert, Reed, Ruth, and Wulf, Alyssa (2001) Lexical variation in African American and white American Sign Language. *American Speech* 76: 339–360.

Lucas, Ceil, Bayley, Robert, Rose, Mary, and Wulf, Alyssa (2002) Location variation in American Sign Language. *Sign Language Studies* 2: 407–440.

Lucas, Ceil, Bayley, Robert, and Valli, Clayton (2001) *Sociolinguistic Variation in American Sign Language*. Washington, DC: Gallaudet University Press.

Lucas, Ceil, Bayley, Robert, Valli, Clayton, Rose, Mary, and Wulf, Alyssa (2001) Sociolinguistic variation. In Ceil Lucas (ed.), *The Sociolinguistics of Sign Languages* (pp. 61–111). Cambridge: Cambridge University Press.

Lucas, Ceil, Goeke, Amber, Briesacher, Rebecca, and Bayley, Robert (2007) Variation in ASL: Two hands or one? Paper presented at the Conference on New Ways of Analyzing Variation 36, University of Pennsylvania.

Lucas, Ceil, Mirus, Gene, Palmer, Jeffrey L., Roessler, Nicholas, and Frost, Adam (2013) The effect of new technologies on sign language research. *Sign Language Studies* 13: 541–564.

Lucas, Ceil and Valli, Clayton (1992) *Language Contact in the American Deaf Community.* San Diego, CA: Academic Press.

McCaskill, Carolyn, Lucas, Ceil, Bayley, Robert, and Hill, Joseph (2011) *The Hidden Treasure of Black ASL: Its History and Structure.* Washington, DC: Gallaudet University Press.

McKee, Rachel, Schembri, Adam C., McKee, David, and Johnston, Trevor (2011) Variable subject expression in Australian Sign Language and New Zealand Sign Language. *Language Variation and Change* 23: 375–398.

Milroy, Lesley (1987) *Language and Social Networks,* 2nd edn. Oxford: Blackwell.

Otheguy, Ricardo and Zentella, Ana Celia (2012) *Spanish in New York: Language Contact, Dialect Leveling, and Structural Continuity.* Oxford: Oxford University Press.

Padden, Carol (1988) *Interaction of Morphology and Syntax in American Sign Language.* New York: Garland.

Palmer, Jeffrey L., Reynolds, Wanette, and Minor, Rebecca (2012) "You want WHAT on your pizza?!": Videophone and video relay service as potential forces on lexical standardization of American Sign Language. *Sign Language Studies* 12: 371–397.

Parnasis, Ila (ed.) (1998) *Cultural and Language Diversity and the Deaf Experience.* Cambridge: Cambridge University Press.

Patrick, Peter and Metzger, Melanie (1996) Sociolinguistic factors in sign language research. In Jennifer Arnold, Renée Blake, Brad Davidson, Scott Schwenter, and Julie Solomon (eds.), *Sociolinguistic Variation: Data, Theory and Analysis* (pp. 229–240). Stanford, CA: Center for the Study of Language and Information.

Poplack, Shana (1980) "Sometimes I'll start a sentence in Spanish and TERMINO EN ESPAÑOL": Towards a typology of code-switching. *Linguistics* 18: 581–618.

Quinto-Pozos, David (2009) Sign language contact and interference: ASL and LSM. *Language in Society* 37: 161–187.

Roy, Joseph (2014) Sociolinguistic statistics: The intersection between statistical models, empirical data, and sociolinguistic theory. In Alena Barysevich, Alexandra D'Arcy, and David Heap (eds.), *Proceedings of Methods XIV: Papers from the Fourteenth International Conference on Methods in Dialectology* (pp. 261–275). Frankfurt am Main: Peter Lang.

Sankoff, David, Tagliamonte, Sali A., and Smith Eric (2005) *Goldvarb X: A Variable Rule Application for Macintosh and Windows* [computer program]. Toronto and Ottawa: Department of Linguistics, University of Toronto and Department of Mathematics and Statistics, University of Ottawa.

Schembri, Adam C., Cormier, Kearsy, Johnston, Trevor, McKee, David, and Woll, Bencie (2010) Sociolinguistic variation in British, Australian, and New Zealand sign languages. In Diane Brentari (ed.), *Sign Languages* (pp. 476–498). Cambridge: Cambridge University Press.

Schembri, Adam C., Fenlon, Jordan, Rentelis, Ramas, Reynolds, Sally, and Cormier, Kearsy (2013) Building the British Sign Language Corpus. *Language Documentation and Conservation* 7: 136–154.

Schembri, Adam and Johnston, Trevor (2013) Sociolinguistic variation and change in sign languages. In Robert Bayley, Richard Cameron, and Ceil Lucas (eds.), *The Oxford Handbook of Sociolinguistics* (pp. 503–522). Oxford: Oxford University Press.

Schembri, Adam, McKee, David, McKee, Rachel, Pivac, Sara, Johnston, Trevor, and Goswell, Delia (2009) Phonological variation and change in Australian and New Zealand Sign Languages: The location variable. *Language Variation and Change* 21: 193–231.

Schiffrin, Deborah (1994) *Approaches to Discourse Analysis*. Oxford: Blackwell.

Schilling-Estes, Natalie (2004) Constructing ethnicity in interaction. *Journal of Sociolinguistics* 8: 163–195.

Shuy, Roger, Wolfram, Walt, and Riley, William (1968) *Field Techniques in an Urban Dialect Study*. Washington, DC: Center for Applied Linguistics.

Shroyer, Edgar H. and Shroyer, Susan P. (1984) *Signs across America*. Washington, DC: Gallaudet University Press.

Stamp, Rosemary, Schembri, Adam, Fenlon, Jordan, Rentelis, Ramas, and Cormier, Kearsy (2011) Lexical variation and change in British Sign Language (BSL): Evidence for dialect levelling? Paper presented at the Sixth International Conference on Language Variation in Europe (ICLaVE), Freiburg Institute for Advanced Studies, Germany.

Stokoe, William C. (1960) *Sign Language Structure: An Outline of the Visual Communication System of the American Deaf*. Occasional Paper Number 8. Buffalo, NY: University of Buffalo.

Tagliamonte, Sali A. (2006) *Analysing Sociological Variation*. Cambridge: Cambridge University Press.

Travis, Catherine (2007) Genre effects on subject expression in Spanish: Priming in narrative and conversation. *Language Variation and Change* 19: 101–133.

Trudgill, Peter (1974) *The Social Stratification of English in Norwich*. Cambridge: Cambridge University Press.

Wolfram, Walt (1969) *A Sociolinguistic Description of Detroit Negro Speech*. Washington, DC: Center for Applied Linguistics.

   (1989) Structural variability in language development: Final nasals in vernacular Black English. In Ralph W. Fasold and Deborah Schiffrin (eds.), *Language Change and Variation* (pp. 301–332). Amsterdam: John Benjamins.

   (1991) *Dialects and American English*. Englewood Cliffs, NJ: Prentice-Hall.

   (1993) Identifying and interpreting linguistic variables. In Dennis R. Preston (ed.), *American Dialect Research* (pp. 193–221). Amsterdam: John Benjamins.

   (1997) Dialect in society. In Florian Coulmas (ed.), *The Handbook of Sociolinguistics* (pp. 107–126). Oxford: Blackwell.

Wolfram, Walt and Schilling-Estes, Natalie (2006) *American English: Dialects and Variation*, 2nd edn. Oxford: Blackwell.

Woodward, James C. (1976) Black southern signing. *Language in Society* 5: 211–218.

Wulf, Alyssa, Dudis, Paul, Bayley, Robert, and Lucas, Ceil (2002) Variable subject presence in ASL narratives. *Sign Language Studies* 3: 54–76.

Zentella, Ana Celia (1997) *Growing up Bilingual: Puerto Rican Children in New York*. Oxford: Blackwell.

5 Discourse analysis and sign languages

Elizabeth A. Winston and Cynthia Roy

Introduction

People often wonder what discourse analysis is and what the field of study includes. As a newer field, discourse analysis is still determining its own boundaries. It is different from traditional linguistics in several ways – it uses natural data for analysis, and it deals with utterances, as opposed to sentences. If you spend time observing everyday talk, you will notice that these utterances rarely look like those grammatical sentences seen in the grammar books and often described in linguistic research about syntax and grammar. In everyday interaction, people do not always use complete "sentences," they leave out information, they add meaning with their voice, or their faces, and they leave their comments unfinished. Yet, we still understand each other. An utterance, then, is the real-life expression of people's thoughts, ideas, and feelings.

Simply put, discourse analysis is the study of language in use. In discourse analysis, we study how people interact by expressing meaning using language within a context. This includes much more than just studying the words or signs that make up an utterance. It includes all the aspects of those utterances: pacing, facial expression, body shifting, gestures, and any other features that add meaning to an utterance. It also includes building understanding one utterance at a time, from beginning to end, in real time.

A major distinction is the difference between *discourse-focused* analyses and *discourse-based* analyses. Both are revealing, and each sheds complementary insights on meaning and interaction. Discourse-focused analyses consider the broader text and context and intentions of interactants, exploring

Acknowledgments: first, we gratefully acknowledge Mark Halley for his work on the figures in this chapter. In addition, we would like to thank Denise Mammen for her assistance with literature searches, formatting and more. We also thank Emily Balzano and Ricardo Ortiz for their assistance. We thank Stacey DeLaune, Hannah Clarke, Damien Spillane, and Nathaniel Muncie for allowing us to film and study their conversations and to use their photos with permission. These conversations were filmed for one of our discourse analysis classes, and we'd like to thank the students who arranged the filming and analyzed these conversations: Connor Gillis, Mark Halley, Darla Konkel, Ami Murray, Corrie Pond, Caitlin Ramsey, and Heather Turrell.

how the parts build the meaning of the whole. Some examples of studies that begin to consider a broader discourse focus, in the discussions if not the methodologies, can be seen in Duchkovsky and Sandler's (2009) analysis of prosodic features in Israeli Sign Language and in Hermann's (2010) analysis of eye blinks and their role in the prosodic structuring of sign utterances in German Sign Language.

Discourse-based analyses on the other hand tend to focus on discrete elements taken from discourse (sign units, space, head nods, leans, etc.). For example, there are studies that investigate eye gaze and verb agreement as discrete features within discourse (Thomson, Emmorey, and Kluender 2006), eye blinks (Wilbur 1994), and utterance boundaries (Brentari and Crossley 2002; Fenlon, Denmark, Campbell, and Woll 2007). These features all contribute to discourse meaning, and such discourse-based analyses are essential for understanding discrete elements of language and interaction; they provide windows into the structures and functions of discourse as a whole. Indeed, focusing on more than one or two discrete elements in an overall text can be an overwhelming task for a single researcher. What remains to be done is to integrate the findings of disparate studies based in discourse and create a discourse-focused understanding of the ways that all the features impact our understanding of meaning in discourse.

The scope of discourse-focused analyses extends beyond the descriptive and utterance level, attempting to ascertain the reasons signers choose to use depiction instead of, or in combination with other linguistic features, and how those uses may change and evolve through an entire discourse or discourse structure. This focus on the larger discourse and its co-occurring structures is at the heart of discourse-focused studies, which search for the intent and impact of the discourse features as well as the specific form and function.

All discourse analysis research, both discourse-based and discourse-focused, reveals important insights for language learners, educators, sociolinguists, and discourse analysts. Collaboratively sharing data that is analyzed from many perspectives, like corpus studies, will allow us to extend de-contextualized information about single discrete features to a broader understanding of all the factors that impact understanding. This, in turn, can be applied to everyday language needs such as language learning and interpreting, two applications that epitomize language in use.

Five important concepts in discourse analysis

In this section we discuss five major concepts that contribute to the study of discourse analysis. Schiffrin (1994) outlines similar ideas, and here they are applied more directly to the study of sign languages.

Idea 1: discourse is interactive

Discourse always has a creator or presenter and an audience and both have an impact on the meaning of the message. Although discourse is often conveniently categorized into monologues and dialogues, in fact there are few, if any, discourse "texts" that have no intended receiver. Discourse that is often labeled "monologue" such as lectures or presentations always occur in some context where an audience will listen or watch it. Presenters frame presentations to the responses and reactions of the audience (Goffman 1981). They pause for laughs or nods of agreement; they scan the audience for signs of understanding. Even "monologues," presented on video with no apparent audience, are presented with the audience and its potential responses in mind. Thus we can explore intent to interact in all discourse.

Likewise, even the most interactive discourse contains types of monologues, where a single participant may continue for substantial periods of time, discussing one or more topics in depth. These segments of discourse can be analyzed both as internal chunks (Labov 1972), and as they impact and influence the responses of other participants.

It is sometimes helpful to think of communication as a cycle. It begins when the first utterance is made and is based on the language choices made by that person. It continues when the other person receives the utterance and uses his or her own understanding of the language choices, context, and content to construct similar meaning. It continues further when that person responds, making their own choices of language features to reflect the underlying meaning, and continues still further when the first interactant receives a response, continues to formulate meaning to create further understanding, and then continues with further talk, or a response (Goffman 1981).

Idea 2: discourse is a series of choices

Keeping in mind that discourse is interactive, and that meaning emerges whether we speak or sign, it is essential to remember that all language production is the result of choices made by the interactants. There is no random use of words or signs. There is no "neutral" facial expression that conveys no meaning. Every aspect of communication has an impact on how that communication is understood, and every aspect of communication occurs due to choices made by the communicators.

That does not mean that each choice is a consciously well-thought-out decision. If it were, we would never have a conversation! But, using our knowledge of language and communication, we base our every understanding on all of our past experience with language and interaction, and try to build discourse meaning as it emerges. And our every response is chosen to reflect our own internal meaning so that the other person can most easily understand what we want to communicate (Grice 1975). Every choice of sign or word, every choice of facial expression, intonation, shift of body stance, or eye gaze communicates something. So, every aspect of communication is part of the study of discourse analysis. Further, every choice is related to the discourse and meaning that has emerged previously, whether a minute ago, or a conversation last week, or last year. These choices create texture and cohesion throughout the text/discourse, and aid the listeners in understanding the underlying coherence of the message as it is created.

Idea 3: discourse meaning emerges

Almost all discourse starts at the beginning and ends at the end. While that may not seem profound, it is an essential understanding for discourse analysts. That is how we first experience it and understand it, sequentially, from start to finish. The first time we see or hear a lecture, read a book, have a conversation, we have only the first utterances to use. We generally do not know what the other person will say next. As we continue our conversation, we can begin to interpret more and more of each other's meaning, but we can never know it at the beginning. In daily discourse we have only real-time, on-line processing to work with. Janzen (2005), and Wilcox and Shaffer (2006) offer insights into ideas of co-construction of meaning in discourse, and bring cognitive considerations to how we analyze discourse. They help us understand that meaning is not a static "thing" transferred like a package of data between people; it is a dynamic, fluid, and amorphous concept that people hope to share in some way as they interact.

Emerging meaning, understood via emerging discourse, is an essential idea in discourse analysis. In linguistics, it is very easy to take an entire text after the fact and analyze it as a whole, but this is only possible after the fact. While we are in the middle of discourse, we have only part of the text, and we build our interpretation of it based only on what we have, not the text as a whole. If presenters never get a chance to finish what they wanted to say, the audience never gets the chance to interpret the full meaning, or guesses must be made at their full meaning. Likewise, others build their understandings of what was intended only to the extent that they are able to interpret all or most of the linguistic and extra-linguistic messages. Even then, as Becker (1995) pointed out, there are exuberances and deficiencies within all our understandings, or interpretations. There are few, if any, studies in sign languages that focus on the understandings of both interactants in discourse. Most focus on specific use of linguistic features, and possibly either the presenter's or the audience's understanding. Exploring both is a challenge for future discourse analysis.

Idea 4: discourse is context, all the parts of interaction

We develop our emerging understanding of the meaning of any interaction by the signals and cues that are part of that interaction, and all of them are important. Each communicative choice that someone makes, from the choice of a topic to a lexical item, from the length of a turn to the length of a pause, contributes to our emerging conceptualization of the meaning. Equally important to our understanding of the meaning is the context of the interaction.

The context in discourse analysis can be separated somewhat arbitrarily into two types: *internal context* and *external context*. Internal context is the text itself: the choice of discourse features, such as symbols (signs or words), the use of different pronouns to reflect different meanings, the choice of and subsequent repetition of lexical items and reference to them, the various choices made in prosody. Also included as internal context are elements such as turn-taking, overlapping talk, and utterances that constitute a pair. These are the kinds of topics that studies of syntax rarely investigate. Discourse analysis finds these topics to be central areas of interest. Each of these contributes cohesive links from previous utterances to subsequent utterances and is intended to help the audience interpret the underlying coherence of the message.

External context is the context that we use to understand discourse meaning around the text. For example, the usual issues of context include the setting, the goal of the interaction, the race, gender, age, and education of each interactant, and the relative status of each toward the other and toward society as a whole. Each of these external forces has an impact on the choices that people make while interacting and on the types and number of cues any given listener or audience member may recognize and use to interpret the speaker's meaning.

Idea 5: natural language data

In discourse analysis we use natural language data. This means that the texts used for analysis are produced in or for real-life settings for a real purpose of communicating. In order to understand how people use language in real life, we need to study it in real life. This makes discourse analysis somewhat challenging. We need to collect data from real conversations, lectures, etc. while trying not to impact those very situations by our data collection, and we do not always get the information we need. For example, if we want to study use of space for mapping time in ASL, we may have to collect hours of data, because temporal maps seem to be relatively rare in ASL. If we want to study how signers ask a favor, we will have to collect video until we gather enough natural examples of asking for favors. Thus, we often arrange for people to be videotaped while just talking about everyday matters, or with real professionals, such as nurses, or police officers, and real patients or witnesses to role-play situations (Metzger 2000), an effort at natural interaction.

Applications of discourse analysis and major ideas

In this next section, we will discuss some of the recent research in signed language discourse as they support the previous claims.

Idea 1: interaction

All interactions include aspects of dialogue and monologue. Often, the distinction is made between conversation – talking between two or more people – and monologues – talk by a single speaker with a largely non-responsive audience or to a camera, with the reminder that all talk is interactive. Conversation is the basic and fundamental way people talk to each other. Conversations include taking turns, overlapping talk, and repetition, while also developing or maintaining relationships, displaying attitudes and gender, while also being polite, or not, being indirect, or not. Analysis of turn-taking in signed languages began with Baker (1977). These findings have been applied to interpreted interaction (Roy 2000; Sanheim 2003). New studies, such as McCleary and Leite (2013), are examining turn-taking in other signed languages, looking at turn transitions and overlapping talk. In their study of Brazilian Sign Language, McCleary and Leite used two cameras to video an everyday conversation, such that they could determine that there are many instances when speakers were not looking at each other as a way of continuing their turn at talk, or resolving overlapping talk quickly and efficiently. They argue for a definition of 'talk' that includes both prosody and gesture.

In any one conversation or talk by a single speaker, examples of specific kinds of discourse features can be found. For example, in any 1–2 minute segment, the following features can be found:

- getting, maintaining, and yielding of turns (turn-taking);
- cohesive markers to provide a link and a guide to importance, background, and changes in the progression of the talk (such as prosody, discourse markers, repetition, and more);
- speaking and acting as others or as self (constructed dialogue, monologue, and action);
- overlapping talk, adjacency pairs, responses, and more.

Thus, discourse as interaction can be and needs to be studied from the larger perspective of how the participants begin, continue, and close interactions within the context of their lives. The interactive nature of communication, whether it be categorized as monologue or dialogue, must be accounted for in all discussions of discourse.

Idea 2: visual imagery: choices with spatial mapping and depiction

The idea of choices in sign languages can be considered by reviewing one aspect of ASL, *visual imagery*, currently discussed using two labels with similar meaning but differing scope: *spatial mapping* and *depiction*. Spatial mapping and depiction are two terms that describe uses of space in ASL and other sign languages from two complementary perspectives. Spatial mapping springs from discourse-focused analyses, looking at the overall use of visual imagery through discourse structures in natural interaction, and generally analyzes larger structures, such as comparisons, temporal mapping, and constructed dialogue (CD) and constructed action (CA) (Roy 1989; Winston 1991), exploring how these may create cohesive segments, and how they map it based on the dynamic construction of meaning in ongoing discourse (Winston 1991, 1993).

Discourse-based depiction

Depiction, as such, occurs in both signed and spoken languages. As used in sign language linguistics, it provides a category label that describes a signer's choices in achieving interactive goals at the utterance level. When choosing to use depiction, a signer wants to portray, in some visually iconic manner, a demonstration of an event, or object, or concept for the audience to use while forming and understanding their own meanings. Depiction is a term brought to us primarily from studies in cognitive linguistics, in which cognitive linguists strive to describe how interactants use cognitive resources to convey meaning in interaction. The descriptions of depiction are generally discourse based, coming from natural data, with the analysis of a discrete feature found within a larger discourse structure. These descriptions usually begin with the discussion of single depicting verbs (also known as classifier constructions), and remain at the utterance level of discourse, often relating back to ideas of grammar (Liddell 2003). Thumann defines it as: "the visual representation of aspects of events, settings, objects, or abstract concepts using components that are accessible in the immediate environment" (2011: 47–48). Discussions of depiction then leap from a discussion of single signs to claims about larger sections of discourse in which depiction occurs (Dudis 2011).

The visual imagery can reflect either concrete events and relationships; those are conceived of as occurring within some setting, called scene depictions – (a bolt of lightning across the sky; two people interacting with each other) or abstract concepts such as sequence lines (e.g., timelines), that are, or can be conceptualized, independently of a setting.

Dudis (2011) for example, offers a description of three ways that a signer might use her body when attempting to convey concepts via imagery in ASL. In Dudis' analysis, the body anchors the visual space in scene depiction, and has three distinct functions – two that are dynamic and one that is static. The body functions dynamically either as a reflection of an entity, or as the vantage point from which a scene is being described. Statically, the body can function as a proxy – used to demonstrate to the audience something that would actually occur on a body – a wound, scar, or other mark. Also quite commonly done for body parts, signers typically use the index and middle fingers pointed downward (Classifier: V) to depict someone's legs (see Figure 5.1). The woman on the right is depicting a woman standing with her legs open as another person is below her (a childhood story of accidentally seeing up a woman's dress). Dudis describes this kind of depiction as, "compared to life-sized the specifications are on a much smaller scale...this scale is small enough to afford a more global viewpoint," (2004: 230).

Discourse-focused spatial mapping

Spatial mapping highlights the importance of space from the perspective of discourse, specifically as signers use it to reflect their conceptions of discourse meaning and structure. Spatial mapping is manifested through signs at the morphemic, syntactic, and discourse levels, and becomes a powerful tool when

Figure 5.1 Example of depiction

it is repeated and used by the signer to build structures called discourse frames. A signer, in reflecting the underlying coherence and establishing expectations in the minds of the receivers, can employ these frames. These frames span sections of discourse larger than an utterance, and occur in at least three types of frames – comparisons, constructed action, and dialogue, and time. For example, a speaker may use a constructed dialogue frame to establish the expectation of two people communicating about something. When the audience realizes that such a frame is being built, they expect specific outcomes from that frame and interpret the meaning based on their understanding of this type of frame. These expectations may or may not be satisfied in the minds of the audience, but they are established and then exploited by the signer (Winston 1993). When spatial mapping is used to help build comparison frames, both present and non-present concrete entities, as well as abstract entities, can be mapped and repeatedly referred to throughout discourse much longer than that one utterance.

Another example of the use of spatial maps can be seen in comparative discourse frames. Winston (1993) analyzes the strategies a signer used to convey a comparison of two abstract entities, ASL and English poetry. In an hour-long lecture, a patterned discourse structure was identified. Repeated spatial references to the entities being compared were interspersed with and interacted with the rest of the text. The pattern typically began with a non-spatial introduction, simply naming an entity or a referent. This introduction was followed by an initial spatial mapping. This mapping had a consistent pattern of production. The first entity was consistently mapped on the non-dominant side; the second entity was consistently mapped on the dominant side. Following the initial mapping, repeated reference to the two entities being compared occurred in the next utterances. Within the frame of comparing the two entities, the signer also shifted between using both sides of the spatial map to refer to the entities and using the central area between two mapped entities. He shifted his focus to the central area to share comments about his mixed emotions about the entities (ASL and English poetry). When those were shared, he could again refer to his comparison by referring to the two sides of the spatial map. The signer could also suspend his map altogether, changing to new topics and using the same physical space for establishing new spatial maps to refer to the new topics. He could then refocus on the comparison spatial maps at any time during the discourse. He did this by re-identifying the entities mapped and their original mapped space.

The comparative discourse frames also had two distinctive patterns used for ending the comparison. One pattern consisted of the opposite pattern of the opening; that is, the entity introduced second was referred to last. Another pattern consisted of both hands pointing to both sides of the map either simultaneously or in alternation. Spatial mapping cues the audience to much larger goals over the course of extended discourse. It is only if and when the analysis of space is extended beyond the level of the utterance, that patterns of larger discourse structures begin to emerge.

All signers use some form of depiction as a part of spatial mapping, and another level of complexity and interest is added when studied through the lens of ethnicity, variation, and/or gender. Metzger and Mather (2004) analyzed nineteen narratives in natural conversations and compared the use of constructed action and constructed dialogue by five black signers and three white signers. Black male signers used more constructed action and constructed action with dialogue, but not constructed dialogue by itself. In McCaskill *et al.* (2011), a study of elicited narratives and narratives in conversation among black Deaf Americans, seem to suggest that black signers use more constructed action and dialogue than white signers, although the authors caution that individual differences were many and more investigation is needed.

As these constructions are identified in stretches of discourse, and observed, noted, and analyzed, and the variety of their composition becomes clear, the use of imagery and dialogue can be seen as rich and plentiful in signed languages. As we keep in mind that all interaction is a series of choices, a signer's decision to use space, whether in the choice to use a simple depicting verb, or to create an entire spatial map comparing two concepts, serves as a cue to the meaning intended.

Idea 3: meaning emerges through cohesion

Meaning is built moment by moment, idea by idea. In order to accomplish that, people choose various linguistic devices, such as depiction described above, to express the meaning and to help others interpret the meaning. Cohesion is the use of such cues to link utterances to help the audience make sense. Cohesive devices refer to those linguistic features that each language uses to link one section of discourse to previous sections. These are the cues that we use to build our understanding of the emerging meaning. There are many cohesive cues that contribute to the overall emergence of meaning in interaction – repeated reference to entities and ideas using both nouns and pronouns (Swabey 2011); use of repetition throughout connected discourse (McCaskill *et al.* 2011), and effective use of prosody to signal such things as openings and closings, topic shift, asides, focus, and jokes. Spatial mapping also creates cohesion, such as in the patterns with comparisons and dialogue and action that were discussed above. In this section, we focus on *prosody* as a cohesive feature to be studied and analyzed.

Prosody can be defined as the combination of features that produce rhythm, accent, or feel of the language, and which allows speakers and signers to reflect their internal focus for any given text or segment of a text. Likewise, it allows the audience to chunk/segment/parse the message in ways that help them interpret the presenter's intended meaning. The challenge of defining and analyzing prosody in any language is that it is produced by so many different features in combinations over a variety of utterances, and is highly influenced by the signer's mental focus at the moment as well as the signer's own signing style.

In sign languages, prosody is anything that impacts the visual image that we interpret for meaning, thus it is essential to consider any visual feature as a possible component of prosody. Many linguists and sociolinguists approach the study of prosody from a perceptual perspective – given that native users identify specific features as prominent or salient, what does that prominence achieve? While it is possible to measure the length of a movement or the exact location of a sign, it is perceptions of prominence that help us identify the features that combine in any given utterance to direct our attention to its meaning. For example, the length of a final hold in a sign only focuses attention on that sign in relation to the length of final holds on every other sign in the utterance. If they are all the same, the length of the final hold is unremarkable; if the final hold is 1 second, and all the other final holds are 2 seconds, the final sign becomes unstressed. If the final sign is held 1 second, and every other sign has no hold or a minimal hold in the transition from one sign to another, then the final sign becomes the focus. So, in studying prosody, it is not only the actual physical production, but the relative types of production within a given series of productions that create the perception of stress, prominence, or focus.

Functions of prosody   When prosodic features co-occur over longer sequences of discourse, they tend to focus the audience on the relative prominence of topics, sub-topics, and asides within the overall discourse structure. For example, the prosodic pattern for listing in English has an upward intonation at the end of each utterance in the list except for the last one, where the intonation falls. "I bought bread, eggs, cheese, and milk" – where the intonation on bread, eggs, and cheese rises, and the intonation on milk falls. This prosodic pattern in English helps the listener predict when and where the list will come to an end. Knowing that the list has ended, the listener will assume that the next utterance moves on to another topic, or sequential sub-topic such as, "then I went home and ate." If the speaker dropped the intonation on milk, then continued the list, the listener would predict that something out of the ordinary was happening next. Likewise, if the speaker did not drop the intonation on 'milk,' the listener would think that the list was unfinished and might ask the speaker what else they bought. Such is the power and function of prosody, to help us chunk discourse, and interpret the prominence/structure intended by the speaker.

Likewise, in signed languages, prosody provides the addressee with a means of chunking and interpreting discourse over larger chunks. ASL is comparable to English in its use of prosody for defining listing – each utterance that lists an item tends to end with an upward movement and slightly longer hold on the last sign of the utterance, until the last item in the list, which tends to have a downward movement on the last sign (or signs) of the final utterance (Winston 2000). Other discourse-level functions of prosody include marking the opening and closing of texts, the segmenting of sub-topics and asides, and the marking of discourse prominence. One of the ASL prosodic features used for marking larger segments of discourse can be seen when signers shift from the naming of an idea to an expansion or explanation of that idea. For example, a signer discussing ASL poetry might sign the first few utterances in fairly central space with relatively little movement, facial expression, head movement, or use of space. But, if the next few utterances compare two aspects of ASL poetry, e.g., its scientific analysis and its art form, the comparison is marked with both spatial mapping and prosodic cues (Winston 1993). When the signer completes the comparison, the summary statement might then be signed with a return to the central space used in the opening of the topic.

Features of prosody   Many features contribute to the prosody of sign languages; some are head movement, eye gaze, eye blink, shoulder movement, torso leans, mouth movements, sign articulation speed and pace, number of hands used, and pauses. More recent studies of prosody in signed languages exist, which tend to recognize the broader discourse context of prosodic cues. Although few are couched in terms of ongoing contextual cohesion, most focus at the utterance level and/or emphasize the need to consider the broader discourse context. In this way, they can be described as more discourse based than discourse focused.

While many of these studies focus on specific features and patterns in sign languages, we are far from having built an understanding of the overall workings of cohesion in sign language discourse. As an example to illustrate this, we highlight some recent work on prosody. Much of it focuses on specific sign categories, such as verbs (Thompson, Emmorey, and Kluender 2006) or prosody at the utterance level (Hermann 2010; Sandler 2009), and are based in discourse data. Others provide extensive overviews of various studies over the years. Only a very few look at cohesive patterns over longer, complete discourse texts. Each contributes pieces to the larger puzzle that is cohesion in signed discourse, but as a whole, discourse analysis has far to go in building a body of literature that explores cohesion and our understanding of how interactants use language to co-construct meaning. Some recent examples of discourse-based prosody research highlight this progress, as well as the need to extend it in many directions.

Thompson, Emmorey, and Kluender (2006) focus specifically on a single prosodic cue, eye gaze, as it interacts with verb agreement in ASL. Future expansions of this type of analysis to other prosodic cues that might also occur would be valuable to discourse analysis. Hogue (2010) also focuses on a single prosodic cue, investigating the interplay of mouth movements and utterance boundaries in ASL. Of course, signals occur within specific signs, or as meaningful markers (e.g., pursed lips or tongue protrusion) added to a variety of signs. They also mark utterance boundaries by their disappearance. For example, the occurrence of tongue protrusion (known as 'th') with the sign DRIVE happens at the end of a clause; when the 'th' disappears, the watcher knows that a new utterance is beginning.

Expanding the scope of analysis beyond the interactions of a single prosodic cue and linguistic forms, Brentari and Crossley (2002) focus specifically on several suprasegmental prosodic cues that interact with signs to signal sentence boundaries. In their study, they analyzed facial prosodic cues, including eye-gaze, eye blink, holds of signs, and other facial cues, as they occurred with or during signs in a one-hour lecture in ASL. They found that these do interact in connected discourse.

Fenlon, Denmark, Campbell, and Woll (2007) also focus their analysis at the sentence level, seeking to identify the cues that signal watchers to the beginnings and ends of sentences in British Sign Language. Their approach, like Brentari and Crossley, analyzes all the prosodic cues that occur at identified utterance boundaries, and emphasize the need to understand the interactions of many differing cues as they co-occur.

Dachkovsky and Sandler (2009) focus primarily at the syntactic level, discussing the interactions of syntax and prosody in Israeli Sign Language, specifically sign language intonation. Although Sandler's work is focused primarily on the interaction of syntax and prosody, she delivers an insightful discussion of the needs to expand exploration of prosody to notions of both form and discourse function. She is one of the few to acknowledge and stress the need to take our understanding of prosody beyond descriptions of its interaction with signs and sentences, and notes that prosody also needs to be analyzed for both its form and its discourse functions.

Herrmann (2010) offers an analysis of eye blinks and other prosodic cues that occur to signal utterance boundaries in German Sign Language. Although her primary focus is eye blinks, she stresses that these must be understood as part of a much more complicated set of interactions of many potential prosodic cues.

Taking a slightly different, and more discourse-focused approach, van der Kooij, Crasborn, and Emmerik (2006) focus on the prosodic cue of body leans in the Sign Language of the Netherlands (SLN), discussing their use to focus the audience on discourse functions, for example new information in the discourse, or information that is particularly salient. This study can be described as more discourse focused, since it interprets this prosodic cue in terms of its functions within an interaction. In addition, the data reflect discourse structures slightly larger than the utterance. However, the data were collected by eliciting sentence pairs, either question and answer, or statement and response, rather than from natural discourse, and the actual scope of the function discussed is generally two utterances.

Two studies provide extensive literature reviews of various prosodic cues: Pfau and Quer (2009) review specific studies of single prosodic cues and range over a wide variety of prosodic cues ranging from lexical to syntactic, and provide an overview of the breadth of possibilities to be explored. The discussion remains primarily at the utterance levels, describing what the prosodic cues look like, rather than describing how they build cohesion across a signed text. Ormel and Crasborn (2012) also provide an extensive literature review of investigations of individual prosodic cues that use the utterance or sentence as the basis of analysis. They focus primarily on phonetic and grammatical aspects of prosody, describing various prosodic cues, and speculating about the need to identify combinations of prosodic cues that will predict sentence boundaries. Their work extends beyond reviews of prosodic cues, however, and includes a section on computer-based technologies that might contribute to the analysis of prosody. Of interest in their broad approach is their recognition of the multiple perspectives needed in studying prosody. While interested in how computers can analyze cues in sign language, they note the essential need for human informants to complete any analysis. They write, "Video analyses and kinematic recordings can provide exceedingly detailed data on each of the possible prosodic cues. However, intuitive judgments can provide information about the actual presence of a prosodic boundary in sign language. Without native informants to confirm the feature extraction data during the initial phase of analysis of (combinations of) features deriving from video analyses, it would be impossible to determine whether the data in fact pointed to boundaries" (2012: 7).

There seem to be two distinct purposes in these studies – to identify prosodic cues that interact at the utterance level or below, and to identify ways to make video analysis of sign languages possible via computer technologies. While studies focused on the first goal add to our overall understanding of prosody in signed languages, since they remain focused primarily at the utterance level, there is still a need to investigate cues in order to expand our overall understanding of cohesion and how it contributes to the ongoing co-construction of meaning through extended discourse.

Idea 4: context: politeness

The idea of context in discourse analysis can be explored by looking at how social knowledge impacts linguistic decisions when speakers engage in specific speech acts, such as requests, rejections, apologies, and more. As speakers interact with others, they do not always recall the specifics of a conversation but they do remember their overall impressions of the other person, whether that person was being friendly or standoffish, rude or polite, knowledgeable or not, and so on. What are the markers of these impressions in sign languages? Do sign languages have strategies for being indirect? And what kind of variations appear in dialects of individual sign languages, such as ASL? What are the internal and external contexts that influence signers' choices as they interact?

For example, one notorious stereotype about Deaf users of many sign languages is that they are blunt or direct, while the corresponding stereotype is that speakers of English are vague or indirect. Roush (1999) considered external context in exploring indirect strategies in ASL. He finds that ASL signers can and do make indirect requests, and, can and do reply indirectly. In fact, they use conventional indirectness and mitigating strategies we find in all languages. In interviews with Deaf speakers, he asked about being direct and his informants told him that, first, direct or blunt comments about appearance are mostly between acquaintances and that Deaf people can be indirect when something is a surprise, or when intended to criticize, as in "I've never seen Deaf people do that" (Roush 2007: 124). Roush also analyzed a commercial videotape with a series of situations where Deaf actors had to make a request to borrow something of value. Roush found that Deaf ASL signers use indirect yes/no questions and used linguistic elements such as the signs DON'T-MIND, ALL RIGHT, and fingerspelled loan signs such as #O-R to appeal to the listener's understanding. ASL signers used statements of regret, excuses, reasons, explanations, alternatives, and negative consequences to make requests as well as to refuse a request. Most of these are accompanied by gestural and facial expressions that express the severity of the request or refusal, or the opposite. Roush claims that the style of talk used by the Deaf participants is indirect rather than direct, and that such indirectness serves to highlight both the interdependence as well as the individual independence among ASL users.

Hoza (2007) considered internal discourse context when examining requests and refusals in both ASL and English. With ASL, he found more indirect refusals than requests but noted that using specific discourse sequences may not have captured that kind of request. He also noted the importance and impact of nonmanual signals in mitigating the impact of refusals; for example, one marker Roush (1999) labeled as polite pucker (*pp*) is used only when impositions are small and the speaker is trying to be cooperative. When the imposition is sufficiently large, the body teeter (*bt*), also identified by Roush, and/or the polite grimace (*pg*), identified by Hoza, marker may be used.

As in any language, elements of sign languages can serve more than one purpose. Hoza (2011) analyzed two particular lexical elements that, while not

Figure 5.2 HEY

Figure 5.3 HEY

serving as content information, do function as both discourse markers and play a role in determining politeness. At the level of discourse, speakers signal how their current utterance relates to the preceding discourse or their intentions for the upcoming discourse. For example, while HEY (Figure 5.2) functions primarily as an attention-getter and conversational opener, it can also function to switch topics (like 'hey' in English) or to express surprise or warning (much like 'oh' in English).

WELL (Figure 5.3), which functions primarily to express hesitation and to hedge, can also function to pause, or express reluctance.

Figure 5.4 WELL

Both also play key roles in politeness functions: HEY when a speaker senses that what they are about to say may seem impolite or is asking too much of someone, as in when a speaker wants to interrupt. WELL, when used for pausing, also marks boundaries in discourse. While WELL functions to express reluctance, it is also used as hesitation when making a request, or when making a rejection can soften the rejection. Nonmanual signals that co-occur with HEY and WELL signal the degree to which the signer is mitigating a request that they will impose on the addressee. (See Figure 4 and Figure 5.)

Idea 5: natural interactions as the data source of choice

Although discourse analysis looks to natural interaction for the preferred source of data, it is often difficult to collect natural data. First, ethically we must inform people that we are collecting data if we are planning to use it for research. This can have an impact on the natural flow of interaction (although, with video becoming so pervasive in our world, people are less and less uncomfortable with video in some cases). In addition, there is now a plethora of video available on the internet that adds more options to our data choices.

Another major challenge for discourse analysts, regardless of type of data, is *transcribing* the data. Transcription is the process of coding and annotating signed language data into written or graphic form so that it can be further studied and analyzed. The goal is to transform the flowing, sequential language data into static, simultaneously available data. The benefits of transforming language data into static, analyzable data is that it can be reviewed, coded, and re-presented for others to access. The dangers of transforming the visual data to graphic form is that (1) we are no longer analyzing the original data; (2) no transcription completely transforms all aspects of the audio or video data; and (3) the nature of the language itself is irretrievably altered. The original is

Figure 5.5 One hand WELL

always the actual language sample. Although transcriptions attempt to represent the features we believe are salient to our analyses, it is in fact secondary data, and it is essential that any analysis is "triangulated back" with the original data, and is not based solely on our secondary data. All transcriptions provide partial views of the data; none represent all aspects of the language. Thus, we need to be careful that our analysis of transcribed data is salient and notable in real time communication.

Given the benefits and challenges of discourse data analysis, transcription is the basis for all discourse analysis. Edwards (2001) sums it up eloquently:

> Recordings are essential tools in discourse research, but are not sufficient by themselves, for the systematic examination of interaction. It is simply impossible to hold in mind the transient, highly multidimensional, and often overlapping events of an interaction as they unfold in real time.
>
> For this reason, transcripts are invaluable. They provide a distillation of the fleeting events of an interaction, frozen in time, freed from extraneous detail, and expressed in categories of interest to the researcher. (321)

Transcribing any natural language is a challenge Transcription practices vary widely, depending on the goals and needs of the researcher and learner. However, there are some more general principles that are applicable to any language, and we need to keep them in mind when we think about transcribing data (Edwards 2001; Johnston 2010). For signed languages comparatively few protocols exist. Most linguists have adopted a type of glossing to represent a basic sign using a parallel spoken language symbol, or word. This system is basic, and often can only be partially understood by the glosser, and barely understood by others. It is not the equivalent of writing a spoken language like English. Moreover, while it is understood to be only a supplement to a signed sample itself, until recently the gloss, sometimes accompanied by photos, has been the only version of data provided in research and textbooks. With the advent of easily accessible video, this is hopefully changing. With the use of systems like ELAN, for example, it is possible to combine both a glossed version, and a simultaneous viewing of the video data.[1] Several more recent studies include the use of ELAN as the transcription tool of choice, because it allows the researcher to view the video in conjunction with the transcription and annotations, it enables easy transcription of multiple layers of features, and results in transcriptions and annotations that are easily manipulated for ease of computer analysis of various pieces of the transcription. It also lends itself to corpus studies, where researchers can share data and compare the various analyses of the same discourse and understand the overlaps, co-occurrences, and correlations between the various features that each has studied.

A problem for transcribing data in any language is that it is often important to transcribe several layers of information as it co-occurs and overlaps. In signed languages, it may be important to know which hand signs what, when both hands are used; which is the dominant hand, and when and how this changes. It may also be important to transcribe the body stance, facial expression, head movement, and eye gaze that co-occur with the language, regardless of whether it is signed or spoken.

Annotation units   Annotation units are the "chunks" or segments of data that are coded in the transcription. Two important considerations are the consistent uniqueness of each annotation label, and the scope, or size of the annotated/annotation unit. The scope, or size, of annotation units is important to determine, as they relate to the goals of the analysis. These can be of many sizes, and longer units may encompass smaller ones. Types of annotations include: features, functions, and structures. For example, it may be important to annotate discourse structures such as utterances, chunks or segments/ topics, introductions or closings, etc. It might be important to annotate the data at the phonemic, morphologic, or lexical level; it may be important to annotate functions of the discourse, such as greetings, interruptions, involvement, or persuasion. It may well be important to annotate for all of these levels in any data set, in order to analyze features that overlap various functions. None of these choices is right or wrong, nor are they mutually exclusive. The choices of what to annotate depend on the specific goals for the analysis of the data.

How to most effectively and clearly transcribe signed language, and especially signed language discourse, has been a difficult question to answer.

Readability   Another consideration for developing transcripts is readability. You always need to be able to read the transcript, and eventually others will, too. Two things to think about: making it visually adequate and

---

[1] ELAN: Max Planck Institute for Psycholinguistics (2011); ELAN – Linguistic Annotator [software]. Available from www.lat-mpi.eu/tools/elan

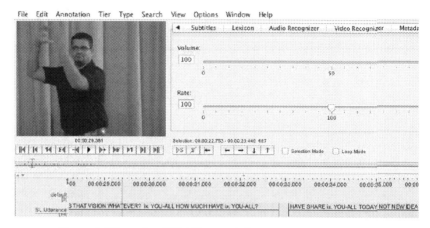

Figure 5.6 Example of ELAN transcription

arranging the annotations for specific reasons (e.g., representing spatial arrangement on the page). If you look at the examples below, you can see the transcription beginning first with no considerations of readability and then demonstrating increasing levels of readability.

Samples: ASL transcription

ASL no readability: This example is a basic transcription of an ASL text with no effort to make it easy to read. (See Figure 5.6.)

RELATEP-MUSIC#WHATTECHNIQUE2h:listofmanythingsPRO.1(B hand)LOOK-FOR+COLLECT(all)PRO.1READ+++WHYWHYPRO.12h-CC:BIG-HEADPMU-SICTECHNIQUENOTPRO.1KNOW-NOTHINGWHEWBUTSELF.1P-O-E-TPRO.1EXPRESSSIGN-ASL[CLEARwithhands]BUTANALYZE2h-PRO.12h-DON'T-KNOWPRO.1SOPRO.1REALHARDTIME++ SELF.1++++2hCL:CCpushaway-ltA-R-Tonlt2hCL:CCpushaway-ltSCIENCEonrt2hCL:CCmoveto rtANALYZErtWHEW PRO.1STRUGGLE+++PRO.12hCL:CC-thbscontactCL:Cseparatert fromcenterCL:CseparateltfromcenterTERRIBLE

Utterance boundaries annotated: Here is the same transcription of an ASL text with minimal readability for linguists.

RELATE P-MUSIC,#WHAT TECHNIQUE, 2h:list of many things, PRO.1(B hand) LOOK-FOR+, COLLECT(all) PRO.1 READ+++. WHY, WHY? PRO.1 2h-CC: BIG-HEAD P-MUSIC TECHNIQUE NOT PRO.1, KNOW-NOTHING,*WHEW! BUT, SELF.1 P-O-E-T,PRO.1. EXPRESS SIGN-ASL [CLEAR with hands]. BUT ANALYZE 2h-PRO.1, 2h-DON'T-KNOW, PRO.1, 'SO'. PRO.1 REAL HARD TIME++ SELF.1++++ 2hCL:CCpush away-lt, A-R-Ton lt, 2hCL:CCpush away-lt.

SCIENCEon rt, 2hCL:CCmove to rt, ANALYZErt. WHEW. PRO.1 STRUGGLE+++, PRO.1 2hCL:CC-thbs contact, CL:Cseparate rt from center, CL:Cseparate lt from center. TERRIBLE!

Utterance boundaries annotated and numbered: In this example the utterances are separated onto separate lines, and numbered, so that they are more easily identified and further annotated. In addition to line numbers, some people might also add time codes to each line.

1. RELATE P-MUSIC,
2. #WHAT TECHNIQUE, 2h:list of many things,
3. PRO.1(B hand) LOOK-FOR+,
4. COLLECT(all)
5. PRO.1 READ+++.
6. WHY, WHY?(rhet. q)
7. PRO.1 2h-CC:BIG-HEAD P-MUSIC TECHNIQUE NOT PRO.1,
8. KNOW-NOTHING,*WHEW!
9. BUT, SELF.1 P-O-E-T,PRO.1.
10. EXPRESS SIGN-ASL [CLEAR with hands]
11. BUT ANALYZE 2h-PRO.1,
12. 2h-DON'T-KNOW, PRO.1, 'SO'.
13. PRO.1 REAL HARD TIME++ SELF.1++++
14. 2hCL:CCpush away-lt,
15. A-R-Ton lt,
16. 2hCL:CCpush away-lt
17. SCIENCEon rt,
18. 2hCL:CCmove to rt,
19. ANALYZErt.
20. WHEW.
21. PRO.1 STRUGGLE+++,over time,
22. PRO.1 2hCL:CC-thbs contact,
23. CL:Cseparate rt from center,
24. CL:Cseparate lt from center.
        _____Y
25. TERRIBLE!

Each of the examples above is an attempt to improve readability. As you read through the various transcriptions, look for this in other transcriptions. And think about how you would make a transcription more readable. Winston (1993) offers a more in-depth discussion of transcription issues for discourse analysis.

To reiterate the importance of transcription, as stated above, transcription is the basis for all discourse analysis: "transcripts are invaluable. They provide a distillation of the fleeting events of an interaction, frozen in time, freed from extraneous detail, and expressed in categories of interest to the researcher" (Edwards 2001: 321). Yet, as much as it supports discourse analysis, it likewise de-contextualizes the transcribed feature(s) from the context in which they are used for communication.

Conclusion

In this chapter we have explored five general principles of discourse analysis and offered some discussion of more recent research into ASL as it reflects those principles. One distinction we have made when describing the field, and related research, is between discourse-focused research that takes a broader perspective on extended language as it is used by signers to interact and discourse-based research that uses natural data while focusing on units of discourse that are analyzed at the utterance level or smaller. Both perspectives and approaches contribute to the still largely incomplete understanding of how ASL signers build meaningful coherence throughout extended discourse.

The early Metzger and Bahan (2001) chapter that we are following up on provides excellent discussion of the discourse analysis work available at that time. Our discussion has focused on expanded understandings of discourse analysis as it has developed from its recent beginnings. It was not our goal to re-cover their discussions, but rather to expand with a review of ongoing explorations into discourse analysis. In this review, we make the distinction between discourse-based analyses, in which analysis focuses on units no larger than utterances, and discourse-focused analyses, in which the analysis looks to larger discourse segments to identify patterns used by signers to accomplish interactive goals. While the former have continued to increase in number, the latter remain rare. Even combining all perspectives brought to the study of discourse, the picture remains sparse, and we would benefit immensely from an expansion of research that explores measurable detail within the broader context of meaning and interaction.

REFERENCES

Baker, C. (1977) Regulators and turn-taking in American Sign Language discourse. In L. Friedman (ed.), *On the Other Hand: New Perspectives on American Sign Language* (pp. 215–236). New York: Academic Press.

Becker, A. (1995) *Beyond Translation: Essays in Philology*. Ann Arbor, MI: University of Michigan Press.

Brentari, D. and Crossley, L. (2002) Prosody on the hands and face. *Sign Language and Linguistics* 5(2): 105–130.

Dachkovsky, S. and Sandler, W. (2009) Visual intonation in the prosody of a sign language. *Language and Speech* 52(2–3): 287–314.

Dudis, P. (2004) Body partitioning in real-space blends. *Cognitive Linguistics* 15(2): 223–238.

(2011). The body in scene depictions. In C. Roy (ed.), *Discourse in Signed Languages* (pp. 3–45). Washington, DC: Gallaudet University Press.

Edwards, J. (2001) The transcription of discourse. In D. Schiffrin, D. Tannen, and H. E. Hamilton (eds.), *The Handbook of Discourse Analysis* (pp. 321–348). Malden, MA: Blackwell.

Engberg-Pederson, E. (1992) Point of view in Danish Sign Language. *Nordic Journal of Linguistics* 15(2): 201–211.

Fenlon, J., Denmark, T., Campbell, R., and Woll, B. (2007) Seeing sentence boundaries. *Sign Language and Linguistics* 10(2): 177–200.

Goffman, E. (1981) *Replies and Responses: Forms of Talk* (pp. 5–77). Philadelphia, PA: University of Pennsylvania Press.

Grice, H. P. (1975) Logic and conversation. In P. Cole and J. Morgan (eds.), *Syntax and Semantics* (vol. III, pp. 41–58). New York: Academic Press.

Herrmann, A. (2010) The interaction of eye blinks and other prosodic cues in German Sign Language. *Sign Language and Linguistics* 13(1): 3–39.

Hogue, R. (2010) OOs and AAs: Mouth gestures as ideophones in American Sign Language, unpublished dissertation, Gallaudet University.

Hoza, J. (2007) *It's Not What You Sign: Politeness in American Sign Language.* Washington, DC: Gallaudet University Press.

(2011) The discourse and politeness functions of HEY and WELL in American Sign Language. In Cynthia Roy (ed.), *Discourse in Signed Languages* (pp. 69–95). Washington, DC: Gallaudet University Press.

Janzen, T. (2005) Introduction to the theory and practice of signed language interpreting. In T. Janzen (ed.), *Topics in Signed Language Interpreting: Theory and Practice* 63: 3.

Johnston, T. (2010) From archive to corpus: Transcription and annotation in the creation of signed language corpora. *International Journal of Corpus Linguistics* 15(1): 106–131.

Labov, W. (1972) *The Transformation of Experience in Narrative Syntax: Language in the Inner City* (pp. 354–96). Philadelphia, PA: University of Pennsylvania Press.

Liddell, S. K. (2003) *Grammar, Gesture, and Meaning in American Sign Language.* Cambridge, MA: Cambridge University Press.

McCaskill, C., Lucas, C., Bayley, R., and Hill, J. (2011) *The Hidden Treasure of Black ASL: Its History and Structure.* Washington, DC: Gallaudet University Press. [book + DVD]

McCleary, L. and de Arantes Leite, T. (2013) Turn-taking in Brazilian Sign Language. *Journal of Interactional Research in Communication Disorders* 4(1).

Metzger, M. (1995) Constructed dialogue and constructed action in American Sign Language. *Sociolinguistics in Deaf communities* 255–271.

(2000) Interactive role-plays as a teaching strategy. In C. Roy (ed.), *Innovative Practices for Teaching Sign Language Interpreters* (pp. 83–108). Washington, DC: Gallaudet University Press.

Metzger, M. and Bahan, B. (2001) Discourse analysis. In C. Lucas (ed.), *The Sociolinguistics of Sign Languages* (pp. 112–144). Cambridge: Cambridge University Press.

Metzger, M. and Mather, S. (2004) Constructed dialogue and constructed action in Conversational narratives in ASL, poster presented at the Conference on Theoretical Issues in Sign Language Research (TISLR 8). Barcelona, September 30–October 2.

Ormel, E. and Crasborn, O. (2012) Prosodic correlated of sentences in signed languages: A literature review and suggestions for new types of studies. *Sign Language Studies* 12(2): 279–315.

118   *Elizabeth A. Winston and Cynthia Roy*

Pfau, R. and Quer, J. (2009) *Nonmanuals: Their Grammatical and Prosodic Rules. Sign languages*. Cambridge, UK: Cambridge University Press.

Pichler, D. C., Hochgesang, J. A., Lillo-Martin, D., and de Quatros, R. M. (2010) Conventions for sign and speech transcription of child bimodal bilingual corpora in ELAN. *Language, Interaction, and Acquisition* 1(1): 11–40.

Roush, D. (1999) Indirect strategies in American Sign Language: Requests and refusals, unpublished master's thesis, Gallaudet University, Washington, DC.

(2007) Indirectness strategies in American Sign Language requests and refusals: deconstructing the deaf-as-direct stereotype. In M. Metzger and E. Fleetwood (eds.), *Translation, Sociolinguistic, and Consumer Issues in Interpreting* (pp. 103–156). Washington, DC: Gallaudet University Press.

Roy, C. B. (1989) Features of discourse in an American Sign Language lecture. In C. Lucas (ed.), *The Sociolinguistics of the Deaf Community* (pp. 231–251). San Diego, CA: Academic Press.

Roy, C. (2000) *Interpreting as a Discourse Process*. New York: Oxford University Press.

Sanheim, L. M. (2003) Turn exchange in an interpreted medical encounter. In M. Metzger, S. Collins, V. Dively, and R. Shaw (eds.), *From Topic Boundaries to Omission*. Washington, DC: Gallaudet University Press.

Schiffrin, D. (1994) *Approaches to Discourse* (vol. VIII). Oxford: Blackwell.

Swabey, L. (2011) Referring expressions in ASL discourse. In C. Roy (ed.), *Discourse in Signed Languages* (pp. 96–118). Washington, DC: Gallaudet University Press.

Thompson, R., Emmorey, K., and Kluender, R. (2006). The relationship between eye gaze and verb agreement in American Sign Language: An eye-tracking study. *Natural Language and Linguistic Theory* 24(2): 571–604.

Thumann, M. (2010) Identifying Depiction in American Sign Language Presentations, unpublished dissertation. Washington, DC: Gallaudet University.

(2011) Identifying depiction: Constructed action and constructed dialogue in ASL presentations. In C. Roy (ed.), *Discourse in Signed Languages* (pp. 46–66). Washington, DC: Gallaudet University Press.

Van der Kooij, E., Crasborn, O., and Emmerik, W. (2006) Explaining prosodic body leans in Sign Language of the Netherlands: Pragmatics required. *Journal of Pragmatics* 38(10): 1598–1614.

Wilbur, R. (1994) Eyeblinks and ASL phrase structure. *Sign Language Studies* 84(1): 221–240.

Wilcox, S. and Shaffer, B. (2005) Towards a cognitive model of interpreting. In T. Janzen (ed.), *Topics in Signed Language Interpreting* (pp. 135–164). Amsterdam/Philadelphia, PA: John Benjamins.

Wilcox, S. and Shaffer, B. (2006) Modality in American Sign Language. In W. Frawley (ed.), *Verbal and Signed Languages: Comparing Structures, Constructs and Methodologies* (pp. 107–131). Berlin: Mouton de Gruyter.

Winston, E. (1991) Spatial referencing and cohesion in an American Sign Language text. *Sign Language Studies* 73(1): 397–410.

(1993) Spatial mapping in comparative discourse frames in an American Sign Language lecture, unpublished dissertation, Washington, DC: Georgetown University.

(1995) Comparative discourse frames in an ASL text. In K. Emmorey and J. Reilly (eds.), *Language, Gesture, and Space* (pp. 85–114). Mahwah, NJ: Lawrence Erlbaum.

(1996) Spatial mapping in ASL discourse. In *Proceedings of the 1996 Conference of Interpreter Trainers Convention* (pp. 1–28). Little Rock, AK.

(1998) Spatial mapping and involvement in ASL story-telling. In C. Lucas (ed.), *Pinky Extension and Eye Gaze* (pp. 183–210). Washington, DC: Gallaudet University Press.

(2000) It just doesn't look like ASL! Defining, recognizing, and teaching prosody in ASL. In *CIT at 21: Celebrating Excellence* (pp. 103–115). Silver Spring, MD: RID Publications.

6 Language policy and planning in Deaf communities

Josep Quer and Ronice Müller de Quadros

Introduction: language policy and planning in Deaf communities

Language policies represent a kind of social intervention in a community. This is not new: for many decades nations and states have been inducing and even forcing people to adopt specific languages or to use specific forms of a language in their interactions. In this sense, the term "language policy" can be used with respect to rather diverse contexts. A language policy will determine decisions regarding the use of languages in a specific country or within linguistic communities (Cooper 1989). To this end, "language planning" will be followed to implement a specific language policy.[1] Haugen (1959) referred in the following way to "language planning" when discussing language intervention in modern Norway:

> Ideas concerning linguistics engineering have here reached out from the quiet studies of linguistics to the market place, where they have affected every citizen and his children. (68)

This passage gives us an idea of what linguistic policy is about: social intervention at the language level. For Haugen, language planning involves developing a normative orthography, grammar and dictionary to establish the prestigious dialect of a language in a specific community. The goal of language planners is to conduct language policies in specific communities. These decisions may or may not coincide with the community's interests in relation to language use, as reported by several researchers, including language planning for Deaf communities (for recent examples, see Behares, Brovetto, and Crespi 2012; Geraci 2012; Meir and Sandler 2008; Quadros 2012; Quer 2012; Schermer 2012a, 2012b). In this seminal publication, Haugen already underscores the question about changes in languages that are driven by political decisions. It is clear that language planning is a complex issue, since it will not only concern linguistic issues with regard to a language and its community, but

---

[1] For recent overviews on language policy and planning, see Spolsky 2004 and Ricento 2006, among others.

120

it will also imply ethical aspects from the community perspectives, together with political ones: language planning means much more than establishing normative language standards, because it incorporates ideological and political stands with respect to a community.[2]

Modifying the existing relations among several languages carries along complexities for the language planning situation. Power relations take different forms in language policies and, consequently, in linguistic planning in each specific context. The goals of language planning can be quite diverse, ranging from turning a multilingual situation into a monolingual one to protecting and revitalizing one or several minority languages in front of the dominant one(s). The goal of the first language planners was to establish one national language in their respective countries through promoting a specific variety as the standard. This type of planning has had direct impact on several sign languages, since by definition a national spoken language directly or indirectly becomes the target of language planning: given that sign languages were not considered national languages, all actions tended to focus exclusively on how to make the national spoken language stronger and to standardize it. The policies were geared toward making the whole population adopt a national language, irrespective of their mother tongue. All other languages, including sign languages, were not respected or even taken into consideration. We see examples of these policies in the era of colonialism around the globe, as well as in the period in which there was a concern to establish "unity" in European countries to reinforce state identity and national frontiers. The values that drove these movements were basically grounded in the desire for political cohesion, and they relied on different instruments, language being one of them (for this perspective on linguistic planning, see Tauli 1968). An interesting example is Indonesian, an introduced national language that derives from standardizing Malay, a traditional lingua franca in the region: despite not being the home language of most Indonesians, who speak one of more than 700 indigenous languages, it is the one used in education and official settings, as Heryanto (1995: 5) explains:

Bahasa Indonesia is a product of language planning, engineering, and development programs *par excellence*. It does not evolve from communal activities in the ordinary lives of its speakers. It has not been a mother tongue to anyone. Speakers of Bahasa Indonesia learn it from authorized institutions and professionals as a language that their mothers do not speak. This language has been unanimously claimed to be the national language of this fourth largest populated country in the globe, even though almost 90 percent of that population do not speak it at home.

---

[2] Several other works started to figure out and address linguistic problems in different countries around the world; for example, Haugen 1966; Fishman 1974; Rubin and Jernudd 1971; Ferguson 1959; Mesthrie 2006; linguistic policies applied to Deaf communities, such as UN declarations and other conventions, will be mentioned later.

This national language, just like the nation itself, is still undergoing an anxious process of being developed. While that process is in progress, the greatest part of the population speak distinct mother tongues, which altogether constitute several hundreds in number. Today these various mother tongues are classified as "local" or "regional" languages, being subordinate [to] or even seen as threats to the national language. Even among the nation's extremely small elite minority who have had access to the prestige and privilege of learning this national language, a very few are considered competent to use it correctly or appropriately.

Language planning involves two different types of intervention: *corpus planning* and *status planning* (Kloss 1969). Corpus planning refers to interventions in the language form (creating or modifying a writing system, creation of neologisms, control of borrowings, standardization, etc.). On the other hand, status planning refers to interventions in the social status of the language and its relation with other languages (the promotion of the language, use in education, media tools, official status, etc.).

Ferguson (1959) drew attention to concerns about multilingualism in language policies by discussing models in which more than a variant of the same language can be present depending on specific contexts. This opened a discussion about the recognition of variants that were not considered before, bringing in the uses, in the plural, of language. He proposed an initial organization of categories: language categories (major, minor, and special status languages); language types (vernacular, standard, classical, pidgin, creoles); language functions (gregarious, official, vehicular, instructional language, religious language, international language, language as the object of teaching). Ferguson himself was not satisfied with these criteria, but it was a considerable change in the way to see languages around the world and to start to recognize a pluralist perspective on languages. For the case of signing communities, this is a relevant change, since multilingualism opened the recognition of human language rights, with consequences for sign languages (at least according to some linguists such as Stokoe 1960) and the Deaf communities themselves.

Specificities of sign language planning

In the last few decades, there has been general recognition of the fact that minority languages exist alongside national or standard languages, due partly to the work of specific communities (users of both spoken languages and sign languages) in raising awareness (for an overview, see Spolsky 2004: 186–216). Minority language communities have fought for their right to use their own language, and therefore languages, in the plural, become part of language planning.

We see this happening among Deaf communities around the world, as they have begun to fight for the recognition of their sign languages and the right to have education and access to all spheres of society in their sign language. They demand the recognition of the bilingual status of the Deaf community, accepting the written (and where possible, the spoken) form of the "national" spoken language as a component of their linguistic background. These claims arose after several decades of oppression marked by the 1880 Milan Conference, in which educators determined that only spoken languages should be taught to Deaf students, prohibiting sign language use at Deaf schools in many parts of the world (Fisher and Lane 1993). The Milan conference considered spoken languages superior for the linguistic and cognitive development of deaf children. At that conference, a very influential language policy based on the oppression of sign languages was established, since the purpose was to replace sign language with the spoken language of the respective countries where education for the deaf was organized. This was a cruel decision serving political and educational perspectives that ignored the cultural and social perspectives of Deaf communities (Duke 2009). The recommendations that resulted from this conference had a huge impact on the Deaf communities around the world for at least a century and its longstanding effects are still perceptible today in the education of deaf children.

Since the languages of Deaf people have been traditionally deprived of recognition as full-fledged languages, sign language users are often not perceived as a linguistic and cultural minority, which hampers their inclusion in comprehensive language policies addressing other language minority groups. They are typically associated with the stigma of disability and, consequently, not granted recognition as users of a minority language. This is the result of the predominant view about deafness, which is the medical one: deafness (and hard-of-hearing-ness) is conceived solely as a physical pathological condition characterized by the lack of hearing (total or partial), which requires the same type of response as other groups with special needs (Fisher and Lane 1993). This view strips Deaf sign language users of their linguistic and cultural identity. The assumption that goes together with this view is that the only way for a deaf person to develop as an individual and to participate in society is by adopting the majority spoken language as the primary means of communication. Such an approach has determined and still determines language policies for signing communities in ways that are detrimental to the individual development of Deaf signers and to the vitality of signing communities as a whole, because it affects the most vital link for sign language transmission: schooling. Given that 90–95% of the deaf children are born into hearing families, the school is for most of them the only way to be exposed to sign language during the first years of their lives, which are crucial for language acquisition (Ferjan et al. 2013; Mayberry et al. 2011; Newport 1990; Padden and Humphries 1988, 2005; Quadros 1997).

Nevertheless, a different view of Deafness, with a capital D, has arisen within Deaf communities as part of their process of empowerment and emancipation: Deaf communities are linguistic and cultural communities where Deaf signers develop their identity. Sign language and the Deaf experience form the basis of such an identity. Social networking through Deaf clubs and activism constitutes the second main line of language transmission from generation to generation, but individual participation in the Deaf community typically starts after adolescence for many Deaf people, when the critical period for natural language acquisition has already passed (Newport 1990; Quadros 1997; Quadros and Cruz 2011; Singleton and Newport 2004).

These basic facts about language acquisition and channels of interaction with the Deaf community have as a consequence that most Deaf people's linguistic biographies are rather diverse, both in their proficiency and use of sign language and the ambient spoken language(s). In this sense, individual variation in sign language competence is affected by type of schooling, age of exposure to sign language, age of entering the Deaf community, degree of identification with Deaf and sign language values, etc. To this we should add regional variation (partly determined by the school attended during childhood, or the Deaf club joined), age (older and younger generations use different varieties of the same language), gender, ethnicity and religion (for an overview, see Schembri and Johnston 2012, 2013; and Chapter 4, this volume). Such variation within a relatively small population presents language policy makers with an additional challenge that is not always addressed or even recognized. Typically, when attempts at sign language recognition are successful, one of the first conditions that policy makers establish is that a standard variety be defined. This was the case, for instance, in the Netherlands, where a special committee was created to study the legal recognition of Sign Language of the Netherlands (NGT): when the committee issued their final report, the government responded with the requirement that there be a standard lexicon as a precondition for legal recognition. Despite the objections raised by researchers and the Deaf community, the standardization process among the existing five regional varieties took place (for details, see Schermer 2012b). Variation within a sign language domain is perceived not as an inherent feature of the richness of the language, but rather as an aspect that can and must be dismissed on practical grounds. However, there have been attempts precisely at preserving linguistic diversity within a sign language domain. One of the best examples is the lexicon project of South African Sign Language, which documents the great lexical diversity among South African Sign languages (Reagan 2001: 162):

[I]n the process of collecting signs for some 2,500 lexical items, only two percent of all the words represented had a single, common sign across all the different Deaf groups, and roughly 10 percent of the words had as few as one or two signed variants . . .

On average, six variants per word were found and the range went as high as 11 variants, each informant having a different sign ... There were also a considerable number of terms for which some informants did not have a sign ... This diversity, although not unexpected, exceeded the original expectations of both the researchers and the deaf individuals involved with the South African Sign Language Research Program (see Penn and Reagan, 1991; 1994; 1995).

An illustrative case is the attempt at creating a pan-Arab sign language reported by Al-Fityani and Padden (2010). The Council of Arab Ministers of Social Affairs, a committee within the League of Arab States, made an effort to devise a sign language shared among the Arab countries by establishing a lexicon that relies on different sign languages across the regions, mostly Lebanese Sign Language (LIU), but also Egyptian Sign Language and Saudi Sign Language, among others. As usual, the motivation for the promotion of this artificial variety is "to meet the needs of integration of deaf persons into society" (Council of Arab Ministers of Social Affairs 2004) by introducing a shared language form, as in the case of Modern Standard Arabic, the literary standard of Arab countries taught in school and used in government and media. This is the only variety shared across the region, because spoken varieties are rather diverse across the twenty-two countries from Morocco to Iraq and are never used in written form. For this reason, diglossia is pervasive in the Arab world and is now replicated with the attempt at introducing the pan-Arab sign language variety. It is used for instance in the sign interpretation appearing in Al-Jazeera newscasts of world events. The attempt at introducing and promoting the use of such an Arab Sign Language, though, goes against the reality of having several differentiated sign languages nationally.

Writing systems

The first language plans established in several countries were concerned with the normalization of a writing form (for example, Haugen 1959). Writing is one of the most powerful instruments used in language planning to standardize a language, because of its central role in education, in mass media and in all forms of formal communication between citizens and administrations. For languages that do not have an established writing system, language planning can include actions of phonological transcription and also the creation of the writing culture through a writing system. Sign languages have no widely adopted writing systems, although attempts have been made to create a specific system to write signed discourse (Sutton's Sign Writing system, Sutton 1981; and Elis system Barros 2008, for example). However, the default policy with respect to writing is to bring literacy to Deaf students through the writing system of the dominant spoken language used in education. Deaf signers that have been introduced to writing systems adequate for sign language transcription tend not to use them on a regular basis in their daily lives, and they rather resort to writing in the spoken language. Nowadays, the widespread use of video recording seems to have further lifted the pressure to "capture" sign language in a written form, because a recording provides direct access to the language fragment and can be as easily reproduced or transmitted.

Ideologies in language planning and language rights

As mentioned above, language policy can have very different ends according to the ideological underpinnings that motivate social intervention at the language level. The default situation is multilingualism, where the role of a language or a group of languages needs to be (re)defined with respect to their social use and official regulation. If the ultimate goal is a monolingual society, the policies will be directed toward depriving all languages other than the official one of recognition and protection, so that their speakers turn into subtractive bilinguals (or multilinguals), the minority languages become recessive in most social spheres and end up being substituted. Sometimes there is no systematic language planning, but social and economic prestige of the dominant language induces speakers of non-dominant languages to adopt the dominant one, which is often presented as the 'common,' shared language of the nation or state, attaching to it values such as neutrality and functionality and presenting it as a prerequisite for social and economic success. In such situations, non-dominant languages remain or become 'home' languages only used for informal exchanges and have low social status, and when their speakers end up adopting the dominant language as their home language, they stop being transmitted and thus their maintenance is threatened. A clear example of this is Spanish speakers in the USA, whose younger generations often end up adopting English even in the private sphere (Fishman 1991). The ideological basis of this approach is language assimilation, based on the assumption that linguistic and cultural unity is a desirable goal in society.

At the other end of the spectrum of types of language policies we find those that foster a multilingual society where different languages receive official recognition and protection and no substantial asymmetries among them are supported. The target of such policies is to promote additive bilingualism/multilingualism, where an individual "adds a second, socially relevant language to [his/her] repertory of skills" (Lambert 1978: 217). The first language of a minority group is not threatened because it is socially prestigious and is supported in different domains such as education or mass media. An example of this would be English-speaking Canadians adding French to their repertoire because of its official status in the country in addition to English.

Monolingual policies were typical of the period of colonialism, where the language of the metropolis was imposed as the prestige language of administration and education and indigenous languages were relegated to informal domains or even minorized. The rise of European nation states followed a similar pattern based on the correlation one state–one language, which has been and still is followed all over the globe to different degrees.

However, after the period of decolonization, a new approach to indigenous and minority languages known as linguistic pluralism emerged, according to which their defense and promotion at different levels is a desirable goal. It emphasizes the language rights of minority groups and it not only accepts but also supports language diversity as a social value. This process is simultaneous with the emancipation movement of oppressed ethnic and cultural minorities. It led to the UN Declaration on the Rights of Persons Belonging to National or Ethnic, Religious and Linguistic Minorities (1992), which attempted to establish human and civil rights of minority groups in order to enhance their protection. Language identity of minority groups is one of the three defining components of a minority group as represented in this text. Article 2.1 establishes the fundamental right to express and enjoy their culture, their religion and their language, thus prohibiting active discrimination against members of such communities on those grounds (i.e., negative language rights). It includes an explicit reference to language use.

Persons belonging to national or ethnic, religious and linguistic minorities (hereinafter referred to as persons belonging to minorities) have the right to enjoy their own culture, to profess and practise their own religion, and to use their own language, in private and in public, freely and without interference or any form of discrimination.

In Articles 4.2 and 4.3 positive language rights are established, with explicit mention of the right to language acquisition of and instruction in the mother tongue:

States shall take measures to create favourable conditions to enable persons belonging to minorities to express their characteristics and to develop their culture, language, religion, traditions and customs, except where specific practices are in violation of national law and contrary to international standards.

States should take appropriate measures so that, wherever possible, persons belonging to minorities may have adequate opportunities to learn their mother tongue or to have instruction in their mother tongue.

Specific reference to the rights of indigenous peoples was made in a subsequent UN declaration, the UN Declaration on the Rights of Indigenous Peoples, in 2007. It further makes explicit the basic language rights that already appeared in the previous declaration and it includes the obligation of the State to provide education in their own language, and the right for the indigenous peoples to control their educational systems and to establish media in their own language:

Indigenous peoples have the right to revitalize, use, develop and transmit to future generations their histories, languages, oral traditions, philosophies, writing systems and literatures, and to designate and retain their own names for communities, places and persons. (Article 13.1)

Indigenous peoples have the right to establish and control their educational systems and institutions providing education in their own languages, in a manner appropriate to their cultural methods of teaching and learning. (Article 14.1)

States shall, in conjunction with indigenous peoples, take effective measures, in order for indigenous individuals, particularly children, including those living outside their communities, to have access, when possible, to an education in their own culture and provided in their own language. (Article 14.3)

Indigenous peoples have the right to establish their own media in their own languages and to have access to all forms of non-indigenous media without discrimination. (Article 16.1)

These declarations have promoted particular legislation and active policies at regional or state level that should materialize those goals. However, the degree of attainment of the goals expressed in the declaration and in legal texts often falls short of the expectations created by them, and sign language communities are not an exception.

As already pointed out above, signing communities have not been approached under the light of language rights until relatively recently because of the usual misconceptions about the nature of sign languages themselves, but also by the strong influence of oralism on policies for deaf individuals. The medical view of deafness has been an obstacle to conceptualizing signing communities as linguistic and cultural minorities: even if sign language is recognized as a proper language, this view does not consider it an adequate means for education and cognitive and personal development, which must take place in the majority spoken language. In terms of language ideology, this amounts to an assimilationist position and it has been dominant for more than a century in education for the deaf. Specific regulations to allow for sign language interpreting services for signers or the inclusion of signed content on television, for instance, have been implemented as instrumental solutions to ensure accessibility rights, and less often as defense of the language rights of signers.

An extreme case of this assimilationist perspective is the creation of manual sign codes of communication intended for the education of deaf children in special schools. A number of different systems have been created in the USA, in particular. The philosophy behind those manual codes is clear: despite using the visual–gestural modality, the only goal is to teach the spoken language (e.g., English), not sign (e.g., ASL). Examples of these sign codes include:

Paget Gorman Sign System in Britain, Australasian Signed English in Australia and New Zealand, and Seeing Essential English (SEE-I), Signing Exact English (SEE-II), and the Linguistics of Visual English (LOVE) in North America (for a detailed overview, see Reagan 2010: 129–154, and Chapter 7, this volume). The property that they all share is that they are intended to represent the structure of English and not of a sign language. For this reason, next to keeping English syntax, even if signs are borrowed from natural sign languages, they are complemented with a whole array of artificial signs to reproduce English grammar in the visual mode. This is the reason why they are known as codes: they were artificially designed and they are no one's natural language. Still, such codes have been the only signed input that many deaf children have had at schools for the deaf in the USA, Australia, and New Zealand. An extreme case of such an approach was the exclusive use of fingerspelling in the classroom, in conjunction with spoken English. This difficult and taxing method, known as the Rochester Method, is now in disuse. To a greater or a lesser degree, however, forms of spoken language in signed form (known as Signed French, Signed Spanish, Dutch with Signs, etc.) have been and are still used in the classrooms with deaf children. This instantiates conscious or unconscious ideology about the primacy of spoken language and low value of sign language, if it is not taught and used at least to the same degree in the educational environment. In other contexts, as in Indonesia, ideological and political decisions bring deaf children into an even more difficult situation: Indonesian, as the national language, is used in education throughout the country despite the fact that it is not the home language for 90 percent of the population; signed Indonesian (SIB, Sistem Isyarat Bahasa Indonesia) is the code used in deaf education, although deaf children do not have contact with that spoken language outside school, but with a different one (Branson and Miller 2004).

Nevertheless, the ideology of multilingualism also had an effect on language policies for sign languages, especially in education. It involved recognizing signing communities as linguistic and cultural communities with an identity that had to be respected and promoted. Sign language is always a minority, threatened language because of historical, cultural, and ideological circumstances and this situation had to be reversed, especially in education. The model that was proposed as most adequate to this end is a bilingual bicultural one, where *bi-* refers to both sign and spoken language, on the one hand, and hearing and Deaf culture, on the other (Mashie 1995; Strong 1995). In some cases, it goes together with the assumption that the Deaf pupil's access to spoken language should be through the written form (writing and reading), thus not prioritizing necessarily the endless resources and time devoted in oralist models to the production and perception of speech. This approach is in line with the perspective taken for linguistic and cultural minorities and is considered to be

130 Josep Quer and Ronice Müller de Quadros

the most acceptable one to the needs and desires of Deaf individuals and communities. In reality, though, the implementation of such models falls short of expectations, mainly because of the lack of sufficient resources and clear directives about sign language use and Deaf culture and identity. It is only a small section of deaf children who enter such bilingual–bicultural programs, because most parents still opt for oral education with no or insignificant presence of sign language. Normally unaware of the reality of sign languages and signing communities, parents easily drop the possibility of trying to communicate with their child in a language they virtually know nothing about and that has a community of users unknown to them. One well-known problem with bilingual–bicultural programs in general is that the professionals that are active in it are hearing second language learners of the language. This has an effect on the language model they offer to the deaf children (for most of them, the only sign language model), as well as on the lack of adult Deaf role models in the learning environment (Shantie and Hoffmeister 2000).

The success of education for deaf children has also been affected for decades by the mainstreaming and inclusive policies for children with special needs that were widely adopted in the 1980s. Its immediate effect was the closing of special schools for the deaf and the integration of deaf children in regular classrooms with some specific support (e.g., sign language interpreter, speech therapist, signing teacher). Schools for deaf children had traditionally offered an environment where children could be exposed to sign language, for even if strictly oralist, it provided continuous opportunities for the children to interact in sign outside the classroom, and sometimes with some Deaf ancillary staff that were employed there. This situation guaranteed exposure to the language and contributed to Deaf identity and socialization. With the immersion of deaf pupils in a mostly hearing class, a language barrier arises that not only reduces sign language input, but also interaction with most peers and the deaf children end up in isolation to different degrees. Since all required resources for the Deaf group are seldom provided for, the actual classroom setting is disadvantageous for the Deaf children.

The UN Convention on the Rights of Persons with Disabilities (approved by the General Assembly on December 13, 2006; entry into force May 3, 2008) directly addresses some of these concerns. Article 24.3 on education urges States to take concrete measures such as:

(b) Facilitating the learning of sign language and the promotion of the linguistic identity of the deaf community;

(c) Ensuring that the education of persons, and in particular children, who are blind, deaf or deafblind, is delivered in the most appropriate languages and modes and means of communication for the individual, and in environments which maximize academic and social development.

Article 24.4 is explicit about the need to employ qualified sign language teachers, including Deaf ones:

In order to help ensure the realization of this right, States Parties shall take appropriate measures to employ teachers, including teachers with disabilities, who are qualified in sign language and/or Braille, and to train professionals and staff who work at all levels of education. Such training shall incorporate disability awareness and the use of appropriate augmentative and alternative modes, means and formats of communication, educational techniques and materials to support persons with disabilities.

And article 30.4, concerned with participation in cultural life, recreation, leisure and sport states the following:

Persons with disabilities shall be entitled, on an equal basis with others, to recognition and support of their specific cultural and linguistic identity, including sign languages and deaf culture.

Despite the clarity of the principles formulated above, educational practice on average is unable to meet those standards partly because of insufficient allocation of human and financial resources, and so-called bilingual bicultural programs for deaf children are far from a model that fully responds to the needs of this school population. This has a negative impact on the outcomes of such models, something that undermines support for them. A further complicating factor that has been added to this scenario is the growing numbers of deaf children with a cochlear implant from a very young age in Western countries: this development is actually increasing the number of hard-of-hearing children in schools where deaf children are concentrated and it increases the pressure to invest extra effort and resources in spoken language teaching for those children. There is a recent controversial proposal by Knorrs and Marschark (2012) that suggests revising the bilingual language policies for the schooling of deaf children in order to meet the challenges of this new scenario, where deaf children attending school are significantly more diverse nowadays.

Among the ideologies of language mentioned by Cobarrubias (1983) we find internationalization, which involves the selection of a language as lingua franca for wider communication, such as spoken English in international contexts. International Sign instantiates the implementation of such a need for communication among signers of different sign languages. It does not have a stable form in practice, as it varies according to the communication setting and the language backgrounds of the participants. Sometimes it has a stronger influence from ASL, some other times it relies more heavily on iconic resources and classifier constructions (see EUD n.d.; Mesch 2010; Rosenstock 2004). The ancestor of its current form can be found in *Gestuno* (1975), a lexicon designed for international communication by the World Federation of the Deaf.

The process of language planning

Language policies that are systematic and take a medium- or long-term perspective are implemented through language planning actions that spread across different stages, which can overlap to some extent. The components of language planning are as follows:

(a) fact-finding;
(b) establishment of goals and outcomes, their articulation and the strategies to achieve them;
(c) implementation; and
(d) evaluation of the planning process.[3]

It seems obvious that before starting language planning design and implementation, information about the state of the language and its community of users needs to be gathered, in connection with the broader linguistic social, economic and political context where the target language is embedded. For instance, facts that need to be collected are number of speakers of each language as first language and as a second language, their social distribution, their sociolinguistic status, the existence of written forms, the breadth of the vocabulary, etc.

The next step involves establishing and articulating goals, strategies and expected outcomes of the language policies. The procedures determined in this phase constitute the core of the process. The most important among those will be presented next. Language selection and minority language treatment are closely interconnected. The former implies the choice of one language variety as national language, for instance. The latter refers to the decisions concerning the use of minority language in public life, most prominently in education and administration, for the sake of their maintenance.

Codification is the main procedure in this phase and is often seen as the central part of corpus planning. It essentially implies establishing the grammar, the vocabulary and the spelling system that will be at the base of the standardized form of the language. Codification appears as one of the main planning activities when a (new) national language is chosen, but it can also be part of the treatment of minority languages. This is typically the case when a minority language starts being used in school as the language of instruction: materials need to be developed that reflect a standardized form for the often coexisting

---

[3] Haugen (1966) discussed language planning as formulation, codification, elaboration, and implementation. Neustupny (1970) brought up the cultivation aspect and Rubin and Jernudd (1971) added the evaluation step, in which the actions implemented on the basis of language planning are analyzed considering their impact on and consequences for a linguistic community according to different criteria (such as language attitudes, uses, status, etc.).

varieties of the same language. In case the language did not have a written tradition, graphization will be the process by which a written code is adopted, created or adapted to the needs of the target language. Intervention at this level can also involve change in the alphabet used for the written form of the language, as in the case of the adoption of the Latin alphabet (instead of the Ottoman Arabic one) for Turkish in the process of language reform launched by Atatürk (Lewis 2002).

Modernization (also referred to as cultivation or elaboration) will be the last procedure in language planning. According to Ferguson (1968: 32), "modernization of a language may be thought of as the process of its becoming the equal of other developed languages as a medium of communication; it is in a sense the process of joining the world community of increasingly intertranslatable languages as appropriate vehicles of modern forms of discourse." This is especially necessary for minority languages that were confined to informal spheres and, when becoming recognized or official, need to expand their usage in a number of new formal discourse contexts. The involved processes are essentially two: lexicon expansion and development of new registers and forms of discourse. Lexical expansion is usually the activity that draws most attention. It basically takes place through compounding of existing words, creation of new ones by derivational processes, and adoption of foreign words (borrowings, calques). This is a process that happens not only in a planned manner, but also spontaneously by language users when faced with the need to express a concept that does not have an established lexical entry. An interesting example of modernization is offered by Hebrew: having survived for 2,000 years as the language of religion and school literacy, it had to undergo significant changes since the end of the nineteenth century, when it started to be revernacularized as the language of the Jewish population in Palestine and later in the state of Israel, founded in 1948. In the process of making it a living language for all aspects of daily life, new words had to be created for many concepts that did not exist in Classical Hebrew. At the same time, the spelling system had to be reformed, for instance, to mark the vowels overtly (Spolsky and Shohamy 1999).

The implementation stage of language planning involves putting the activities into practice. It requires mobilizing human and financial resources, and preparing, sequencing, and coordinating the planned activities with the planning agents and the linguistic community.

After the planned actions have taken place, the process needs to be evaluated. This is an often neglected aspect of language planning, although it is of great importance to be able to plan follow-up procedures and activities that complement or correct the achieved outcomes. However, next to a number of notable exceptions, long-term language policies are rare and they are often driven by short-term political agendas, misguided assumptions and a range of extra-linguistic factors. Users of the language might also be reluctant to adopt the proposed new standardized forms, for instance, clinging to their local varieties or to direct borrowings from other languages where a more "genuine" form had been proposed by the planners. In addition, language planning mostly affects formal registers of the language, while informal spoken usages remain more easily free from that influence.

Sign languages have not been the object of global language planning, but as a consequence of their emancipation and social and legal recognition in some countries they have undergone some of the processes just mentioned, especially corpus planning.

Even before any formal planning takes place, informal activities originating in the community itself are deployed. The most common one is the elaboration of dictionaries, as if that were the best way to preserve the language. Typically, they are bilingual dictionaries between the ambient spoken language and the sign language and are organized according to the list of spoken words.[4] Dealing with new terminology is an important part of lexical fixation and expansion. Language planning can design actions to control lexical influence from other languages. A clear example of this is found in France, where borrowings are rejected in formal French and newly created French words are expected to replace them, against the general trend that English words are borrowed for information technology terms, for example (perceived as corrupt French by purists, as the label *Franglais* intends to reflect). New terms like *mouse*, *delete*, and so on, are incorporated in some languages applying morphological changes when needed, like in Brazilian Portuguese *deletar* (with the verbal morphology morpheme for verbs in this language), or even adopted directly from English without morphological adaptation as in the case of *mouse*. However, for French, this is much more controlled and restricted, and for example the neologism *logiciel* for 'software' is broadly employed, while *le week-end* has supplanted the allegedly more genuine form *la fin de semaine*. In this case, the goal is to "maintain," to "preserve" the purity of the language, avoiding any "contamination" by other languages. The Turkish language reform that took place around the foundation of the Republic of Turkey by Atatürk undertook the replacement of loanwords from Arabic and Persian with Turkish-based equivalents (either neologisms or revived old forms) (Lewis 2002).

In some ways, we can see this happen in some sign languages as well, and in two different directions. In Brazil, for example, some Deaf people do not

---

[4] There are important exceptions, such as the ASL dictionary by Stokoe *et al.* (1965) and the British Sign Language dictionary by Brien (1992), structured according to the organizational principles of the phonology of sign language. Moreover, current digital lexicography allows much more easily for a non-biased organizational principle, as access to the lexicon can proceed according to the principles of both signed and spoken languages.

accept borrowings from Portuguese, especially older Deaf people. By contrast, more and more Deaf people are becoming bilinguals in Brazil and Brazilian Sign Language (Libras) experiences a strong contact with Portuguese that influences neologisms in Libras through fingerspelling, initialization, calque, etc. Words from Brazilian Portuguese like *bar* 'bar,' *sol* 'sun,' *nunca* 'never' are partially or completely fingerspelled in the corresponding Libras signs. This kind of sociolinguistic phenomenon arising from language contact has also been reported in other sign languages (for example in ASL and English by Davis 1989; Lucas and Valli 1992; see also Chapter 3, this volume). There is no planning regarding neologisms in Libras, but the social conflicts show worries about how this happens in the terminological development in this sign language.

A different kind of lexical borrowing that can take place is the one between sign languages. It is often the case that when faced with a new concept or with a proper name lacking a sign in their language, they might adopt a foreign sign as the first option. ASL sometimes has this role as source language for loan signs, given its significant international presence and its influence on International Sign. Lexical borrowing between closely related languages, such as Catalan Sign Language vis-à-vis Spanish Sign Language, can be consciously avoided by signers on the basis of linguistic identity and purity.

The creation of neologisms is always a sensitive activity in language cultivation or modernization (see above). Since in the case of sign languages, there is often no authority to create and sanction neologisms, this task is usually carried out by groups of experts that try to respect the structural properties and the lexical wealth of the language. Attempts at steering language use in the community with the introduction of neologisms are not always successful. Neologisms usually confront signers with new lexical entries that do not belong to their lexical repertory and that seem to be imposed by groups of experts and researchers (often hearing) and only used by interpreters. Evaluating the success of terminological proposals is of paramount importance in order to be able to revise the proposed terms if they get rejected in actual use.

A very powerful step toward corpus planning that actually incorporates elements of the fact-finding phase is the ongoing development of sign language corpora for a number of sign languages. They are conceived as both a representation of the language at a certain stage and as a tool for the subsequent description and analysis of its grammar and lexicon that must support many language planning activities, such as the development of teaching materials or language tests. Most of the ongoing corpus projects attempt to cover the variation that exists in the signing community on the basis of regional, age, gender, or discourse-type variation. Such corpora can also be seen as a way to document a type of language that in general lacks systematic records, by means of collecting spontaneous or semi-spontaneous discourse from a representative number of users (for a recent overview, see van Herreweghe and Vermeerbergen 2012).

The typical scenario for sign languages is that language planning activities take place in an ad hoc fashion in order to respond to the practical needs that arise on the go. It is only recently that new legislation for some sign languages explicitly establishes the need for sign language planning. In the cases of Catalan Sign Language (LSC) and Spanish Sign Language, the legal texts designate the organizations in charge of establishing the norms for the standard (Institut d'Estudis Catalans, the Catalan Academy of Sciences and Humanities, for LSC) or for leading the language planning geared at the normalization of the language (Centro de Normalización de la Lengua de Signos Española, for LSE). Sometimes the existence of such a center does not derive from specific sign language legislation, but simply from administrative decisions, as in the case of the Gebarencentrum (Sign Language Center) in the case of the Netherlands, which is the designated body for standardization of Sign Language of the Netherlands (NGT) (see Schermer 2012b).

However, moves toward standardization also happen as a consequence of language related activities that are not conceived of as language planning. In Brazil, for instance, a university-level e-learning system including several states of the country that has Deaf students as the target was set up some years ago: as a consequence of that, some sort of standardization of the lexicon is taking place, even though the glossaries used in the program include the variants used across the country for each sign when they are available. The inclusion of the variants of the same sign is part of language planning, since it values these variants, but still choosing one of them when signed materials are produced makes one of the variants stronger than the others. It is hard to make uniform decisions regarding terminology and grammatical usages of a specific language when they are associated with media materials, media tools, and education.

However, current technologies pave the way for some forms of participation by language users. A very simple example is represented by the possibility of contributing online lexical variants of those that are already stored in a lexical database, or commenting on them. This is the case of the lexical database for Auslan (Johnston 2001). Such a perspective on language planning and standardization is the one proposed by Dotter (2006: 116) under the label 'soft standardization':

'Soft' means that the sign language communities accept that there is a standard to be taught to learners but that the individual signers or groups are not forced to give up their variants, so that – like in most spoken languages – there is more than one 'variant' or 'register' of the respective signed language.

Standardization of the lexicon of sign languages always has to face the tension between the existing variation and the imposed choice for a consensus form to be adopted in teaching, interpretation, and media. This was explicitly addressed, for instance, in the process of standardizing the lexicon of Sign Language of the Netherlands (NGT), as described in Schermer (2012a, 2012b). Since the need for a standard form typically comes from hearing parents of deaf children, teachers of the deaf, interpreter trainers but also from political and administrative spheres, it is often felt by the Deaf community as imposed on them by the needs of the hearing and this might lead to rejection, as in the case of the Flemish Deaf Community in Belgium (see van Herreweghe and Vermeerbergen 2009), which after a debate in 1997 turned down the plan to have the language standardized from above.

If we put aside the knowledge about the lexicon, a major gap in knowledge in the process of codification of sign languages is grammar. Research is still fragmentary and there are only a few cases of more or less global descriptions of the grammar of particular sign languages (Austrian Sign Language (Skant *et al.* 2002), Catalan Sign Language (Quer *et al.* 2005), German Sign Language (Eichmann *et al.* 2012; Papaspyrou *et al.* 2008), Sign Language of the Netherlands (Bos and Kuiken 2002), Spanish Sign Language (Herrero Blanco 2009), among others). This major task lying ahead is currently being addressed by the European COST project SignGram that aims at creating a blueprint in order to develop sign language reference grammars.

Policy and legislation

Laws are imperatives: they are created to determine specific rules to be followed by people. Laws and official regulations effectively have impact on the ways that languages will be used in a country. The existing legal regulations are used to drive language planning. Deaf communities have long strived for the legal recognition of their languages and for the protection of their rights as signers and as citizens. As mentioned above, nowadays there exist international recommendations about human language and minority rights, some of them making explicit reference to sign language and signers, as well as several national or local official proceedings that are intended to support language policy. In the past few decades, a number of sign languages have been recognized in constitutional texts, specific laws or indirectly through other legal proceedings related to education for deaf children, sign interpreting, accessibility provisions for deaf individuals, etc. Sometimes the recognition has been only political, but it has secured funding for research projects or centers that have an impact on policies for sign language (for an overview, see Krausneker 2009 and Schermer 2012a; for a number of recent case studies, see Quer and Quadros 2012).

Apart from the UN declarations referred to above, European institutions have featured prominently in the promotion of legal recognition of sign languages internationally (see Wheatley and Pabsch 2010). In 1998, the European Parliament issued a resolution on sign languages to promote official recognition of sign languages in the member states, as well as initiatives to ensure education and interpretation in sign language, among other aspects. In 1992 the Council of Europe passed the European Charter for Regional or Minority Languages, which is intended "on the one hand to protect and promote regional and minority languages as a threatened aspect of Europe's cultural heritage and on the other hand to enable speakers of a regional or minority language to use it in private and public life. Its overriding purpose is cultural. It covers regional and minority languages, non-territorial languages and less widely used official languages" (www.coe.int/t/dg4/education/min-lang/aboutcharter/default_en.asp). Despite the obvious applicability to sign languages, no explicit mention of them appears in the Charter. Only Recommendation 1492 (2001) by the Parliamentary Assembly of the Council of Europe on the rights of national minorities includes the following explicit proviso for sign languages:

give the various sign languages utilised in Europe a protection similar to that afforded by the European Charter for Regional or Minority Languages, possibly by means of the adoption of a recommendation to member states.

This led to Recommendation 1598 (2003) on the Protection of sign languages in the member states of the Council of Europe. The text states that official recognition will help improve the current situation of sign languages and their users in the continent, thus showing confidence in the role of legislation as a language planning tool. Similar calls have been made from within the signing communities as well, as in the 2010 Brussels Declaration on Sign Languages in the European Union adopted by the National Associations of the Deaf in the Member States (www.eud.eu/uploads/brussels_declaration_English.pdf).

European-level recommendations have resulted in some cases in national and regional legislation for sign languages. This is the case of Spain, where in 2007 the Parliament issued a law that, among other regulations about accessibility for deaf people, recognizes both Spanish Sign Language (LSE) and Catalan Sign Language (LSE) for the first time in legal proceedings. The level of recognition, though, does not amount to granting them the status of official languages, which the Constitution reserves for Spanish and the three co-official languages (Catalan, Basque, and Galician) in their respective territories. The Spanish law does establish the creation of a center to implement language planning for LSE and leaves the regulation of LSC to the Catalan Administration. The Catalan Autonomy Law from 2006 stated the right to use LSC and the need to protect and teach it, but it will only be in the Act on

Catalan Sign Language, passed in 2010 by the Catalan Parliament, that a full-fledged recognition of the language and the rights of their users takes place. The perspectives taken by the Spanish and the Catalan legal texts are significantly different, as the former adopts an accessibility view, while the latter takes an exclusively linguistic and cultural point of view. This has probably to do in part with the influence of oralist lobbies during the drafting period, but also with the long tradition of language planning for a minority language in the case of Catalonia (Quer 2012). A related development is the process of legal recognition of Italian Sign Language (LIS): in 2011 the bill incorporated a change in the name of the language from *lingua dei segni italiana* to *linguaggio o tecnica comunicativa mimico-gestuale* (lit. 'mimed–gestural language or communication technique'), together with other misconceptions about access to spoken language with current audiological technology and about confrontation between oralist and signing deaf people. Again, the political sphere turned out to be very sensitive to the pressure from groups defending the medical view of deafness (and sign language).

In Brazil, there is a specific law that recognizes Brazilian Sign Language as a national language (Law 10.436/2002, called the Libras Law) and a decree that establishes a plan to implement the Libras Law (Decree 5.626/2005), a kind of language planning document. These official documents had a real impact on Deaf communities around the country, since they establish, for example, that all degrees in different areas that train teachers at the undergraduate level (*licenciaturas*) must include Libras as a subject in their curriculum. This decision had several consequences for the recognition of the positive status of Libras in Brazil. One of them was that the creation of programs to train Libras teachers became urgent, since they were needed for the several open positions in all universities around the country. To this end, the first Brazilian Sign Language Program was created in the academic domain of Languages (*Letras-Libras*) (where the same kind of language programs called in Brazil *Letras* 'Languages' are taught and studied, including Portuguese, English, Spanish, French studies, and so on). This first program started with a proposal to have students graduate in the whole country through an e-learning system. From 2005 to 2013, more than 1,000 students graduated in Brazilian Sign Language, across fifteen states of the country, with an undergraduate four-year program. More than 70 percent of these graduated students were Deaf, since the Decree included an affirmative action article that gives priority to Deaf students in the programs that train Libras teachers. In 2013, a government decision approved the opening of the Libras Program in at least one public university in each of the twenty-seven federal capitals of the country. The plan has set the goal to have these programs established by the end of 2015.

These actions carried along several consequences for the Deaf community in Brazil. Libras has become a very well-known language and people recognize this language as one of the languages used in Brazil. Many hearing people became interested in learning the language and Deaf people started to become very proud of their language. Nevertheless, there are also some other conflicts that result from this process. One of them, for instance, is the question to whom Libras belongs. Deaf people started to be worried about the ownership of the language. They have the feeling that they may lose this property to hearing people, since they are teaching "their" language to many hearing people and several of them are becoming good signers. This is very subtle, but it is a special issue about attitudes that must be discussed with the Deaf community and Deaf intellectuals in Brazil. Another consequence of the Libras Law is the increase in the number of Libras teachers hired at the university and also professors that started to be required to work in these sign language programs. For example, at Universidade Federal de Santa Catarina, the first one to open this program in 2006, there are twenty-two full-time tenured or tenure-track positions hired to work as university professors and researchers in the Brazilian Sign Language Program and in the Libras curriculum for other education programs at the university (e-learning and regular face-to-face programs) in 2013. From these twenty-two full-time professors (all have at least a master's degree), fourteen are Deaf professors and eight are full bilingual hearing professors.

On the other hand, in the same country where all these positive actions to implement a language policy in favor of Brazilian Sign Language have taken place, there are also other laws that conflict with it, making it hard for Deaf children to have access to full bilingual education. This other law is related to general accessibility to education and forces all regular schools to have students with disabilities in the same school. This is applied to Deaf children as well, without paying attention to their specific language needs. The government states that this educational system is the one to be followed and believes that for Deaf children, the presence of Brazilian Sign Language interpreters will be enough to observe the Libras Law. This is a problem, because there are several schools with a few or even with only one Deaf child and this does not guarantee a full bilingual education, or a successful Deaf education, since all these schools function with Brazilian Portuguese, that is, the teachers and staff members speak this language, the materials and school signage are all in this language, the communication is in this language, even in some cases in which sign language interpreters are present. The consequences are far-reaching for Deaf children and for the Deaf community, since they do not have contact with their language and Deaf peers.

These examples from Brazil, Catalonia, Italy, and Spain clearly illustrate the fact that legal recognition of sign languages is a significant step forward in the right direction, and it has immediate impact on status planning. However, the full exercise of the rights established in legal texts is not immediate or straightforward. Language planning as designed in those texts requires a commitment to allocate human and financial resources in order to deploy the actions required to reach the goals. It has become clear to Deaf communities that legal recognition is only a first step that opens up a whole range of new possibilities, and that actual implementation of the provisions in the legal texts also needs to be fought for.

REFERENCES

Al-Fityani, K. and Padden, C. (2010) Sign languages in the Arab world. In D. Brentari (ed.), *Sign Languages: A Cambridge Language Survey* (pp. 433–450). Cambridge: Cambridge University Press.

Barros, M. E. (2008) ELiS – Escrita das Línguas de Sinais: proposta teórica e verificação prática, Ph.D. thesis, Programa de Pós-Graduação em Linguística. Universidade Federal de Santa Catarina.

Behares, L. E., Brovetto, C., and Crespi, L. P. (2012) Language policies in Uruguay and Uruguayan Sign Language (LSU). *Sign Language Studies* 12(4): 519–542.

Bos, H. and Kuiken, F. (2002) *Basisgrammatica Nederlandse Gebarentaal.* Amsterdam/Bunnik: University of Amsterdam/Dutch Sign Language Centre.

Branson, J. and Miller, D. (2004). The cultural construction of linguistic incompetence through schooling: Deaf education and the transformation of the linguistic environment in Bali. *Indonesia. Sign Language Studies* 5(1): 6–38.

Brien, D. (ed.) (1992) *Dictionary of British Sign Language/English.* London: Faber and Faber.

Cobarrubias, J. (1983) Language planning: The state of the art. In J. Cobarrubias and J. Fishman (eds.), *Progress in Language Planning* (pp. 3–26). Berlin: Mouton de Gruyter.

Cobarrubias, J. and Fishman, J. A. (eds.) (1983) *Progress in Language Planning.* Berlin: Mouton de Gruyter.

Cooper, R. (1989) *Language Planning and Social Change.* Cambridge: Cambridge University Press.

Council of Arab Ministers of Social Affairs (2004) Background paper on the international convention for the protection and promotion of the rights and dignity of persons with disabilities. Available at www.un.org/esa/socdev/enable/rights/contrib-arab1.htm

Davis, J. (1989) Distinguishing language contact phenomena in ASL interpretation. In C. Lucas (ed.), *The Sociolinguistics of the Deaf Community* (pp. 85–102). San Diego, CA: Academic Press.

Dotter, F. (2006) 'Soft' standardization of sign languages? *Veröffentlichungen des Zentrums für Gebärdensprache und Hörbehindertenkommunikation der Universität Klagenfurt* 8: 98–118.

Duke, Irene (2009) *The Everything Sign Language Book*, 2nd edn. Avon, US: Adams Media.

Eichmann, Hanna, Hansen, Martje, and Heßmann, Jens (eds.) (2012) *Handbuch Deutsche Gebärdensprache. Sprachwissenschaftliche und anwendungsbezogene Perspektiven.* Seedorf: Signum Verlag.

EUD [n.d] International Sign Disclaimer. European Union of the Deaf. Available at www.eud.eu/International_Sign_Disclaimer-i-206.html

Ferguson, C. A. (1959) Diglossia. *Word* 15: 325–340.

(1968) Language development. In J. A. Fishman, C. A. Ferguson, and D. G. Jyotirindra (eds.), *Language Problems of Developing Nations* (pp. 27–36). New York, London: Wiley.

Ferjan Ramirez, N., Leonard, M. K., Halgren, E., and Mayberry, R. I. (2013) The neural correlates of childhood linguistic isolation. In S. Baiz, N. Goldman, and R. Hawkes (eds.) *Proceedings of the 37th Boston University Conference on Language Development* (vol. I, pp. 110–121). Boston, MA: Cascadilla Press.

Fisher, R. and Lane, H. (1993) *Looking back: A Reader on the History of Deaf Communities and their Sign Languages.* Seedorf: Signum Verlag.

Fishman, J. A. (1974) Language planning and language planning research: The state of the art. In J. A. Fishman (ed.), *Advances in Language Planning* (pp. 15–33). The Hague: Mouton de Gruyter.

(1991) *Reversing Language Shift: Theory and Practice of Assistance to Threatened Languages.* Clevedon, UK: Multilingual Matters.

Geraci, C. (2012) Language policy and planning: The case of Italian Sign Language. *Sign Language Studies* 12(4): 494–518.

Haugen, E. (1959) Planning in modern Norway. *Anthropological Linguistics* 1(3): 68–81.

(1966) *Language Conflict and Language Planning: The Case of modern Norwegian.* Cambridge, MA: Harvard University Press.

Herrero Blanco, Ángel (2009) *Gramática didáctica de la lengua de signos española (LSE).* Madrid: S.M.

Herreweghe, M. van and Vermeerbergen, M. (2009) Flemish Sign Language standardisation. *Current Issues in Language Planning* 10(3): 308–326.

Herreweghe, M. van and Vermeerbergen, M. (2012) Data collection. In R. Pfau, M. Steinbach, and B. Woll (eds.), *Sign Languages (Handbooks of Linguistics and Communication Science, HSK* (pp. 1023–1045). Berlin: Mouton de Gruyter.

Heryanto, A. (1995) *Language Development and Development of Language: The Case of Indonesia.* Pacific Linguistics, Series D86, Department of Linguistics, Research School of Pacific and Asian Studies. Canberra: Australian National University.

Johnston, T. (2001) The lexical database of Auslan (Australian Sign Language). *Sign Language and Linguistics* 4: 145–169.

Kloss, H. (1969) *Possibilities on Group Bilingualism: A Report.* Quebec: International Centre for Research on Bilingualism.

Knorrs, H. and Marschark, M. (2012) Language planning for the 21st century: Revisiting bilingual language policy for deaf children. *Journal of Deaf Studies and Deaf Education* 17(3): 291–305.

Krausneker, V. (2009) On the legal status of sign languages: A commented compilation of resources. *Current Issues in Language Planning* 10(3): 351–354.

Lambert, W. E. (1978) Some cognitive and sociocultural consequences of being bilingual. In J. E. Alatis (ed.), *Georgetown University Round Table on Language and Linguistics* (pp. 214–229). Washington, DC.

Lewis, G. (2002) *The Turkish Language Reform: A Catastrophic Success.* Oxford: Oxford University Press.

Lucas, C. and Valli, C. (1992) *Language Contact in the American Deaf Community*. New York: Academic Press.

Mahshie, S. (1995) *Educating Deaf Children Bilingually*. Washington, DC: Laurent Clerc National Deaf Education Center.

Mayberry, R. I., Chen, J.-K., Witcher, P., and Klein, D. (2011) Age of acquisition effects on the functional organization of language in the adult brain. *Brain and Language* 119: 16–29.

Meir, I. and Sandler, W. (2008) *A Language in Space: The Story of Israeli Sign Language*. New York: Lawrence Erlbaum.

Mesch, J. (2010) *Perspectives of the Concept and Definition of International Sign*. World Federation of the Deaf. Available at www.wfdeaf.org/wp-content/uploads/2012/03/Perspectives-on-the-Concept-and-Definition-of-IS_Mesch-FINAL.pdf

Mesthrie, R. (2006) Language, transformation and development: A sociolinguistic appraisal of post-apartheid South African language policy and practice. *Southern African Linguistics and Applied Language Studies* 24(2): 151–163.

Neustupny, Jiri V. (1970) Basic types of treatment of language problems. *Linguistic Communication* 1: 77–98.

Newport, E. (1990) Maturational constraints on language learning. *Cognitive Science* 14(1): 11–28.

Ngcobo, M. N. (2013) *Language planning, policy and implementation in South Africa*. Accessed 12/08/2013 www.academia.edu/1123928/Language_planning_policy_and_implementation_in_South_Africa

Padden, C. and Humphries, T. (1988) *Deaf in America*. Cambridge, MA: Harvard University Press.

(2005) *Inside Deaf Culture*. Cambridge, MA: Harvard University Press.

Papaspyrou, C., von Meyenn, A., Matthaei, M., and Herrmann, B. (2008) *Grammatik der Deutschen Gebärdensprache aus der Sicht gehörloser Fachleute*. Seedorf: Signum Verlag.

Penn, C. and Reagan T. (1991) Toward a national policy for deaf education in the 'new' South Africa. *South African Journal of Communication Disorders* 38: 19–24.

(1994) The properties of South African Sign Language: Lexical diversity and syntactic unity. *Sign Language Studies* 85: 319–327.

(1995) On the other hand: Implications of the study of South African Sign Language for the education of the deaf in South Africa. *South African Journal of Education* 15: 92–96.

Quadros, R. M. de (1997) *Educação de surdos: a aquisição da linguagem*. Porto Alegre: Artes Médicas.

(2012) Linguistic Policies, Linguistic Planning, and Brazilian Sign Language in Brazil. In *Sign Language Studies, Special Issue on Language Planning for Sign Languages*. 12.4: 543–564.

Quadros, R. M. de and Cruz, Carina (2011) *Línguas de Sinais: Instrumentos de Avaliação*. Porto Alegre: ArtMed.

Quer, J. (2012) Legal pathways to recognition of sign languages: a comparison of the Catalan and Spanish sign language acts. *Sign Language Studies* 12(4): 565–582.

Quer, J. *et al.* (2005). *Gramàtica bàsica LSC*. Barcelona: FESOCA-Universitat de Barcelona. Available online at http://blogs.iec.cat/lsc/grammar-2/?lang=en

Quer, J. and Quadros, R.M de (2012) *Sign Language Studies, Special Issue on Language Planning for Sign Languages* 12(4).

Reagan, T. (2001) Language planning and policy. In C. Lucas (ed.), *Sociolinguistics of Sign Languages* (pp. 145–180). Cambridge: Cambridge University Press.

(2006) Language policy and sign languages. In T. Ricento (ed.), *An Introduction to Language Policy: Theory and Method* (pp. 329–345). Oxford: Blackwell.

(2010) *Language Policy and Planning for Sign Languages.* Washington, DC: Gallaudet University Press.

Ricento, T. (ed.) (2006) *An Introduction to Language Policy: Theory and Method.* Oxford: Blackwell.

Rosenstock, R. (2004) An investigation of international sign: Analyzing structure and comprehension, Ph.D. dissertation, Gallaudet University.

Rubin, J. and Jernudd, B. (eds.) (1971) *Can Language Be Planned?* Honolulu: University Press of Hawaii.

Schembri, A. and Johnston T. (2012) Sociolinguistics aspects of variation and change. In R. Pfau, M. Steinbach, and B. Woll (eds.), *Sign Languages (Handbooks of Linguistics and Communication Science, HSK)* (pp. 788–816). Berlin: Mouton de Gruyter.

(2013) Sociolinguistic variation and change in sign languages. In R. Bayley, R. Cameron, and C. Lucas (eds.), *The Oxford Handbook of Sociolinguistics* (pp. 503–524). New York: Oxford University Press.

Schermer, T. (2012a) Language planning. In R. Bayley, R. Cameron, and C. Lucas (eds.), *Sign Languages (Handbooks of Linguistics and Communication Science, HSK)* (pp. 889–908). Berlin: Mouton de Gruyter.

(2012b) Sign language planning in the Netherlands between 1980 and 2010. *Sign Language Studies* 12(4): 467–493.

Shantie, C. and Hoffmeister, R. J. (2000) Why schools for deaf children should hire deaf teachers: A preschool issue. *Journal of Education* 3(182): 37–47.

Singleton, J. L. E and Newport, E. (2004) When learners surpass their models: The acquisition of American Sign Language from inconsistent input. *Cognitive Psychology* 49: 370–407.

Skant, A., Dotter, F., Bergmeister, E., Hilzensauer, M., Hobel, K., Krammer, I., Okorn, C., Orasche, R., Ortner, and Unterberger, N. (2002) *Grammatik der Österreichischen Gebärdensprache. Veröffentlichungen des Forschungszentrum für Gebärdensprache und Hörgeschädigtenkommunikation der Universität Klagenfurt: Band 4: 2002.* Klagenfurt: ZGH.

Spolsky, B. (2004) *Language Policy.* Cambridge: Cambridge University Press.

Spolsky, B. and Shohamy, E. G. (1999) *The Languages of Israel: Policy, Ideology and Practice.* Clevedon, UK: Multilingual Matters.

Stokoe, W. C. (1960) *Sign Language Structure: An Outline of the Visual Communication Systems of the American Deaf, Studies in linguistics: Occasional papers (No. 8).* Buffalo: Dept. of Anthropology and Linguistics, University of Buffalo. [reprinted *Journal of Deaf Studies and Deaf Education* 10(1) 2005]

Stokoe, W. C., Casterline, D. C., and Croneberg, C. G. (1965) *A Dictionary of American Sign Language on Linguistic Principles.* Washington, DC: Gallaudet College Press. [reprinted in 1976 by Linstok Press]

Strong, M. (1995) A Review of bilingual/bicultural programs for deaf children in North America. *American Annals of the Deaf* 140(2): 84–94.

Sutton, V. Signwriting system. At www.signwriting.org (accessed August, 28 2013).

(1981) *Sign Writing for Everyday Use*. La Jolla: Deaf Action Committee for Sign Writing.

Tauli, V. 1968. *Introduction to a Theory of Language Planning*. Uppsala: Almqvist and Wiksell.

UN Convention on the Rights of Persons with Disabilities www.un.org/disabilities/convention/conventionfull.shtml

Wheatley, M. and Pabsch, A. (2010) *Sign Language Legislation in the European Union*. Brussels: EUD.

Joseph C. Hill

Introduction

In May 2011, a major controversy erupted in Italy regarding the official recognition of the sign language used by Italian Deaf people (see Nassisi 2010; La protesta 2011; LIS Subito! n.d.; Searls 2011). Since the 1980s, this sign language has been recognized in the Italian Deaf community as Lingua dei Segni Italiana (conventionally abbreviated as LIS, not LSI, which would follow the conventions of spoken and written Italian) which is translated as Italian Sign Language, but the name of the language is not widely known among hearing people in Italy. Leaders of the Italian Deaf community had been working to achieve the official recognition of LIS to affirm its language status and its essential role in supporting for Deaf people's access to information in education, employment, and service. The leaders were close to getting official recognition when one house of the Italian Parliament, the Senate of the Republic, approved the bill in recognizing LIS and it only needed approval from the other house of the Italian Parliament, the Chamber of Deputies, in order to pass the bill (La protesta 2011). In May 2011, the Chamber of Deputies revealed a change in the bill in calling what they thought was a more accurate name for the sign language: Linguaggio Mimico-Gestuale (LMG) (Searls 2011). The English translation of the name is "language of mime and gesture" with the meaning of *language* as a particular communication activity (e.g., baby talk or technical jargon) rather than a full-fledged linguistic system. The former name had reflected and affirmed the linguistic status of the sign language, but the new name was an implicit rejection of that status. The Parliament was willing to pass the bill with the new name, but the Deaf community refused to accept the name and called for keeping the former name which reflected the actual nature of LIS (LIS Subito! n.d.). Despite the intervention by the leaders of the Italian Deaf community and academics and researchers in LIS- and Deaf-related fields, the call for retaining the former name went unheard; instead, the Parliament drafted a new bill with the support of medical professionals that required speech and hearing interventions for deaf children, including the use of

146

cochlear implants, in order to ensure proper educational and language developments for them (LIS Subito! n.d.).

In November 2012, a single petition was submitted to We the People, which is a section of the White House government website for American citizens to submit their petitions to the policy experts in the Obama administration. The petition called for American Sign Language (ASL) to be officially recognized as a community language and as a language of instruction in schools that serve deaf and hard-of-hearing children. To receive a response from the White House, the petition must reach 25,000 signatures; over 27,000 signatures were obtained in less than a month and it caught the media attention including *USA Today* and the *Washington Post*. During the summer of 2013, the White House made an official response to the petition saying that "there shouldn't be any stigma about American Sign Language" and that they "reinforce its importance in numerous federal laws, regulations, and policies." This might be taken as a positive sign of support for ASL, but a closer look on their statement revealed a service-oriented view of ASL as an auxiliary aid to help with the access to employment and education. The petition called for a federal recognition of ASL as a legitimate language on American soil; the White House responded by saying it was legally protected as an accessible communication for deaf and hard-of-hearing people in America. The intentions of both parties were completely mismatched. In addition, the fact that English is also not federally recognized as the national language in US and that there are over 300 languages in the country (Shin and Kominski 2010), it is doubtful that Congress would be willing to consider drafting a bill to recognize languages in the USA and its territories.

These stories are the reality for the Deaf communities in Italy, America, and many other countries whose sign languages are largely ignored, viewed as an impediment to spoken language development, questioned as legitimate languages, or used as communication support systems instead of languages in their own right. The reality is the outcome of attitudes about sign languages has necessarily been driven by ideologies concerning the fundamental nature of sign language and their basic suitability for use by humans, i.e. (1) whether humans should be allowed to communicate with their hands as opposed to their voices and what it means if they do; (2) what it means when humans cannot hear; and (3) what the implication of deafness is for society. These ideologies parallel those concerning the suitability of non-standard and non-written varieties of spoken languages but are unique in that they get at the basic issue of language modality, which is an information-encoded form of sensory perception that is used in a communication exchange. Spoken languages are of the aural–oral modality which is the predominant form of communication in the world, whereas sign languages are of the visual–kinetic modality which is typically associated with deafness. According to people who subscribe to the medical model of deafness, deafness is conventionally seen as a physical impairment that severely affects one's life, but there is also the cultural model of deafness which attributes a positive meaning to deafness (Lane 2002; Lane *et al.* 1996). The cultural model reflects Deaf people as a linguistic and cultural minority whose primary languages are sign languages. Notwithstanding, deafness has historically been seen as a medical problem that needs to be remedied and that means the medical model is much more prevalent than the cultural model. The medical model creates a conditional existence of sign languages of Deaf people, meaning that if deafness were to be completely cured, sign languages would lose their usefulness and Deaf cultures, which are intimately related with sign languages, would be drastically affected. Such ideologies undercut the language status of sign languages, and the ideologies have governed the formal recognition of sign language at local, national, and international levels, such as that of the United Nations (see Monaghan 2003; Reagan 2010).

Language status is determined by the majority recognition, extent of language use, social capital of the language users, and other favorable sociocultural and socio-economic conditions and the status clearly influences the perceptions of language or language variety. The attitude studies of language varieties whose language status is well established are likely to be different from the attitude studies of language varieties whose language status is still in question (i.e., pidgins, creoles, and sign languages). In the former case, speakers of one spoken language may question the prestige of another language but the belief of the language status of the other spoken language as "a real language" is rarely questioned. In the latter case, the language status of pidgins, creoles, and sign language are often questioned because of how the societal ideologies about language condition people's thoughts about what real languages are.

In *The Sociolinguistics of Sign Languages* volume edited by Ceil Lucas, a chapter written by Burns and her colleagues (2001) provides an excellent coverage on language attitudes involving the studies on sign languages and Deaf communities. Little has changed in terms of the contribution of the studies of language attitudes toward sign languages and Deaf communities, but this chapter offers important insights into the role of standardization and stigmatization in the maintenance of language attitudes, the underlying attitudes in educational policies on communication in deaf education, and the relationship between social identities and language attitudes. The discussion will include the language attitude and linguistic studies of sign languages as well as spoken languages to support the understanding of the issues.

Role of standardization and stigmatization in language attitudes

Attitude is defined as "a psychological tendency that is expressed by evaluating a particular entity with some degree of favor or disfavor" (Eagly and Chaiken 1993: 1) and it is very much part of every aspect of life and society but it is not always on the conscious level of awareness nor is it always visibly or, at least, publicly expressed in a particular context. A particular entity that is under attitudinal evaluation is termed as an "attitude object" (Eagly and Chaiken 2007: 583). Attitude objects may be conceptual (e.g., ideology, belief, knowledge) or tangible (e.g., a house, a car, a person, an animal) and the objects may be individual (e.g., the current US president, a reality TV star) or collective (e.g., college students or the US Congress) (Eagly and Chaiken 2007). Attitudes are generally formed and expressed in one or more types of evaluative responses toward attitude objects: affective, cognitive, and behavioral. An affective type has to do with our feelings toward attitude objects; a cognitive type deals with our knowledge and belief about attitude objects; and a behavioral type focuses on our reactions toward attitude objects.

In this case, a language is an attitude object and the scope of attitudes has narrowed to language attitudes which encompass affective, cognitive, and behavioral types of evaluative responses toward particular language varieties (that is, languages, dialects, pidgins, and creoles) based on stereotypical perceptions of social groups who use those varieties (Campbell-Kibler 2009; Garrett 2010; Preston 2002). Responses toward language varieties, which are attitude objects, are based on two perceptions: a sensory perception of linguistic items in a language variety and a stereotypical perception of a social group that uses these items. Linguistic items can range from phonology (in the specific sense) to discourse (in the broadest sense). For example: on the phonological level, a community produces a vowel in a word differently from another community (i.e., vowels /ɛ/ and /ɪ/ in pin); on the lexical level, how two mutually intelligible linguistic communities use different words to refer to the same objects (i.e., soda/pop/coke, sofa/couch/davenport); and on the grammatical and discourse levels, how a community has a sentence that is different from that in another community that produces the same meaning (i.e., "She *is usually* home at 7"/"She *be* home at 7"). Attitudes toward language varieties are generally influenced by the process of language standardization (Garrett 2010: 7) and prestige, which is acquired through the process of standardization in a given society in a given time, is often associated with a social group with weighty influence in the society (Milroy 2001).

Ideologies as the underpinning of standardization in sustaining language attitudes

Majority or socially dominant language varieties gain the status of "standard" after years of use and acceptance (or in some cases, enforcement) by most members within a given society. These varieties are normally favored over minority or socially subordinate language varieties because of their association with social, economic, and educational privileges. This does not necessarily mean that all members of the majority have acquired these privileges due to their use of the majority language. A person from a less-privileged background can use the majority varieties proficiently, and people detecting acceptable linguistic markers in the person's language may assume that the person has a good social standing. In this sense, the perception of standard varieties generates a stereotypical image of a person or group enjoying the benefits of the community. Some members of the minority may have negative attitudes about the majority language varieties and hold positive values of cultural and familial ties for their own varieties, but they still view the majority language as a desirable commodity. There is a pressure in various forms for the minority to conform to the majority by adopting the majority's way of life including using their language if they want to acquire the favorable conditions. Minority members develop different strategies to deal with two distinct varieties (be they mutually intelligible or not) that would eventually affect their cultural identity, language proficiencies, and the nature of language varieties themselves.

A standard language variety is not inherently prestigious; it simply acquires prestige when its "speakers have high prestige, because prestige is attributed by human beings to particular social groups and to inanimate or abstract objects, such as Ming vases and language varieties, and it depends on the values attributed to such objects" (Milroy 2001: 532). In this sense, the standard variety carries *overt prestige* (Wolfram and Schilling-Estes 2006: 184). That is, members of a society make a mental association between a majority's variety and social prestige; minority language users usually aspire to gain proficiency in the standard language or, at least, acknowledge that the prestige associated with that language is associated with social, economic, and educational success. Even though a minority's variety may be recognized as a natural linguistic system by both majority and minority communities, the minority's variety is not as prestigious in the majority based on the majority's attitudes toward the variety and the perception of the minority's social status. In spite of the stigmatized status of the minority, the minority members and their variety are able to endure the problems of stigma because their language variety is just as important as their social identities. Language and culture are interconnected in a way that they reinforce one another so it makes sense that the stigmatized variety is persistently favored by the minority. The persistence is due to *covert prestige* (Wolfram and Schilling-Estes 2006: 184) which explains the existence of the stigmatized variety because it is part of the cultural properties. Even with the covert prestige that functions as a protective factor for the variety, the minority members cannot help but feeling insecure about their language variety.

Linguistic insecurity as a result of stigmatization

Language attitudes can affect dialects as much as they can languages that are mutually unintelligible. Dialects are more than language variants with differences in linguistic structure; they are the cultural symbols of social groups and the status of social groups is dependent on major social characteristics. Even if the dialects are minimally different on the phonological level, the association of marked phonetic sounds with the stigmatized group is enough to generate negative attitude toward the language variant. Speakers of stigmatized dialects deal with their linguistic insecurity in different ways: they may accept their status and attempt to work toward a standard variant; they may deflect the negative attention by being critical of another dialect; they may defend their dialect and proclaim it as part of their cultural make-up; or they can fight for recognition of their dialect as a legitimate variant.

From the linguistic perspective, dialects are structurally related varieties that have certain distinctive phonological, lexical, morphological, and syntactical features. By the linguistic definition of *dialect*, that includes standard language varieties that are highly favored in a society as well as nonstandard language varieties with stigmatized linguistic features. However, dialects receive attitudinal evaluations just as languages based on certain linguistic features (known as 'markers') and the social status of people speaking the dialects. The general definition of *dialect* is strictly reserved for language varieties that are different from standard varieties and the particular meaning of "different" is varieties that are considered nonstandard. There seem to be two meanings of *dialect* in the general perspective: one referring to a group of people who use the language differently from the local, native community of language users and another referring to language varieties that are socially stigmatized (Wolfram and Schilling-Estes 2006). According to the second meaning, standard varieties should not be called dialects because they are free of socially disfavored linguistic features. Some linguistic features are stigmatized when they are strongly associated with groups of people who are in an unfavorable social status with respect to region, race, ethnicity, class, religion, and even generation.

Preston (1996) studied language attitudes related to regional dialects and measures the subjects' opinions of language correctness in each US region based on their stereotypical knowledge of regional dialects. From the study, Northern (i.e., Midwest, New England, and Middle Atlantic states) and Southern dialects were polar opposites in terms of social-related adjectives. Northern speakers were perceived as "proper," "intelligent," and "cold" based on their speech and Southerners were perceived as "informal," "undereducated," and "friendly." For Northern speakers, linguistic insecurity was never an issue because they are protected by their *standard* dialect in the US even though some adjectives such as "cold" were not flattering. In addition, the finding from the study is that Northern speakers were clearly prejudiced against the Southern dialect based on the judgment scale of language correctness and the affective scale which indicates their feelings about language varieties. For a group of speakers with a stigmatized dialect, linguistic insecurity may affect their perception of correctness of the dialect as in the case of Indiana, where Midwest speakers assume that their dialect is comparable with the Southern dialect but never with the Northern speech because the speech is already in a "correct" form. Also, with linguistic insecurity, a group of speakers may line up with prestigious speakers and become increasingly critical of other regions with a comparable dialect in order to deflect negative perceptions. However, this is not true for all stigmatized dialects. Southerners know that their dialect attracts negative attention and they are aware of the stereotypes of Southern speech and culture, but solidarity based on their cultural pride keeps them from being crippled by linguistic insecurity. Their regional difference is part of their cultural identity and they may even promote Southern stereotypes such as 'gentlemanliness' and 'hospitality.' They may rate their own speech as 'incorrect,' reflecting linguistic insecurity but they rate it high on the affective ('pleasantness') scale, based on group solidarity. Even when the difference between dialects is minimal on the phonological level, stigmatized phonological markers in one variety will elicit negative reactions. For instance, in Illinois, North Midland is considered a prestigious English dialect and the South Midland dialect has a linguistic feature that contrasts with the North Midland dialect, an intrusive /r/. For North Midland, the /r/ appearing in the word "wash" as in "warsh", for example, is too "Southerner" or "farmer" which is considered to be a negative social trait in the US, which is the basis for the stigmatization of the South Midland dialect (Frazer 1987).

Language varieties with socially disfavored features may not be forever stigmatized. The attitude toward a language variant changes as the social setting changes. For example, Quebec French was formerly stigmatized but is now considered the standard variety in Quebec, Canada. From the 1960s to the 1980s, sociolinguistic studies of speakers of Quebec French showed that the speakers were linguistically insecure because of three major factors: the support from the French government for Standard European French, the notion of the compromised quality of written and spoken French due to the influence of Quebec French, and the specifications from the officials of language planning policy and publications on the acceptable language use in accordance with Standard French (Evans 2002). In recent years, the signs of linguistic insecurity have been disappearing because of the growth of the local pride in Quebec French and the clamor for the acceptance of their dialect.

The case of stigmatization and standardization in the American Deaf community

Deaf ASL signers are able to acquire language, traditions, and social behaviors that are the common features of American Deaf culture, but the channels of language acquisition are largely different from those in the mainstream society. Whereas spoken languages are transmitted from generation to generation within families, most Deaf people acquire sign language from other Deaf people and teachers because their hearing parents do not sign (e.g., Lane *et al.* 1996). While the existence of deaf people has been acknowledged by the wider community, Deaf culture is an unfamiliar concept to most hearing people. Deafness is largely defined as a physical disability that can be assisted with modern technology and accommodation such that people who are deaf can be realigned within mainstream society (Lane 2002). It has not widely been understood that deafness can also be a cultural attribute of a Deaf community and that deaf people have their own languages which are distinct from spoken languages. In addition, they unconsciously adhere to the definition of 'culture' as one's membership in a group, more specifically, as belonging to a family within a community where language, tradition, and social behaviors are shared and passed on from adults to children in successive generations through familial relationships (Baynton 1996: 2).

Historically, the cultural attributes of Deaf communities arose within educational institutions for deaf children where community members acquired and used sign languages, formed lifelong friendships, and developed their identities as deaf people. In a world without these institutions for deaf people, Deaf communities would not be easily formed and sign languages would not be used as widely as they are today (Monaghan 2003: 20). After the founding of the first American public institution for the deaf, the American School for the Deaf (ASD), in Hartford, Connecticut in 1817, a sign language was developed from a mixture of French Sign Language (the native language of the school's first deaf teacher), the indigenous sign language of Martha's Vineyard off Massachusetts, the indigenous sign language of Henniker, New Hampshire, and deaf children's home signs[1] (see Lane *et al.* 1996: 56–58). The sign language continued to flourish through generations of deaf children at ASD and other institutions for the deaf. Some of those deaf children became teachers and served as the sign language models for deaf children at these schools. Some deaf graduates had deaf and hearing children to whom they passed on their sign language. The

---

[1] Home-sign is a system of gestures spontaneously created in a single family with at least one deaf family member (typically a child). Since family members do not know sign language, they invent gestures to communicate with their deaf member (Goldin-Meadow and Mylander 1994).

founding of other institutions for the education of deaf children spread southward and westward from the first school in Hartford and Deaf communities formed around the schools to maintain community ties (Lane *et al.* 1996; Padden and Humphries 1988). With geographical separation, dialects of the sign language emerged in different communities as it would happen to any natural language with the same geographical condition.

Until the early 1960s, this language was simply called "the sign language" (Padden and Humphries 2005). It finally received a name when William C. Stokoe, Carl Croneberg, and Dorothy Casterline published the first linguistic analysis of what they called American Sign Language. Linguistic work on ASL and the new official name of the language should have been a moment of celebration for the American Deaf community because it validated the linguistic status of ASL, but instead it was a moment of anxiety, confusion, and anger (Liddell 2003: 4; Padden and Humphries 2005: 125–128). The stigmatization of ASL had been maintained for a long time by both hearing and deaf people until its status quo was challenged by the validity of ASL as a natural linguistic system. Anxiety emerged because it was a struggle for the community to understand ASL as more than just a way to communicate with hands and eyes and equate its linguistic status with that of English that had been long held as standard. Confusion occurred because it was difficult for them to discuss it as a language in the midst of a few label changes from *the sign language* to *American Sign Language* to *Ameslan*[2] to *ASL* (Padden and Humphries 2005: 126–127). Anger arose because the belief about ASL as an imperfect system was challenged and Stokoe was attacked by people inside and outside of the American Deaf community out of anxiety about the proclamation of ASL as a valid linguistic system and its role as a medium of instruction in the education systems for deaf children (Padden and Humphries 2005). At this point, the ideology of language had shifted and language attitudes toward ASL changed with it. That led to more positive changes with the language status of ASL in the next decades in the American Deaf community and the surrounding public.

ASL is now a popular language that is studied as a foreign or second language in secondary schools and post-secondary institutions (Padden and Humphries 2005; Rosen 2010). Deaf community members have metalinguistic awareness of signing varieties (Baer, Okrent, and Rose 1996) and there is a general perception of a Standard ASL variety. In 1965, Carl Croneberg wrote an essay describing the kinds of variation in ASL in the US and the standard variety of ASL that emerged at Gallaudet University. Croneberg (1965) explicitly stated: "the body of signs used at Gallaudet, then, must contain the main base of what we call *standard ASL*" (319, my emphasis).

---

[2] The term was coined by Louie J. Fant (1972).

In the recent decades, certain features of ASL have been implicitly or explicitly promoted through ASL dictionaries, ASL instructional videos and textbooks, ASL courses, ASL video media, ASL assessment and language instruction programs. The promotions are part of the process of standardization for ASL to preserve ASL forms and features and prevent the incorporation of English-based items. The standardization of ASL is the basis for the perceptions of Standard ASL so any signing variety that is perceived to have marked English features are stigmatized in the American Deaf community (Johnson and Erting 1989). Manually Coded English (MCE) is a stigmatized signing code that is not a full-fledged language system like ASL. A number of MCE systems were created in the US, but a few of them are still practiced in educational settings for deaf students, so the acquisition of MCE is sustained as long as the students remain exposed to it.

MCE systems, also known as "artificial sign systems," can be used with or without voice and they are typically used in simultaneous communication programs (Power and Leigh 2011: 39).[3] For the sake of simplicity, only SEE1, SEE2, and Signed English will be discussed. MCE systems are designed in a particular way so that the essential features of English can be expressed visually, but the systems differ from one another in their philosophy of how English should be expressed. In SEE1, signs are designed to correspond with English morphemes or root words irrespective of conceptual meanings. For example, the English word "butterfly" is conveyed through two separate signs, BUTTER and FLY.[4] SEE2 developed from SEE1 with a special concentration on the conceptual meanings of independent words and morphemes of English to which the signs corresponded. For example, SEE2 has one conceptual sign for "butterfly" instead of the two signs used in SEE1 (Gustason et al. 1993). Signed English is designed to be used with some of the fourteen markers to make it less cumbersome for children and adults to learn (Bornstein et al. 1983). In fact, Signed English users are encouraged to use as few as four markers (i.e., possessive, irregular plural, irregular past tense, and progressive tense) within a context (Bornstein et al. 1983: 6). MCE systems like SEE2 and Signed English are the instructional tools that are intentionally designed with the purpose of developing English skills in deaf and hard-of-hearing children.

With MCE, ASL, and contact signing (see Chapter 3, this volume) coexisting in the community, perceptual issues have emerged concerning what ASL

---

[3] Simultaneous communication is the means of communication in a way that a person can sign and speak at the same time. MCE systems are typically used in this manner since they are based on English but, with ASL, it is difficult to express oneself clearly through simultaneous communication. See Tevenal and Villanueva 2009 for further discussion.

[4] It is a convention in sign language studies to use capital letters for English words (glosses) that represent ASL or MCE signs.

should be and who tends to use it with whom. Also, relevant here is the fact that English is favored above all the other languages in American society, thus affecting the perception of ASL. ASL is in a very interesting position because it is often still not recognized by the hearing majority in the USA as a language (and it is stigmatized in some places) but it is recognized as a language by most people who are involved in or with the American Deaf community and it has prestige in that community. With the history of suppression and misconceptions of ASL, the language status of ASL is still largely uncertain in the US and in some parts of the American Deaf community. In addition to the skepticism about the status of ASL as a language, different forms of manually coded English (MCE) were introduced in place of ASL as a medium of instruction for deaf and hard-of-hearing children and that has resulted in a contact variety of ASL (see Lucas and Valli 1992). However, the standardization of ASL is ongoing by the way of dictionaries, textbooks, curriculum, and language proficiency assessments and the status of ASL as a language has been gaining recognition in some parts of the country. For example, a few states such as Alabama, Maine, Colorado, and Rhode Island have recognized ASL as a natural and legitimate language of the American Deaf community in their legislation while some states and the District of Columbia, rather than recognize ASL as a fully developed language of the Deaf community, *only* legislate ASL for two purposes: as a foreign language that can (or in some cases, *may*) be studied and accepted for credit in schools and universities and as a communication accommodation with the provision of ASL interpreters (Reagan 2010). So with the double status of ASL (prestigious and stigmatized), it may lead to a wide range of judgments of what linguistic features constitute ASL (as opposed to the contact variety and MCE) and of its legitimate status as a language.

Underlying language attitudes in educational policies

In deaf education, the language of classroom instruction is intricately linked with language acquisition and exposure for deaf and hard-of-hearing students because schools are usually the primary places for students to acquire a language in a variety of communication modes: sign, speech, or sign-supported speech modes. Behind every language of instruction, there is an educational philosophy that explains the choice of the language and the values that teachers and administrators want to instill in their students. If the language of instruction is a sign language, the teachers and administrators may have the same respect for sign languages as they do for spoken languages and convey the positive values of a sign language by using it with their deaf and hard-of-hearing students. The positive values can be, for example, the status of a sign language as a true language, the awareness of linguistic and cultural values of a sign language, the pride of being bilingual with spoken/written and sign languages, and the sense of being normal with the use of a sign language. If the medium of instruction is strictly in an oral or sign-supported speech mode, the teachers and administrators may not have as much respect for sign languages as they have for spoken languages and they convey the negative values toward a natural sign language by using only a speech-based communication method with their students. The negative values can be the unacknowledged status of a sign language as a true language, the perpetuation of the misconceptions of a sign language, and the indignity of using a sign language. If the language of instruction contains both speech and sign components, it depends on how the teachers and administrators convey the message to the students with their actions and use of the two languages.

Changes in deaf education that influence the communication outcomes

Through many years of existence, schools for the deaf have long been considered to be the crucibles for the acquisition and maintenance of sign language (Lucas *et al.* 2001: 52) and Deaf communities have typically formed in the regions where special schools or education programs for deaf children were established (Monaghan 2003: 20). The special schools or program provides a rich language environment with sign language being used among deaf and hard-of-hearing peers and school staff. A new cohort of Deaf students who had little or no knowledge of sign language prior to the beginning of their formal education usually acquired sign language in the company of older Deaf peers. This is known as "horizontal transmission" which is normal for the cohorts of deaf and hard-of-hearing children at special schools as opposed to "vertical transmission" which is normal for hearing communities in which hearing children typically acquired their first language from their family.

In the 1970s, educational laws and regulations that enforced the inclusionary practices for deaf and hard-of-hearing students to attend regular schools with or without communication accommodation initiated a worldwide trend of educational mainstreaming that affected the enrollment at the schools of the deaf. In the USA, it started with the passage of Public Law 94-142 (the Education of All Handicapped Children Act of 1975). In Italy, a similar trend emerged in the late 1970s with the passage of the legislation on the mainstreaming of children with disabilities, including deaf and hard-of-hearing children (Geraci *et al.* 2011: 532). In New Zealand, the mainstream placement of deaf and hard-of-hearing children became increasingly favored starting in the 1980s (McKee and McKee 2011: 492).

With the increase of mainstreaming, the role of the schools for the deaf has become increasingly smaller as a source of sign language input for deaf and hard-of-hearing children. For instance, before the 1960s, almost 80 percent of the deaf children in the US attended residential schools for the deaf (Lane *et al.* 1996: 244); by 2010, the percentage had declined to 24.3 (Gallaudet Research Institute, 2011). Similar figures can be found throughout the world with some percentages of deaf and hard-of-hearing children enrolled at the schools for the deaf extremely low. Legal developments in deaf education have observable effects on the provisions of communication access for deaf and hard-of-hearing people. In deaf schools (including residential schools and special educational centers for the deaf), deaf and hard-of-hearing students enjoy common communication advantages that are accessible to them, but in the mainstream settings, deaf and hard-of-hearing students may not have the same advantages. Mainstreamed students tend to be widely distributed among neighborhood schools and the schools have an extremely low number of deaf and hard-of-hearing students relative to the rest of the school population (Mitchell and Karchmer 2006: 95 and 99). Communication methods are highly individualized based on the needs of mainstreamed deaf and hard-of-hearing students and the decisions made by parents and educator. The intentions behind the methods are to place mainstreamed students in the least restrictive environment and to have them function as if they are no different from their regular peers, but the actual effects of mainstreaming are the minimization of the social ties between deaf and hard-of-hearing students and the impression of the importance of using a language of the majority, not of the minority.

The case of English and American Sign Language as languages of instruction

In many ways, English is the standard language of the United States, and non-English languages (e.g., Spanish, Chinese, Navajo) are generally relegated to a secondary status. Not only is English highly valued in the country, the Standard English variety is highly favored over other English varieties (e.g., African American English, Appalachian English, Chicano English). In that sense, one must be proficient in Standard English in order to be a productive and respectable member of American society. In the second half of the twentieth century when the ban on sign language in the classroom started to be lifted, several educators developed communication tools in order to provide complete access to English by manual means.

MCE systems are typically used as instructional tools in deaf education programs within regular schools because it is easy for hearing instructors to use them with speech and they are believed to be useful tools in exposing deaf and hard-of-hearing students to English. Deaf schools typically use ASL for deaf and hard-of-hearing students although some instructors might use MCE or contact signing. Recall that before the 1960s, 80 percent of deaf and hard-of-hearing students attended deaf residential schools. Since the advent of mainstreaming, the number of deaf schools has been decreasing and the majority of deaf and hard-of-hearing students now attend mainstream programs (Karchmer and Mitchell 2003; Lane et al. 1996; Mitchell and Karchmer 2004, 2006). The implication of the student demographics in terms of communication exposure is that since the combination of speech and signs, most likely simultaneous communication, are used in some mainstream programs, more deaf and hard-of-hearing students have been exposed to them.

As for deaf and hard-of-hearing students, Kannapell (1985, 1989) investigated sociolinguistic profiles and attitudes of deaf students with respect to the modes of communications and relevant cultural identities in the American Deaf community. Kannapell studied the sociolinguistic characteristics of deaf Gallaudet University students with the purpose of finding a relationship between the students' exposure to modes of communication in their educational programs and their attitudes about ASL, English, and Deaf culture.

In the first phase, Kannapell found that the significant social variables relating to deaf students' attitude about ASL and English were, in order of importance, the number of years spent at a school for the deaf, the age of sign language acquisition, the age of onset of hearing loss, and the hearing status of parents and siblings. Also, she found that the subjects who were culturally Deaf held positive attitudes toward ASL and borderline attitude toward English, while the subjects who were hard-of-hearing or oral deaf held positive attitudes toward English and its signing forms.

In the second phase, the finding was that the students' self-evaluations of communication skills (i.e., ASL, PSE,[5] MCE, lip-reading, speech, reading, and writing) were similar to the communication professionals' evaluations of the students' communication skills. Also, the students who rated themselves higher in ASL proficiency tended to rate themselves lower on other areas except for PSE.

In the third phase, it was found that the students had a good understanding of the linguistic differences between ASL, PSE, and English but the students had interesting opinions about ASL and English, for example, that ASL was a language but its grammar was not proper like English; ASL had a bad effect on English skills; ASL was important for Deaf children but speech must be taught in order to fit in with the mainstream society; and ASL was used by less educated Deaf people (Kannapell 1989: 203). The implication of the study was that language planning in education programs had a considerable effect on deaf students' identities and attitudes and Kannapell strongly encouraged the need

---

[5] PSE is an abbreviation of Pidgin Signed English. It is a colloquial term for contact signing, but it is a misnomer because of the misapplication of the word "pidgin" (see Lucas and Valli 1992).

of positive promotion of ASL in order to instill positive attitudes toward ASL in deaf students. She believed that her study "indicates that language control is a powerful tool in the education of deaf children. Language planning means identity planning" (1989: 207).

The study was carried out in 1985 and there have been many changes since that time, including the emergence of the bilingual–bicultural (or 'bi–bi') philosophy. This approach takes the view that deaf children can learn effectively through their visual channel with ASL as the medium of instruction and English in various forms (Easterbrooks and Baker 2002: 15). To put it in practice, teachers are expected to be proficient in ASL and learn visual strategies to facilitate deaf children's learning. There is interest among researchers in understanding the impact of the bilingual–bicultural philosophy on the academic performance of deaf and hard-of-hearing children, but in spite of the interest, few studies have been done (Geeslin 2007: 12).

In the study by Ward Trotter (1989), the argument was that the language attitudes of teachers influenced their relationship with and evaluation of deaf students and that would have an effect on classroom interaction and the students' education. Based on her experience in a teacher-training program, Ward Trotter hypothesized that the language attitudes of the teachers were shaped by their teacher-training programs with the philosophy about appropriate modes of communication for deaf students and the misconceptions about ASL. She employed the modified matched-guise technique with the videotapes of ASL-like and English-like signings. For the videotapes, she filmed three signing models twice in ASL and Signed English interviews. The ASL interview was done with a deaf native ASL user and the other interview was done with a hearing signer who used Signed English. Once the signing interviews were taped, Ward Trotter then employed the matched-guise technique with the video samples of ASL and English-based signing. In addition to the matched guise, she used a semantic differential scale with rating for the video samples of signing. Student teachers were chosen as the subjects of the study because they would be "the most idealistic and flexible" (1989: 219) about ASL in comparison to veteran teachers of the deaf. The result of the study was mixed but from a certain viewpoint, English-based signing samples received higher ratings than ASL samples. The reasons for the mixed results were as follows: the modified matched-guise technique for the videotapes was not sensitive enough to measure the subjects' attitudes; the subjects were still in teacher-training so their language attitudes about ASL and English were partially developed; and their signing receptive skills were mediocre so they might not do the task successfully. Nonetheless, the higher ratings for the English-based signing described the teachers' attitudes toward ASL as a medium of instruction for deaf and hard-of-hearing students.

Relationship between language attitudes and social identities

Linguistic items and markers usually evoke a stereotypical image of a social group of similar characteristics that use the items. For example, the grammatical construction of "She be home at 7" is a typical and acceptable construction in African American English (AAE) but it is not typical or acceptable in Standard English. Variants of a linguistic item are forms that are perceived to constitute a particular linguistic community and the variants are used by members of a social group to identify speakers who are socially similar or different; in other words, the variants carry social meaning for people to implicitly perceive and inform each other of their social characteristics (Campbell-Kibler 2009; Garrett 2010). Social meaning may elicit different evaluative responses toward a person's language and, in a social context, influences a social standing of members of a linguistic community.

Social interpretations and perceptions of language users and linguistic forms

People are aware of distinctive linguistic forms in language varieties in their community and the forms carry social meanings from which people can infer other people's social backgrounds and communities, but the connection between social groups and linguistic forms is usually stereotypical. With the power of stereotype, their perceptions of the distinctive forms can be influenced by their knowledge of one's social background. For example, Niedzielski's study (1999) found that a geographic label, *Michigan* and *Canada*, influenced the subjects' perception of nonstandard vowels in a Detroit native's speech. The vowels in the Michigan dialect are different from those of Standard American English (SAE), but Niedzielski found that they were not perceptible to Detroit-resident subjects. When Detroit-resident subjects were informed that the speaker was from Michigan, the majority of them reported that the vowels in her speech were part of SAE, but when the speaker was found to be Canadian, the subjects noticed the nonstandard vowels in her speech, even though the speaker was a Detroit native.

We have seen how language attitudes toward specific dialects of American English can result in stigmatizing and stereotypic of whole groups of people. However, few dialects in the US have been met with as much derision and criticism as African American English (AAE). AAE is a legitimate language variety with certain phonological, morphological, lexical, and semantic markers used by African-American speakers in urban and rural communities (e.g., Green 2002). Not all African-Americans speak AAE nor is it strictly exclusive to African-Americans. Like with any language variety, anyone can acquire it as long as they have access and exposure to the variant, but for AAE, the typical language group is African-Americans (e.g., Green 2002).

Oppression of AAE speakers also can be found in educational systems. For example, in 1995 to 1996, of the major ethnic groups of students enrolled in the public schools in Oakland, California, the African-American group had the lowest grade point average (GPA), 1.8. Ogbu (1999) attributed this to the difference in language use, since teachers used Standard English as the medium of instruction and African-American students used AAE. Moreover, African-American students were treated differently when they were tested for English language proficiency. Students from other language groups (e.g., Cantonese, Tagalog, West African) were tested and classified as Fluent English Proficient (FEP) or Limited English Proficient (LEP) and black students were tested and classified as FEP or Speech Impaired (SI). Predictably, the former group was more successful in education than African-American students because they received necessary treatment to make sure that they were proficient in English in order to get the education they needed. African-American students were expected to be proficient in English simply because they were Americans. If they did not use the standard dialect, they were perceived as speech impaired. Flowers (2000: 230) listed the following assumptions of language deficiency in African-American students using AAE in the classroom:

- African Americans use an inferior linguistic system that must be remedied before they can actively participate and learn in a classroom.
- The African American language is not a legitimate way of communicating in American society.
- The African American language is viewed as being used by individuals who are less intelligent and/or academically inferior.

Despite the pressure against AAE, it still exists because of the cultural solidarity of African-American speakers. By using AAE, the speakers reveal their cultural ties with other AAE speakers. If an African-American speaks Standard English with AAE speakers, it may represent a cultural distance from African-American culture. At worst, the choice of Standard English may be perceived as a cultural insult and the speaker may be accused of trying to be "white." This indicates linguistic insecurity relating to power structure or, more generally, socio-economic status. AAE is associated with African-American speakers who are institutionalized into the lower socio-economic status relative to the speakers of Standard English who tend to be in the higher socio-economic status. For an African-American to speak Standard English then is much more than just talking differently: it is a display of a dominant social identity that is disagreeable to AAE speakers. It can represent a threat against cultural solidarity.

Linguistic and social realities of Deaf community members

The attitudes toward signing varieties are tied to the perceptions of social identities related to deafness and signing abilities. The social identities in the American Deaf community are as follows: *Deaf* as a person with an entrenched cultural identity and a carrier of ASL; *hard-of-hearing* as a person with residual hearing and speech capacity and possible signing proficiency in whatever mode: ASL, contact signing or MCE; *oral deaf* as a person with little or no hearing but has a strong preference in oral communication over signing for daily use; *late-deafened* as a person who possessed normal hearing and speech abilities before losing them due to medical conditions, e.g., illness, genetic predisposition, or accident; and *hearing* as a person with normal hearing and speech abilities in contact with a Deaf community in whatever role.[6] Although the identities listed above are presented in a simple manner, they are not as clean and fixed as they appear in the American Deaf community or, generally speaking, all Deaf communities in the world. Throughout the world, deaf identities and a notion of Deaf culture may not be the same in all Deaf communities because "the nature of deaf and Deaf identity in a given community depends on the forms of community and language" and with respect to forms, "the form any sign language takes is intertwined with the nature of the community that uses it" (Monaghan 2003: 20).

Notwithstanding the complexity of deaf identities, the use of ASL is one qualifying property (i.e., shared language) signaling membership in the American Deaf community (Kannapell 1994). Other properties such as a collective name, sense of community, shared and distinct values and customs, culture knowledge, history, social structures, and arts underpin a Deaf identity (Leigh 2009). Even Deaf children are aware of the importance of language use to their social identities (Johnson and Erting 1989). It is through interaction that the children develop their social identity based on language use and form, and their interactions form the language attitudes that lead them to favor a group that uses the language form more like theirs. Deaf children who are proficient in ASL communicate and associate with each other more often than do Deaf children who are less proficient in ASL (Johnson and Erting 1989). To sum up the discussion on social identities, the use of ASL, contact signing, or MCE is a signal carrying social meaning for others to infer one's membership in social groups in the American Deaf community.

ASL signers have a general understanding that the social identity of an addressee/interlocutor influences a signer to choose a signing variety that aligns with the supposed communication preference of the addressee/

---

[6] See Kannapell 1994 and Leigh 2009 for further discussion on various identities in the Deaf community.

interlocutor. For example, Deaf signers use ASL with each other but often consciously or unconsciously switch to contact signing or Signed English when a hearing signer joins in their conversation. When the hearing signer leaves, Deaf signers may revert back to ASL. However, a study by Lucas and Valli (1992) has shown that a social identity is not a significant factor on the change of signing between interlocutors. Lucas and Valli found that some Deaf signers will use ASL with a hearing person, and some Deaf signers will use contact signing or even MCE signing with other Deaf signers. Other factors that influence signing choice with an interlocutor, include formality of the setting, familiarity with an interlocutor, and pride in one's membership in a social group.

Not only did Lucas and Valli (1992) examine the signers' choice of signing type in various situations, they also examined the issues of how the signers' signing was perceived. Lucas and Valli had a panel of ASL language professionals judge a total of twenty clips of different signers as 'ASL' and 'not ASL.' The experts were unanimous in their judgments with five clips as 'ASL' and the rest as 'not ASL.' The same clips were tested on Deaf signers who had no linguistic training as "naïve" judges and their judgments were not always in accordance with the master judges. The difference in results led Lucas and Valli to explore possible correlations with the judges' social characteristics. For example, on a particular clip, all master judges agreed that it was 'not ASL,' but 37 percent of white naïve judges judged the clip as 'ASL' and 82 percent of black naïve judges judged as 'ASL.' The discrepancy in judgment between white and black naïve judges could be related to the salience of linguistic structures in their perception. For instance, a signer in the clip used contact signing with English word order, but also used key ASL features such as eye gaze, referential spaces, and body shift. The saliency of these key ASL features in the black judges' perception despite the obvious presence of English could account for the discrepancy in the results.

As a follow-up to the interesting difference in perception of signing between white and black judges in Lucas and Valli's study, Hill (2012) investigated the effects of social information on deaf subjects' perception of signing produced by other deaf signers. The subjects were grouped by age (*young and old*), race (*black and white*), and age of sign language acquisition (*early and late*); the number of social groups based on the social characteristics was eight. There was a collection of videos containing various signing types (i.e., *Strong ASL, Mostly ASL, Mixed*, and *Non-ASL*) for the deaf subjects to view and they were asked to classify the signing as "*ASL*" or "*Not ASL.*" From the subjects as a whole, there was a systematic agreement of the responses with the highest proportion of *ASL* responses for *Strong ASL*, the second highest for *Mostly ASL*, the 50:50 proportion for *Mixed* and the lowest proportion for *Non-ASL*. A further analysis on the difference between *Strong ASL* and *Mostly ASL*

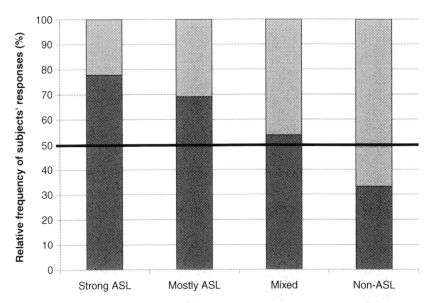

Figure 7.1 Relative frequency of ASL (dark gray) and non-ASL (light gray) responses from all subjects

revealed that the relative frequencies of ASL responses were significantly different (see Figure 7.1). In the subsequent analysis, the social groups' relative frequencies of *ASL* and *Non-ASL* responses for each signing type were compared. The frequencies were not found to be significantly different for *Strong ASL*, *Mostly ASL*, and *Mixed* except for *Non-ASL* where the difference was significant for three social groups (Older Black Non-Native, Older White Non-Native, and Younger Black Native) that perceived *Non-ASL* as a mixture of ASL and English while the other groups perceived it as English-based signing. This indicated that with the presence of English-based forms in the signing, some social groups might have different ideas of how much English was acceptable in the contact form of signing based on their social and communication backgrounds.

Hill's study was repeated but with a change in the procedure: the inclusion of social information that might influence deaf subjects' perception of signing produced by other deaf signers. This study was innovative in a sense that there was no prior socio-perception study on sign language that was similar to Niedzielski's Michigan dialect study. The social information included the types of school (*mainstream* versus *deaf school*), family hearing status (*deaf* versus *hearing*), and types of education (*high school* versus *college*). The first two social information relevant as social traits in Deaf communities but the type of education might not be relevant but could explain the perception of signing related to register. The social information did not have to be necessarily true. The goal was to observe possible changes in the signing perception when the deaf subjects learned the social background of other deaf signers. As a result, there were some changes in the subjects' responses but the changes were not systematic. The interpretation was that all signing types could be perceived differently due to relevant social information and the changes in responses could go in either direction. There were uncontrolled variables in the study, for example, the effect of the subjectivity of social information for the subjects, the effect of the social diversity of the subjects, the effect of narrative content produced by the signers in videos, and fatigue effect in the subjects' participation.

Studies of language attitudes on sign language

Since the 1960s, a matched-guise technique (MGT)[7] designed by William Lambert has been a classic technique that has been employed to this day to capture subjects' language attitudes indirectly. The questionnaire is an indirect method of gathering targeted attitudinal reactions on the use of language or dialect with controlled speech samples and no visual information about speakers. The technique involves using speech samples from bilingual (or bi-dialectal) speakers that are disguised as two separate speech samples from individual monolingual speakers. The technique leads experimental subjects to assume that the separate samples spoken by polyglot speakers are spoken by monolingual speakers. After listening to the samples, the subjects are asked to fill out a questionnaire to evaluate the personality traits of the speakers including *height, good looks, leadership, sense of humor, intelligence, religiousness, self-confidence, dependability, entertainingness, kindness, ambition, sociability, character,* and *likability.* This technique could be useful in examining attitudes toward sign languages, but a challenging part about the technique is that signers must be visible to deaf subjects; the signers' appearance could not be disguised. Ward Trotter (1989) (the study described above) and Fenn (1992) have managed to get around this problem with a modified matched-guise technique by employing signers who were similar in appearance but signing differently.

Hill (2012) followed the spirit of the technique in examining deaf subjects' attitudes toward signing types, but instead of disguising the deaf signers as

---

[7] MGT is effective for several reasons: it makes the subjects focus on the use of languages or dialects rather than speech traits; it controls the variability of voice quality, pitch, and timbre between two language variants uttered by the same person, and it effectively elicits from subjects' pre-existing social assumptions with languages or dialects.

similar people, Hill changed the questionnaire to include social information that was relevant to the American Deaf community. The subjects in the study viewed videos of eight deaf signers and were asked to classify the signers by type: *ASL*, *Mixed*, and *Signed English*. Following the classification of the signing types, the subjects were asked to give evaluative ratings of the signers in terms of aesthetics, purity, fluency, leadership, identity, education, and intelligence. The findings were that signing perceived as *ASL* was evaluated positively on all social and language evaluation scales; signing perceived as *Mixed* received mixed evaluations from the subjects except for the scale of smoothness in signing, Deaf identity, education, and intelligence; and signing perceived as *Signed English* evaluated negatively on all social and language evaluation scales except for the scale of smoothness in signing, education, and intelligence. There were three evaluations that were considerably positive for all signing types: smoothness, education, and intelligence. It was possible that smoothness had two interpretations for the subjects: that the signing was fluent with no hesitation or excessive pauses, or that thoughts were expressed clearly with strong points regardless of hesitations. For education and intelligence, there were two possible reasons for most subjects to give positive or neutral evaluations: that education and intelligence had no bearing on forms and features in the signing; or that the subjects were hesitant to reveal their bias against the signers due to the visibility of the signers' identity.

Hill's questionnaire study was followed by a qualitative study involving the discussion of comments about the same eight signers' signing derived from the interviews with a group of sixteen deaf and hard-of-hearing subjects with diverse backgrounds. The comments were organized on each linguistic level from phonological (specific level) to discourse (general level) and comments that were para-linguistic or non-linguistic were grouped as 'other.' Also, the comments were grouped as 'positive' or 'negative' based on the manner of how the subjects described the forms and features and the adjectives they used in their descriptions.

For ASL signing, most comments on almost all linguistic levels were positive. There were a few comments about atypical forms or features the subjects described as "errors" (e.g., lack of facial expression, idiosyncratic facial expression, and word choice) or as English (e.g., initialized handshapes and English-like phrases). Even though ASL was viewed positively, there were a few comments about ASL as not having word order. As for para- and non-linguistic features listed as 'other,' there were some positive comments about clarity of signing, identity (i.e., Deaf identity), composure, personality, and signing style, but there were some negative comments on some of the same features in addition to a few others, for example, "low intelligence," and "grassroots" identity (as to mean working-class or vocational trained group).

For Mixed signing, there were both positive and negative comments on almost linguistic levels. The positive comments were on forms and features that were typical of or standard in ASL and the negative comments were on forms and features that were English based or were viewed as errors (e.g., "sloppy handshape," "choppy signing," "unusual combination of words," "weak classifiers"). Even with the negativity about English-based forms and features, there were few comments about it having appropriate English word order. As for other features that were para- or non-linguistic, the signers were described positively as confident, comfortable, clear, skillful, or negatively as being hearing, unclear, uncomfortable, and possessing sub-standard ASL skills.

For Signed English signing, most comments were negative on all linguistic levels but there were some positive comments. The positive comments were based on forms and features that were typical of or standard in ASL and the negative comments were about English-based forms and features, errors, and reduced presence of necessary ASL forms and features in signing. As for para- and non-linguistic features, the comments were mostly negative. While there were a few positive comments about the clarity of signing in the English-influenced style preferred by a few subjects, the signers perceived to be using Signed English were viewed to be unclear, unconfident, late-deafened, or affected by a medical condition such as Usher syndrome I.

Following the qualitative analysis of the subjects' description of the linguistic forms and features, a linguistic analysis of ASL-dominant and English-dominant signing was completed to uncover the actual linguistic forms and features in term of initialized signs, nonmanual signals, use of classifiers, indicating and locative verbs, and word order. The ASL-dominant signing as shown through the video of three signers out of eight was found to have no initialized signs, a significant amount of nonmanual signals, a productive use of classifiers and dynamic verbs (indicating and locative) in relation to the signing space, and ASL word order. The findings supported the majority of subjects who perceived the signing of these three signers as ASL. However, a small number of subjects felt that the signing was mixed because they were not satisfied with the use of classifiers and nonmanual signals. The English-dominant signing as shown through the video of the other three signers of the eight was found to have initialized signs, a reduced amount of nonmanual signals, a lack of classifiers, fewer instances of indicating and locative verbs and dominant English word order including the English function words. A minority of the subjects perceived the signing as Signed English, but a majority of the subjects perceived it as Mixed. Fewer subjects perceived it as ASL. A possible reason for the English-dominant signing to be viewed as Mixed was that it was not strictly English due to the presence of ASL-related nonmanual signals and indicating and locative verbs.

Conclusion

In summary, three basic issues were raised in this chapter pertaining to attitudes about sign languages: (1) whether humans should be allowed to communicate with their hands as opposed to their voices and what it means if they do; (2) what it means when humans cannot hear; and (3) what the implication of deafness is to the society. The case of the controversy about LIS in Italy exemplifies the first issue regarding how language is typically expressed. LIS does have linguistic properties as any natural language whether it is spoken or signed, but the fact that the Chambers of Deputies wanted to rename it as Linguaggio Mimico-Gestuale instead of using this name Lingua dei Segni Italiana which spoke volumes to how they viewed the language expressed through signs. This view is not limited to Italy, however. It is also shared by the rest of the world.

People of the world should not be blamed for possessing this view of speech as a language because deafness is not a common disability and the probability for the hearing majority being deeply familiar with deaf people in their lifetime is low. That is related to the second issue: what it means when humans cannot hear. They may assume what it is like to be deaf by imagining missing their hearing sense. This is a deficit perspective that defines their treatment and their interaction with deaf people as in the case of the White House response to the survey that requested the official recognition of ASL as a community language and as a language of instruction. The White House administration missed the cultural undertone of the message and assumed ASL as a service-oriented accommodation for deaf people in education and employment.

This leads to the third issue: what implication of deafness is to the society. Speaking is a human behavior; the fact that language and culture have long been associated with speech is the basis for the ideology that speech is the normal mode of communication. Signing is also a mode of communication, but it is usually assumed as a communication aid that helps circumvent the inability to communicate through speech. If there were a way to alleviate deafness, signing would be rendered unnecessary. For some hearing people, signing is an object of fascination simply because it is a different and enjoyable way to communicate. In either case, the cultural and linguistic components of signing remain hidden to the public and even to some deaf and hard-of-hearing individuals in a signing community. In most parts of the world, a small percentage of deaf and hard-of-hearing individuals were born to deaf or hard-of-hearing parents whose primary language is sign language and another percentage of the individuals acquired sign language or signing systems at educational institutions. Deaf and hard-of-hearing individuals are fortunate to have been exposed to some forms of signing as the accessible medium of instruction in schools, but the attitudes of educators and administrators toward sign languages may not necessarily be positive or supportive. It is common that educators and administrators are guided by the educational principle of normalization to help deaf and hard-of-hearing individuals to function in a mainstream society. By normalization, it means that a language of a majority is the rule and actions should be taken to make instructions available on that language in whatever form, be it oral, written, or signed. As a result, this relegates sign language to a stigmatized or, in a relatively neutral sense, secondary status.

Even with the lower status of sign language, sign language exists due to covert prestige espoused by a community of deaf and hard-of-hearing individuals. Sign language is a cultural symbol that reminds deaf and hard-of-hearing individuals that they are still humans and that there are people who are like them. There are hearing allies who believe that sign language has natural language properties and know that language development in deaf and hard-of-hearing children can and has been done with sign languages. A community of deaf and hard-of-hearing individuals that uses sign language as a community language bear social characteristics that all language communities exhibit, e.g., beliefs, values, traditions, communication practices, social identities, varieties of sign language, and ideologies of sign language. These characteristics have been studied, but it is usually the case that a certain social group of the community members are studied more than other social groups based on a system of social-based privileges in a Deaf community.

The racial and ethnic groups have different social practices from the American Deaf community and that can make their signing quantitatively and qualitatively different. For instance, a study on African-American ASL signing, called Black ASL, has covered different linguistic aspects that make this ASL variant quantitatively and qualitatively different from mainstream ASL based on the social practices and socio-historical foundation of African-American community (McCaskill *et al.* 2011). McCaskill *et al.*'s study of Black ASL enjoys the steady media interest since its publication in 2011 because it is new and different, but the truth is that the African-American variety has been around for generations and it was seldom studied due to the system of privileges until recently and the publication of Black ASL was picked up by the public via news stories and shared postings on social media. This kind of public attention is a fortunate event, but still, there is a question whether it will translate into further research on the attitudes expressed by a group of African-American deaf and hard-of-hearing individuals and other social groups about Black ASL. There are also other ASL varieties based on social differentiation that need to be studied as well. With the existing literature on language attitudes toward sign languages, enough is known about the effects of an ideology of spoken language on sign language in a respective community, but not much is known about language attitudes expressed by different social groups within a Deaf community toward their own signing varieties and those of others. A look into language attitudes within Deaf communities in the world is the next step that needs to be taken. Perhaps future findings from eventual studies of language attitudes within sign language communities will make deaf and hard-of-hearing signers seem more human in the public eye and the common ideology of language may no longer be singly defined by one communication mode that is speech.

REFERENCES

La protesta dei sordomuti, la lingua dei segni deve avere la stessa dignità di quelle parlate (2011) *La Repubblica*, May 30. Online: www.repubblica.it/solidarieta/volontariato/2011/05/30/news/la_protesta_dei_sordomuti_la_lingua_dei_segni_deve_avere_la_stessa_dignit_di_quelle_parlate-16977846/index.html

Baer, A. M., Okrent, A., and Rose, M. (1996) Noticing variation in ASL: Metalinguistic knowledge and language attitudes across racial and regional lines. In L. Byers and M. Rose (eds.), *Communication Forum, School of Communication, Student Forum* (pp. 1–33). Washington, DC: Gallaudet University Department of ASL.

Barnes, S. L. (2003) The Ebonics enigma: An analysis of attitudes on an urban college campus. *Race Ethnicity and Education* 6(3) (2003): 247–263.

Baugh, J. (2007) Attitudes towards variations and ear-witness testimony: linguistic profiling and voice discrimination in the quest for fair housing and fair lending. In R. Bayley and C. Lucas (eds.), *Sociolinguistic Variation: Theories, Methods, and Applications* (pp. 338–348). Cambridge: Cambridge University Press.

Baynton, D. C. (1996) *Forbidden Signs: American Culture and the Campaign against Sign Language*. Chicago, IL: University of Chicago Press.

Bornstein, H., Saulnier, K. L., and Hamilton, L. B. (1983) *The Comprehensive Signed English Dictionary*. Washington, DC: Gallaudet University Press.

Campbell-Kibler, K. (2009) The nature of sociolinguistic perception. *Variation and Change* 21: 135–156.

Croneberg, C. G. (1965) Sign language dialects. In W. C. Stokoe, D. C. Casterline, and C. G. Croneberg (eds.), *A Dictionary of American Sign Language on Linguistic Principles* (313–319). Silver Spring, MD: Linstok Press.

Eagly, A. and Chaiken, S. (1993) *The Psychology of Attitudes*. Orlando, FL: Harcourt Brace Jovanovich College Publishers.

(2007) The advantages of an inclusive definition of attitude. *Social Cognition* 25: 582–602.

Easterbrooks, S. R. and Baker, S. (2002) *Language Learning in Children Who Are Deaf and Hard of Hearing: Multiple Pathways*. Boston, MA: Allyn and Bacon.

Eckert, P. (1997) Age as a sociolinguistic variable. In F. Coulmas (ed.), *The Handbook of Sociolinguistics* (pp. 151–167). Oxford: Blackwell.

Evans, B. E. (2002) An acoustic and perceptual analysis of imitation. In D. Long (ed.), *Handbook of Perceptual Dialectology* (vol. II, pp. 95–112). Philadelphia, PA: John Benjamins.

Fant, L. J. (1972) *Ameslan: An Introduction to American Sign Language.* Acton, CA: Joyce Media Inc.

Fenn, A. (1992) *A pilot study on sign language attitudes*, unpublished thesis, Gallaudet University, Washington, DC.

Flowers, D. A. (2000) Codeswitching and Ebonics in urban adult basic education classrooms, *Education and Urban Society* 32(2): 221–236.

Fordham, S. (1999) Dissin' 'the Standard': Ebonics as Guerrilla Warfare at Capital High. *Anthropology and Education Quarterly* 30: 272–293.

Frazer, T. C. Attitudes toward regional pronunciation. *Journal of English Linguistics* 20(1): 89–100.

Gallaudet Research Institute (2011) *Regional and National Summary Report of Data from the 2009–2010 Annual Survey of Deaf and Hard of Hearing Children and Youth.* Washington, DC: GRI, Gallaudet University. Retrieved March 4, 2012, from http://gri.gallaudet.edu/Demographics/2010_National_Summary.pdf

Garrett, P. (2010) *Attitudes to Language.* Cambridge: Cambridge University Press.

Geeslin, J. D. (2007) Deaf bilingual education: a comparison of the academic performance of deaf children of deaf parents and deaf children of hearing parents, unpublished dissertation, Indiana University.

Geraci, C., Battaglia, K., Cardinaletti, A., Cecchetto, C., Donati, C., Giudice, S., and Mereghetti, E. (2011) The LIS corpus project: A discussion of sociolinguistic variation in the lexicon. *Sign Language Studies* 11(4): 528–574.

Goldin-Meadow, S. and Mylander, C. (1994) The development of morphology without a conventional language model. In V. Volterra and C. J. Erting (eds.), *From Gesture to Language in Hearing and Deaf Children* (pp. 165–177). Washington, DC: Gallaudet University Press.

Green, L. J. (2002) *African American English: A Linguistic Introduction.* Cambridge: Cambridge University Press.

Gustason, G. and Zawolkow, E. (1993) *Signing Exact English.* Los Alamitos, CA: Modern Signs Press, Inc.

Hill, J. (2012) *Language Attitudes in the American Deaf Community.* Washington, DC: Gallaudet University Press.

Johnson, R. E. and Erting, C. (1989) Ethnicity and socialization in a classroom for Deaf children. In C. Lucas (ed.), *The Sociolinguistics of the Deaf Community* (pp. 41–83). San Diego, CA: Academic Press.

Kannapell, B. (1985) Language choice reflects identity choice: a sociolinguistic study of deaf college students, unpublished dissertation, Georgetown University.

(1989) An examination of deaf college students' attitudes toward ASL and English. In C. Lucas (ed.), *The Sociolinguistics of the Deaf Community* (pp. 191–210). San Diego, CA: Academic Press.

(1994) Deaf identity: An American perspective. In C. Erting, R. C. Johnson, D. L. Smith, and B. D. Snider (eds.), *The Deaf Way: Perspectives from the International*

Conference on Deaf Culture (pp. 44–48). Washington, DC: Gallaudet University Press.

Karchmer, M. A. and Mitchell, R. E. (2003) Demographic and achievement characteristics of deaf and hard-of-hearing students. In M. Marschark and P. E. Spencer (eds.), *Oxford Handbook of Deaf Studies, Language, and Education* (pp. 21–37). Oxford: Oxford University Press.

Lane, H. (2002) Do Deaf people have a disability? *Sign Language Studies* 2(4): 356–379.

Lane, H., Hoffmeister, R., and Bahan, B. (1996) *A Journey into the DEAF-WORLD*. San Diego, CA: Dawn Sign Press.

Leigh, I. (2009) *A Lens on Deaf Identities*. Oxford: Oxford University Press.

Liddell, S. K. (2003) *Grammar, Gesture, and Meaning in American Sign Language*. Cambridge: Cambridge University Press.

LIS Subito! [n.d.] retrieved September 13, 2011 from Movimento Lingua dei Segni Italiana Subito! Online: www.lissubito.com

Lucas, C., Bayley, R., and Valli, C. (2001) *Sociolinguistic Variation in American Sign Language*. Washington, DC: Gallaudet University Press.

Lucas, C. and Valli, C. (1992) *Language Contact in the American Deaf Community*. San Diego, CA: Academic Press.

McCaskill, C., Lucas, C., Bayley, R., and Hill, J. (2011) *The Hidden Treasure of Black ASL: Its History and Structure*. Washington, DC: Gallaudet University Press.

McKee, D., McKee, R., and Major, G. (2011) Numeral variation in New Zealand Sign Language. *Sign Language Studies* 12(1): 72–160.

McKee, R. and McKee, D. (2011) Old signs, new signs, whose signs? Sociolinguistic variation in the NZSL lexicon. *Sign Language Studies* 11(4): 485–528.

Milroy. J. (2001) Language ideologies and the consequences of standardization. *Journal of Sociolinguistics* 5(4): 530–555.

Mitchell, R. E. and Karchmer, M. A. (2004) When parents are deaf versus hard of hearing: Patterns of sign use and school placement of deaf and hard-of-hearing children. *Journal of Deaf Studies and Deaf Education* 9(2): 133–152.

(2005) Parent hearing status and signing among deaf and hard of hearing students. *Sign Language Studies* 5(2): 231–244.

(2006) Demographics of deaf education: More students in more places. *American Annals of the Deaf* 151(2): 95–104.

Monaghan, L. (2003) A world's eye view: Deaf cultures in global perspective. In L. Monaghan, C. Schmaling, K. Nakamura, and G. H. Turner (eds.), *Many Ways to Be Deaf: International Variation in Deaf Communities* (pp. 1–24). Washington, DC: Gallaudet University Press.

Nassisi, S. (2010) Lingua dei segni, ancora ritardi la legge è ferma in commissione, *La Repubblica*, December 27. Online: www.repubblica.it/solidarieta/volontariato/2010/12/27/news/lingua_dei_segni_ancora_ritardi_la_legge_ferma_in_commissione-10633842/index.html

Niedzielski, N. (1999) The effect of social information on the perception of sociolinguistic variables. *Journal of Language and Social Psychology* 18: 62–85.

Ogbu, J. U. (1999) Beyond language: Ebonics, proper English, and identity in a black-American speech community. *American Educational Research Journal* 36(2): 147–184.

Padden, C. and Humphries, T. (1988) *Deaf in America: Voices from a Culture.* Cambridge, MA: Harvard University Press.

(2005) *Inside Deaf Culture.* Cambridge, MA: Harvard University Press.

Power, E. and Leigh, G. (2011) Curriculum: Cultural and communicative contexts. In M. Marschark and P. E. Spencer (eds.), *Oxford Handbook of Deaf Studies, Language, and Education*, 2nd edn (vol. I, pp. 32–46). Oxford: Oxford University Press.

Preston, D. R. (1996) Where the worst English is spoken. In E. W. Schneider (ed.), *Focus on the USA* (pp. 297–360). Amsterdam: John Benjamins.

(2002) Language with an attitude. In J. K. Chambers, P. Trudgill, and N. Schilling-Estes (eds.), *The Handbook of Language Variation and Change* (pp. 40–66). Oxford: Wiley-Blackwell.

Reagan, T. G. (2010) *Language Policy and Planning for Sign Languages.* Washington, DC: Gallaudet University Press.

Rosen, R. (2010) American Sign Language curricula: A review. *Sign Language Studies* 10(3): 348–381.

Searls, D. B. (2011) A commentary on the recent controversy to recognize Lingua dei Segni Italiana. June 1. Online: www.discoveringdeafworlds.org/component/k2/item/4-when-your-voice-is-no-longer-your-own-a-commentary-on-the-recent-controversy-to-recognize-lingua-dei-segni-italiana.html

Shin, Hyon B. and Kominski, Robert A. (2010) *Language Use in the United States: 2007.* American Community Survey Reports, ACS-12.

Stokoe, W. C., Casterline, D., and Croneberg, C. (1965) *A Dictionary of American Sign Language.* Washington, DC: Gallaudet College Press.

Tevenal, S. and Villaneuva, M. (2009) Are you getting the message? The effects of SimCom on the message received by deaf, hard of hearing, and hearing students. *Sign Language Studies* 9(3): 266–286.

Thumann-Prezioso, C. (2005) Deaf parents' perspectives on deaf education. *Sign Language Studies* 5(4): 415–440.

Ward Trotter, J. (1989) An examination of language attitudes of teachers of the deaf. In C. Lucas (ed.), *The Sociolinguistics of the Deaf Community* (pp. 211–228). San Diego, CA: Academic Press.

Wolfram, W. and Schilling-Estes, N. (2006) *American English*, 2nd edn. Oxford: Blackwell.

Index

Printed in the United States
By Bookmasters